Edinburgh Law an

Two wee

<u>day loan</u>

Edinburgh Law and Society Series
Editors: P. Young and B. Brown

The Edinburgh Law and Society Series promotes scholarship that makes a significant contribution to exploring the inter-relations between legal and social spheres. It publishes empirical and theoretical work informed by classical traditions and contemporary developments in the social sciences, philosophy and political theory.

Forthcoming

P. Young *Punishment, Money and Legal Order*
S. Frith *Music and Copyright*

What's Wrong with Rights?

Problems for Feminist Politics of Law

ELIZABETH KINGDOM

EDINBURGH UNIVERSITY PRESS

© Elizabeth Kingdom 1991

Edinburgh University Press
22 George Square, Edinburgh

Set in Linotron Plantin
by Koinonia, Bury, and
printed in Great Britain by
The Alden Press Limited, Oxford

British Library Cataloguing
    in Publication Data
Kingdom, Elizabeth
    What's Wrong with Rights?
Problems for Feminist Politics of Law
I. Title II. Series

ISBN 0 7486 0250 X

Contents

A Note from the Series Editors

We are very pleased that Elizabeth Kingdom's *What's Wrong with Rights?* will launch the Edinburgh Law and Society series. Elizabeth Kingdom's contributions to British debates on feminist use of rights are increasingly cited, not only for what she has to say on rights discourse as such, but also because of the high standard of theoretical analysis she has long brought to feminist accounts of law. Further, in the present context of debate about feminist jurisprudence, her views offer a quite different perspective from those of Catherine MacKinnon and Carol Gilligan.

This volume brings together much of Elizabeth Kingdom's work on the subject, together with some previously unpublished pieces. Many of the pieces are on the subject of reproductive rights, an area often over-shadowed by the focus on discrimination, or considered solely in relation to abortion. The issues, specific and general, are rigorously stated and argued, and legal matters are dealt with in ways that, we believe, will be accessible to lawyers and non-lawyers alike. We feel this is an important book.

Beverley Brown
Peter Young
Series Editors

Preface

The first of the pieces appearing in this collection was published in 1980, and the last was completed in 1990. For the greater part of those ten years, pointing out the dangers and limitations of essentialist theories of law and the pitfalls of rights discourse did not attract feminist, socialist or popular, never mind academic support. Indeed, the very use of terms such as essentialism and rights discourse, even its seemingly less theoretically contentious equivalent, rights talk, could attract hostile comment. It was clear to me, however, that adherence to the familiar discourse of rights was less of a help than a hindrance in the articulation of feminist objectives. Happily, in the latter part of the 1980s, some feminist academics and activists involved in legal and political struggles recognised the strength of this position and became increasingly alert to the need for caution in the use of rights talk.

This change in feminist politics of law is welcome. But rights discourse flourishes in legal and political debates and disputes. It is ironic, then, that just at the time when some feminists are becoming aware of the need to identify alternative ways of constructing feminist politics in relation to law, so they have to analyse how feminists can respond to political initiatives which are ineluctably framed in terms of rights. It would be a crude mistake, therefore, to suppose that feminists should now implement a mechanical search-and-destroy strategy for instances of rights discourse. Although the term rights discourse is a singular noun and may on that account suggest that it refers to a homogeneous legal–political vocabulary, it is used in this book in its proper sense – to insist that the discourse of rights is neither univocal nor unified, and that it refers to diverse formulations and practices. Feminists must acknowledge that diversity in their vigilance for the anti-feminist potential of rights discourse. Indeed, the specific and complex nature of appeals to rights constitutes a recurring theme of the essays in this book.

All the essays were produced either for publication or for a conference and can therefore be read on their own, but they do comprise a coherent collection. The opening essays show how essentialist theories of law and general concepts of rights are theoretically flawed and constitute an obstacle to working out feminist policies and objectives. This theme is further substantiated by scrutiny of the inauspicious career of rights talk in the essays dealing with the specific issues of abortion, sterilisation and cohabitation. In the course of these essays, strategies for the reconceptualisation of rights are offered for consideration, with particular regard for how formal declarations of rights pose special problems for feminists.

These essays all address legal issues of importance to feminists, but it will be apparent that the collection is neither a legal textbook nor a feminist handbook. Some of the essays are, of course, law-dependent, but none of them pretends to be a comprehensive account of the current state of the law in a particular field. For this reason, I have not attempted to bring up to date every aspect of law which I have touched on since 1980. I have changed legal references where they are blatantly out of date and where my argument accordingly needs fresh support, and sometimes I have replaced the original examples with more topical illustrations. But the book is primarily intended to exhibit some of the specific ways in which feminist interventions in legal politics have been hampered by inadequate theories of law and of women's position in relation to law. Accordingly, feminists will be disappointed if they hope for a primer on feminist legal struggles or for instruction in how to criticise law if you are a feminist. In that respect, the collection is not a book of feminist dogma. On the contrary, my aim is to show that it is certain types of dogma – some feminist, others not – that have delayed recognition of the fact that appeals to rights cannot be assumed to advance the cause of feminist politics in relation to law and that their use may be serious tactical error.

Acknowledgements

I am grateful to the following for permission to use the material indicated: the Editors of *m/f* for the first version of Chapter 1 (*m/f*, 4: 1980); the Editorial Group of *Politics and Power* for the first version of Chapter 2 (*Politics and Power*, 3: 1981); Julia Brophy and Carol Smart for Chapter 3 (Brophy and Smart, eds., *Women in Law*, Routledge and Kegan Paul: 1985); the Editor of *Journal of Law and Society* for the first version of Chapter 4 (*Journal of Law and Society*, 12, 1: 1985) and for the first version of Chapter 5 (*Journal of Law and Society*, 15, 1: 1988); Franz Steiner Verlag Wiesbaden GMBH for the Note to Chapter 4 (Mark Occleton, ed., *Medicine, Ethics and Law*, 1987); Robert Lee and Derek Morgan for the first version of Chapter 7 (Lee and Morgan, eds., *Birthrights: law and ethics at the beginning of life*, Routledge: 1989); and Aberdeen University Press for part of Chapter 8 ('Gendering rights', in A. J. Arnaud and E. Kingdom, eds., *Women's Rights and the Rights of Man*, 1990).

Table of Cases

Table of Statutes

Introduction

The title of this collection of essays sets up the paradox that there is something wrong with rights. This is more than a verbal paradox. To put the paradox in terms of strategy, this book addresses the question of whether the invocation of rights should continue to be a feature of feminist politics of law. The question constitutes an immediate dilemma for feminists. On the one hand, feminists have traditionally made their political demands in terms of rights, and their achievements have formed the basis for much contemporary feminist politics of law. Furthermore, other radical and progressive thinkers have recently intensified campaigns for rights, for example in their support for Charter 88 and for a UK Bill of Rights. On the other hand, feminist academics and activists are becoming sceptical about the usefulness of traditional appeals to rights for the achievement of feminist goals in relation to law (cf. Smart 1989: 138–59; Women's Reproductive Rights Campaign (WRRC) 1990: 4)

The essays in this collection give reasons why feminists should hesitate before expressing their political strategies in terms of rights. Appeals to rights, however attractive at first sight, frequently conceal inadequate theories of law in relation to women's social position. Typically, these theories are essentialist. In this book, essentialism has a very simple meaning, and it is best explained initially through a conventional feminist understanding of essentialism.

Rosemary Pringle has provided a brief but useful account of the type of feminist essentialism 'which takes for granted the unity of both gender categories and the law'; this essentialism 'pits masculine law against the unity of women and of feminist law' (1990: 229). One example is the theory that law systematically oppresses women by giving expression to male interests. This type of feminist legal essentialism would certainly be included in the meaning of essentialism used in this book, but it would not exhaust it. Here essentialism refers to any theory of law which seeks to identify the essential feature or features of law. For example, it would refer to theories of law which claim it to be the revealed word of God or the embodiment of liberal moral values, and it would refer to theories of law which claim it to be essentially rational, and to theories of law which claim it to be essentially neutral. Quite simply, it refers to theories of law which claim it to be *essentially* anything. In this book, it refers in particular to all those theories of law which are reductionist in that they attempt to reduce law to non-legal elements. The main examples considered here are classical Marxism, where law is reduced to economic relations, and feminist theories according to which women's oppression by law is attributed to some general principle, such as patriarchy or male bias.

Chapters 1 and 2 exhibit the main problems of these essentialist theories, both in relation to the Marxist reduction of law to economic relations and in relation to the analogous feminist reduction of law to patriarchy or to male bias, theories which have been of great importance for socialist feminists in particular. First, the references to economy, to patriarchy and to male bias are so abstract and general that far from explaining specific events and outcomes in legal contexts, they explain them away by reference to non-legal elements. In the feminist theories, the logic of these essentialist theories is an opening tirade against patriarchy or male bias followed by a catalogue of legal specimens. By diverting attention from the specific workings of the law, the generality of these theories becomes an obstacle to working out the direction and detail of those feminist policies and objectives which have to engage with legal mechanisms. A further effect of the generality of these theories is that they cannot prevent the appeals to rights which they generate from being used in ways which run counter to those feminist objectives.

Substance to this last problem of essentialist theories is afforded by scrutiny of the inauspicious career of rights talk in the chapters on specific legal–political issues: abortion, sterilisation, cohabitation, the use of the distinction between equal and special rights in the context of the legal regulation of human reproduction, and formal declarations of rights. Chapter 3 shows how feminists' demand for a woman's right to choose has been situated in the essentialist frameworks of Marxist and feminist theories of reform and revolution, so that the demand cannot operate in the sphere of practical feminist politics of law. In the Note to Chapter 3, an analysis of 'the Bobigny affair' is an object lesson on the problems of relying on rights discourse. The burden of this Note is what I call 'the attraction of opposite rights', the phenomenon whereby the invocation of one right attracts the invocation of another – irreconcilable – right, occasioning interminable rights wrangles. Feminists are increasingly alarmed at the way in which the politically powerful slogan of a woman's right to choose has facilitated the placing of the abortion issue squarely on the territory of women's rights *versus* men's (fathers') rights and fetal rights. Chapter 4 and the Note to Chapter 4 provide another salutary warning against the careless use of rights discourse. Here, in the context of legal attitudes towards sterilisation for contraceptive and eugenic purposes, I follow the vicissitudes of what might appear to be the feminist-friendly human right to reproduce and reveal how its invocation harks back to some less than friendly, indeed, atavistic rights.

Chapters 5 and 6 are about socialist and feminist politics of cohabitation. In Chapter 5, my main purpose is to argue for the legal recognition of cohabitation contracts. In keeping with the rubric of this book, I am more concerned to identify the complex legal materials which have to be assembled to develop a socialist feminist politics of cohabitation than to pitch into the game of moral claim and counter-claim for and against cohabitation contracts. Indeed, I conclude that, contrary to what might be expected, there are positive dangers in arguing for cohabitation contracts in terms of the moral value of equality, in terms of equal rights. Problems with equality, and specifically with equal rights claims, emerge in Chapter 7. This chapter is concerned with some of the rights which are claimed in the context of birth, pregnancy and parenthood. I examine the way in which feminist disillusion with demands for equal rights in the context of American constitutional politics has produced a strategy which focuses on the claim that differences between men and women warrant not equal rights but special rights. My argument is that this strategy, far from being a remedy for the problem of equal rights, is its redescription, and that feminists should look elsewhere for ways to enter feminist policies into formal declarations of rights.

Different problems for feminists in connection with formal statements of rights are discussed in Chapters 6 and 8. Chapter 6 makes the key point that in English law rights are not given, not directly conferred, but constructed. Accordingly, I review some of the different ways in which 'cohabitation rights' – a bogus term, really, since there is no clearly defined set of such rights in English law – are constructed. With its critique of the distinction between rights and discretion and its argument for minimising the scope for judicial discretion, it paves the way for Chapter 8. Chapter 8 deals with feminist responses to formal declarations of rights. It reviews some powerful arguments for why feminists should not become embroiled in the legal politics of formal declarations of rights, not least the experience of feminists in other countries. But the chapter ends on the suggestion that there may be political arguments for supporting the campaign for a UK Bill of Rights which override the dangers of rights discourse in this context.

Now, it might seem that the conclusion to Chapter 8 flatly contradicts my argument in the preceding chapters. My constantly reiterated warnings to feminists about using rights discourse now look like crying wolf. For of course it would be an example of essentialism to claim that rights talk necessarily obstructs the advancement of feminist politics, and that it should on that account be abandoned. But none of the essays proposes a total embargo on appeals to rights. All the essays commend caution in the use of rights talk and thorough analysis of how rights have featured – their past and present excursions and pathologies – in the legal–political contexts of importance to feminists. Chapter 8 is important, then, not only because it deals with a neglected area of feminist politics of law in the UK, but also because its conclusion draws attention to the fact that feminists cannot always choose the political ground of their struggles. Depending on the legal–political contexts, feminists may have more or less room for flexibility with respect to the terms in which they present their policies. For example, they would find it much easier to abandon their appeal to a woman's right to choose than to persuade nation states and international lawyers of the shortcomings of rights discourse in the context of formal declarations and conventions of rights.

There is no snap answer, then, to the question of whether rights should continue to be used in feminist politics of law. Rights may well feature ineluctably in certain legal-political contexts, and it is so convenient to use the phrase 'women's rights' that it will probably withstand any amount of feminist theorising and disillusion. In Chapter 2, however, I argue for the reconceptualisation of 'women's rights' in terms of the discourse of women's capabilities, capacities and competences, and Chapter 7 shows how that type of reconceptualisation would work in the context of birthrights. I should stress that the proposal to reconceptualise women's rights is not a philosophical exercise. First, it is not to be understood as the decree that henceforth the phrase 'women's rights' and all entries of the words 'right' and 'rights' be removed from feminists' legal-political thesaurus. Nor is it to be understood as a philosophical proposition of the formal equivalence of the two discourses, as if women's rights were ontological entities whose properties could be transferred in a philo-sophical experiment to the different ontological entities of capabilities, capacities and competences. In that respect, Michael Freeman is mis-taken when he attributes to me an interest in finding out if the right to reproduce exists (Freeman 1988: 70–1). In this book. I am concerned not with whether rights exist, whatever that may mean, but with how rights are constructed, with what transpires when they are claimed, countered or refused, and with whether feminists should continue to employ them as a matter of strategy and tactics. The proposal to reconceptualise women's rights is one means – and there may well be others – by which feminists can turn their attention away from abstract and moralistic rights and so formulate their policies in realistic terms. In this way, the proposal has the status of a heuristic, a sort of intellectual and political knee-jerk, for resisting the attractions of rights discourse and for working out tactics in less risky terms.

In saying that there may be other ways in which women's rights could be reconceptualised, I must guard against another, more serious misinterpretation. This is that when I argue for a heuristic to help feminists to correct the looseness of the phrase 'women's rights', and when I argue for caution in the use of rights discourse, I am one of the 'fem-crits'. This unattractive term has been used to describe not only those feminists who have allied themselves to the critical legal studies movement but also the work of radical feminists such as Carol Gilligan and Catherine MacKinnon (Stark 1990: 56). Although I cannot do justice to their work here, a brief description of it is necessary in order to distance myself from it.

Gilligan and MacKinnon have argued, in their different ways, that emphasis on rights reflects male values and male power (Gilligan 1982: 164; MacKinnon 1983: 644). In Gilligan's critique of the presumptions of the psychology of moral discourse, the ethic of rights and the ethic of justice comprise the male voice, whereas the female voice is the ethic of care. Her research leads her to the conclusion not that the male voice should be suppressed to make way for the muted female voice, but that properly adult moral conceptions integrate both ethics (1982: 105). Gilligan's work has generated much debate and criticism in feminist politics of law (cf. Daly 1989). For example, Ann Scales comments that Gilligan's work 'tempts one to suggest that the different voices of women can somehow be grafted onto our right- and rule-based legal system' (1986: 1374). Scales is opposed to what she sees as the facile idea that the incorporation of the female voice into a rights-based system could be anything other than mere incorporation, arguing that the inevitable result is the further repression of the contradictions between the two voices (1986: 1373 n. 37, 1391–2).

For similar reasons, MacKinnon has no time for equal but different voices. For her, preoccupation with equality as a matter of what differences between men and women are reasonable or unreasonable is 'part of the way male dominance is expressed in law' (MacKinnon 1987: 44). More seriously, as Scales has paraphrased MacKinnon, 'from such viewpoints we cannot see that male supremacy is a complete social system for the advantage of one sex over another' (1986: 1382). For MacKinnon, it is sexuality that creates the social beings defined as women and men (1982: 516) and it is sexuality that is the form of power which institutionalises male dominance and female subordination (1986: 533). A key mechanism for the institutionalisation of this male power is the law's claim to gender-neutrality and objectivity, epitomised in the appeal to abstract rights (MacKinnon 1983: 658).

Even from this sketch of their views, the essentialisms of Gilligan and MacKinnon will be apparent. For Gilligan and MacKinnon, legal politics and practice are explained by reference to the dominance of male sexuality, and rights discourse is accordingly male. Nothing could be further from my argument in this book. For although Carol Smart (1986: 121) has suggested that Gilligan, MacKinnon and I arrive at a similar position about rights through very different avenues, our different starting-points mean that we have different routes and, since I would resist the idea of a destination, different stopping-off points. Gilligan and MacKinnon both start from a theoretical position which postulates non-legal elements – sexuality and male power – perpetually intervening in law and by various devices constantly regenerating men's social dominance. On this view, there is nothing to be learned about the legal career of rights: rights can safely be presumed to be the necessary concomitant or expression of institutionalised male power. It follows that feminists need waste no time on strategic questions of whether rights should continue to feature in feminist politics of law.

In contrast, however much I appreciate the fem-crits' achievements in giving recognition to the importance of feminist politics of law, I resist their critiques of legal politics and jurisprudence. This is because the value of exposing the essentialism of law's claimed gender neutrality and objectivity is wasted if what is substituted is some new form of essentialist discourse, whether expressed in terms of different voices or in terms of male power. An example here is Zillah Eisenstein's rejection of the essentialist relegation of sex equality to economic or legal issues, followed swiftly by her assimilation of it to the discourse of the pregnant body and her situation of that discourse within the wider 'phallocratic' discourse and the triumph of the phallus (1988: 1–4, 28). Similarly, even Smart's critique of MacKinnon's essentialism, backed by her own recognition of law's plurality, is nonetheless dependent on the essentialist concept of law's power as derived solely from its self-confirming claim to singularity and unity (Smart 1989: 4).

It is much easier, of course, to detect essentialism in others than to avoid it oneself. Just as socialists were once pestered to say what, following their critique of capitalism, they would put in its place, so feminists who publicly reflect on the shortcomings of traditional feminist appeals to rights will be under pressure to find discourses of comparable theoretical respectability, and to latch on to more sophisticated forms of essentialism. Fortunately for the development of feminist politics of law, the anti-essentialist critique is itself gaining ground, at least among academic feminists. My collection of essays is a contribution to that critique, submitted in the certainty that any traces of essentialist theory in them will be swiftly detected.

1

Women in Law

Introduction

In *Sexism and the Law* Albie Sachs and Joan Hoff Wilson (1978) collect materials from legal and non-legal sources to provide a record of judicial initiatives and responses regarding the legal status of women in Britain and the United States from the mid 1850s onwards. Each main Part of the book is divided into a chapter on legal history and practices in Britain and a corresponding chapter on the United States.

In Part One, 'The Male Monopoly Cases', Sachs and Wilson chart the unsuccessful campaign of seven women to enter the University of Edinburgh's Medical School in 1869, and they map the early history of the issue of whether or not a woman could count as a person in law. This is followed by a history of the question of whether or not American women could count as citizens. Among other things, Sachs and Wilson show that the legal position of women was probably stronger in the early colonial period than in the late 1800s. They explain – by referring to the constitutional rights of female bartenders and jurors – that whereas discrimination on a sexual basis in the United States is in certain conditions illegal, it is still not unconstitutional. Part Two, 'Judges and Genders: a New Look at Family Law', begins with a brief examination of the conceptualisation of women, mainly married women, in early and current legislation. It proposes that transformations in family law must be seen as corresponding to changes in the character of the monogamous nuclear family. A rather more detailed analysis is then given of aspects of family law in the United States. Part Three, 'The Legal Profession', investigates both the obstacles facing women when they seek entry into parts of the legal profession in the two countries, and the immense professional and personal difficulties they experience if they are successful. Part Four, 'Equal Opportunity ... and Beyond', is concerned with the passing of British and American acts seeking to combat sex discrimination; it briefly evaluates their legislative strengths and weaknesses and their effectiveness in, if not eliminating, then reducing sex discrimination. There are two Appendices. The first gives 'Landmark Decisions and Legislation' and the second asks 'How Many Women?' work in the legal professions. Throughout the book there are suggestions for the continuing fight against sex discrimination and a great many references to pertinent court cases, Royal Commissions, newspaper articles, feminist literature and academic works.

There is no doubt that the enormous variety of materials, familiar and overlooked, which Sachs and Wilson have collected will fill gaps in many people's knowledge of legal practices regarding women. But it is also clear that the authors do not intend these materials to be considered as a mere collection of materials for *ad hoc* browsing. In the crucial first ten pages of the Introduction to Part One, Sachs and Wilson briefly defend the assumption underlying their investigation of what came to be called 'the persons cases'. It is that 'the generalised and mythical pronouncements about females masked specific and discoverable material interests that the judges as upper-class males shared generally with members of their class and gender' (1978: 8). Sachs and Wilson claim that judges and legal experts have 'hidden material interests' and that they are 'tenacious defenders of unfair material advantage' (1978: 8–9). This underlying assumption in fact permeates the whole book, as does the claim that these material or economic interests provide the means for understanding the patterns of behaviour and beliefs which the book investigates. And the general justification for the whole enquiry is the authors' claim that 'in a modern society it is the law above all that defines social issues and constructs models of appropriate and inappropriate behaviour' (1978: ix).

Further evidence of the fact that Sachs and Wilson intend their collection of legal materials to be seen as more than a source book can be found in their discussion of the male monopoly cases in Britain. These are the legal battles which took place from the 1860s onwards over whether women could be included in the category of persons, the supposedly gender-neutral term used in statutes relating to, for example, the regis-tration of doctors, jury qualification, and candidature for municipal and county councils.. In their study of these cases, Sachs and Wilson are concerned with specific sets of beliefs about the legal profession. Their first concern is to challenge the conventional notion that judges are impartial. Their second task is to explode the myth of legal practitioners' male protectiveness, or chivalry, both towards potential and actual female colleagues and towards all women wanting greater involvement in public life. Their third objective is to probe the extent to which, in spite of the removal of all formal legal disabilities, the judiciary and the legal profes-sion have sustained male domination. These themes reappear in the discussion of the male monopoly cases in the United States about whether American women qualified for legal status as citizens. They recur, though less noticeably, in the remaining parts of the book. The Conclusion emphasises that, contrary to legal mythology, legal systems do not evolve 'according to inherent principles of logic and procedure' and that, again contrary to legal mythology, the legal profession has not acted 'as the guardian of the individual as against public power' (1978: 25–6). The final paragraph is a careful balance between pessimism and optimism about future campaigns on both sides of the Atlantic for the elimination of gender discrimination and inequality in legal contexts.

The materials which Sachs and Wilson have put together, then, are clearly not intended to be seen as a mere chronology of legal and related events. On the contrary, they are presented from the point of view of a theoretico-political position which, for convenience, can be called their basic position. This basic position is that sex discrimination against women in the context of law is best explained by reference to a specific type of bias on the part of male judges and legal experts, which is not simply a bias against women *per se* but which derives from their concern to protect their economic interests. For Sachs and Wilson these economic interests have the additional characteristic of being upper-class interests.

Sachs and Wilson acknowledge, in passing, that their basic position is controversial. For example, they point out that it means rejecting any contemporary theory of male supremacy which appeals to essentially biological differences between men and women (1978: 8–9). Similarly, they recognise that it means rejecting psycho-sexual theories designed to explain social behaviour. This is because such theories cannot explain 'why elderly judges more concerned with longevity than virility should have repeatedly turned down women's claims' (1978: 11). Sachs and Wilson feel that their basic position is preferable because, among other things, 'it is the one that appears to throw most light on the question of why women were so resolutely kept out of the professions' (ibid.).

It is unfortunate that Sachs and Wilson do not acknowledge the full extent of the controversial nature of their basic position. There are general theoretical problems with the use of 'interests' to explain social pheno-mena. Parveen Adams and Jeff Minson (1978) have shown how the construction of the categories of 'men' and 'women' as undifferentiated, and of the category of 'women's interests' and 'men's interests' are an impediment to political calculation and reduce the evaluation of feminist struggles to the vacuous confirmation of the ever-present threat of men's interests and to the equally vacuous celebration of the eternal justice of fighting for women's interests. Following this type of argument, there is an additional problem with the way in which Sachs and Wilson identify the economic interests of male judges as being upper-class interests. Such a position is bound to produce discrepancies. Either there is some economic difference between all men and all women, or an explanation of bias in terms of economic interest requires a supplementary account of sexist bias, in which case economic interest is not the source of sexism. Further, if upper-class interest is isolated, then, again, it would seem that no distinction could be made between the treatment of non-upper-class men and all women.

Sachs and Wilson cannot claim that such problems are incidental to the substance of the book, because they constantly refer to their basic position. It is most unfortunate, then, that they refer to it not as something to be debated and clarified by the collected materials but as a given position which automatically explains particular examples of discrimination. For example, Sachs and Wilson claim that in the persons cases in Britain 'male ideology ... *rationalised* legal disabilities imposed on women in terms of each sex having dominium in its separate sphere' (1978: 52, emphasis added). Here there is a hint, but only a hint, of a theory about the relation between male beliefs and legal practices. Another example is provided by the description of an important and unfavourable ruling on maternity disability insurance in the United States. The description is mostly in terms of useful information about particular cases and various congressional and public responses to them. But the claim is also made that the ruling 'represented a clear victory for male supremacy and the brand of capitalism on which it is based in the United States' (1978: 154). There is no further discussion of this large and contentious claim. It is simply assumed that the way in which male supremacy is 'based on' a certain form of capitalism is clear and that the ruling in question is an expression of that relation.

Other examples could be given of how Sachs and Wilson refer fleetingly to their undeveloped but seemingly crucial basic position. What should also be noted is their heavy use of irony and sarcasm. For example, American courts 'admitted' that women were citizens (1978: 101), British judges 'did not actually say that they counted women among their best friends, but ...' (1978: 53) and, in connection with the appeal to evolutionary theories to explain male ascendancy, 'it is rather unconvincing to suggest that it is the inheritance of the qualities needed to bash in an antelope's head that explains why only males sit as judges in the House of Lords' (1978: 11). There is hardly a component of the book that does not rely on such devices for casually reminding the reader of the authors' basic position.

Now, the objection to these devices is not that Sachs and Wilson write in a style which is unorthodox in academic works, nor that much of what they write is journalistic. The objection is that the use of these devices undermines any serious approach to the development of a feminist analysis of law. It is almost as if the moment such an analysis is intimated, it is deliberately averted in favour of a flourish or a punchline. Here is a further example taken from the discussion of the persons cases in Britain.

The vigour of the campaigns against male monopoly needs to be understood in terms of male obduracy rather than of female destructiveness, and research should be directed at the husband's actual self-interest rather than the spinster's alleged rage. It is not, of course, suggested by this that male stubbornness flowed from some constitutional or biological characteristic, but rather that it arose out of the material and social advantages that flowed from possession of a male biology. (1978: 64)

Sachs and Wilson clearly believe, here, that there is a connection between a psychological characteristic, an economic interest, and a biology. But what kind of connection is it? A psychological characteristic 'arises' from the economic interest, and the economic interest 'flows from' biology. But how precisely does that contention relate to the earlier claim in the Preface that behaviour and beliefs must be attributed 'primarily' to hidden material interests? Until the metaphors of arising and flowing are replaced by something more specific about the mechanisms of male stubbornness, the reader is in no position to assess the claim that research should be directed to the actual self-interest of the husband, nor, indeed, to envisage how that research might even be initiated. To put the point more generally, until certain aspects of the basic position adopted by Sachs and Wilson are clarified, and some of its problems identified and tackled, it is impossible to make a rigorous assessment either of the materials which have been selected in accordance with it or of the proposals and recommendations made in the light of it.

These problems need not affect the usefulness of the book as a preliminary source book for courses or projects in social policy, law and women's studies. But it is already clear that Sachs and Wilson have a wider concern, and there are at least three more indications of this. First, as noted above, they state in their Preface that 'in a modern society it is law above all that defines social issues and constructs models of appropriate and inappropriate behaviour'. The precise meaning of 'above all' is not given, but one can surmise that it is intended to attribute to law pre-eminence, if not strict determinacy, in the construction of social practices. Secondly, Sachs and Wilson request the reader's serious consideration of the social dangers of the presence of sexism in legal life (1978: ix). Thirdly, they claim the issue of sexism as an area of scholarly concern, and they propose a definition of sexism.

By sexism we mean the tendency to think about and behave towards people mainly on the basis of their gender, to generalise about individuals and groups on the grounds of their biology rather than to recognise their actual interests and capacities. ... As scholars we are happy to use such a term. (Ibid.)

Given these three indications of the seriousness with which Sachs and

Wilson would like the book to be read, it is reasonable to infer that they would also see it as at least pertinent to the development of a socialist feminist analysis of law. This inference is all the more reasonable since, although law has long been dismissed by sections of the left and of feminism as being irredeemably reactionary and therefore politically impenetrable, legal practices are increasingly being seen as a site of feminist intervention and the place to press demands for rights. Sachs and Wilson themselves provide many references for this trend, and I have discussed elsewhere issues about the legalisation of rights in the context of Marxist politics (Kingdom 1980).

The contribution which Sachs and Wilson can make to that trend, however, is limited by the absence of a developed account of their basic position. On the other hand, their faint but frequent clues and allusions to it suggest a congruence between it and two traditions of analysing law. The first is classical Marxism and the second is legal realism. In what follows I situate the basic position of *Sexist Bias and the Law* in relation to those traditions. Then, on the assumption that the development of a socialist feminist analysis of law requires a critique both of influential theories of law and of the pertinence of them to socialist feminist politics, I will set out some of the problems of any theory of law which incorporates elements of classical Marxism and legal realism. This introduces the particular problems of a theory of law, such as the one adopted by Sachs and Wilson, which sees it as the expression of male partiality based on economic and class interest.

It is not possible here to do justice to the many and varied legal practices described by Sachs and Wilson. That is because their description of them persistently tempts and demands discussion of the wider theoretical issues which they themselves see as crucial to the interpretation of specific legal practices and which have repercussions for the production of recommendations and policies. The following section introduces these wider perspectives with a brief study of Engels' critique of certain simplistic analyses of the relation between law, economy, and the consciousness of jurists. The second section takes further the discussion of jurists' consciousness as typified by Jerome Frank's version of legal realism. The third section resumes the question of the relation between law and economy, and the final section examines the legal and political effects of the way in which Sachs and Wilson conceptualise impartiality and the law. I argue that acceptance of their way of linking economic interest and male partiality in the context of law can, ironically, lead to the adoption of positions which may reproduce the very legal ideologies which help to perpetuate that partiality.

Law, economy and the consciousness of jurists

In a letter written in 1890 to C. Schmidt, Engels discusses the limitations of seeing law as no more than the faithful reflection of economic conditions. He argues that 'in a modern state, law must not only correspond to the general economic condition and be its expression, but must also be an *internally coherent* expression which does not, owing to inner contradictions, reduce itself to nought' (Engels 1970: 686–7). The 'ideological outlook' produced by this requirement is then able, according to Engels, to react back on the economic basis and, within limits, modify it. But this ideological outlook is not an element in the consciousness of jurists. Indeed, Engels argues, the jurists' conception of legal right could no more tolerate the theory of legal principles as the reflection of economic relations than it could tolerate the theory that 'a code of law is the blunt, unmitigated, unadulterated expression of the domination of a class' (ibid.). On the contrary, Engels remarks, jurists turn their attention to the establishment of what they take to be *a priori* principles operating within the legal sphere.

In this highly condensed statement of classical Marxist theory of law, Engels raises a number of questions which are crucial for immediate purposes. First, what is the force of his phrase 'in a modern state'? Engels might be suggesting that law cannot be seen as having the same function in states of different epochs, or he might be suggesting that in modern states there are particular problems about how law is characterised by jurists. Secondly, Engels' use of the term 'must' is vague. He might be claiming that there is a necessary relation between general economic conditions and the law, namely that the economic is expressed in the law. On such a view, law is the perfect register of the economic and must take the form imposed on it by the economic. Alternatively, Engels might be claiming that there are constraints imposed on law by conditions other than economic conditions, such as ideological conditions. Given what follows immediately in the quotation, it is the first alternative that seems most plausible. This is because the relation between law and economy is characterised as 'having to be' expressed in an internally coherent form, with this requirement in turn producing a certain ideological outlook. But this interpretation will make it difficult for Engels to sustain the claim that law has the ability to react back on the economic. For if legal ideology is ultimately the perfect register of the economic, how does legal ideology acquire the power to affect the economy in any way which is not already determined by the economic? On the other hand, if terms such as 'correspond', 'produce' and 'react back' are not to be interpreted as describing necessary relations between law, economy and legal ideology, then it follows that it is always *a priori* and dogmatic to insist that it is the economic that will explain the law and to rely on the law/economy relation as an explanation of legal ideology.

All these and many related questions have been the subject of debate in Marxist and feminist critiques of law in recent years. Rosalind Coward (1978) gives a useful organisation of them. It is unlikely that they will be answered by a fresh bout of speculation on what Engels really meant. Engels' letter is used here both to air these issues and to provide a theoretical setting for them as sketched in *Sexism and the Law*. There are two broad issues. First there is the issue of the relation between law and economy, an issue which Sachs and Wilson give only the slightest indication of being contentious. This will be discussed in the third section below. Secondly, and this is perhaps the more immediately instructive part of Engels' letter, there is the issue of jurists' consciousness – how judges, magistrates, lawyers and legal experts are supposed to think and what they are supposed to believe. This is examined in the next section, but there is a point in Engels' letter which provides a useful introduction to that issue.

Engels, we have already seen, offers one account of the dissociation of jurists or legal practitioners from economic considerations and their subsequent devotion to the polite rough-and-tumble of what might be called legal truth tables – that is, the perpetual refinement of what they take to be the 'harmonious system of law' and the professionally protected activity of scanning the body of law for inconsistencies.

Now, there is no obvious reason why the legal profession's separation from considerations of economy should take the form of their conceptualising law as a harmonious system. After all, it could equally well take the form of conceptualising law as the revealed but not necessarily consistent word of God. But Engels' letter does point to what is certainly a recurring theme in most forms of jurisprudence, namely the claim or rebuttal of law as being governed by a set of consistent principles. To illustrate this theme, jurisprudence can be pragmatically defined as the study of law from one of three points of view: the scientific, the philosophical, and the realistic.

Where the jurisprudential approach is scientific, the task is to tease out hidden relations between professional pronouncements. Such a process might be loosely characterised as culminating with the discovery that 'if all rulings on this subject were reducible to one, it would be this'. The aim of such an activity would be to produce either a rational technique for drafting statutes or a rational model of law. Where the jurisprudential approach is philosophical, jurisprudential activity is characterised by the heuristic that law – in the form of statutes and opinions – can be justified by reference to what might be called the higher courts of ethics or religion. From this point of view, law always has to be shown to be consistent with general principles or values.

Whether scientific or philosophical, such jurisprudential analyses attempt the extrapolation from sheer description of legal practices to some more general and more internally consistent analysis of law. To return to Engels, his letter is an attack on both forms of jurisprudence. In particular, he is concerned to demolish the idea that law is a body of beliefs, practices or decisions which comprises a paradigm of rigour, either in the sense of internal consistency or in the sense of scrupulousness in application.

It could well be Engels' demolition of jurisprudence that Sachs and Wilson have in mind when they rail against myths of impartiality and chivalry in law and when they attack the idea of law evolving according to 'inherent principles of logic and procedure'. But their basic position is equally reminiscent of yet another more elaborate, very influential, and similarly unacknowledged demolition. That demolition is the form of jurisprudence which studies law from a realistic point of view – legal realism.

Bias and law

The sub-title of *Sexism and the Law* is *A Study of Male Beliefs and Judicial Bias*.[1] To understand the full implications of the claim made by Sachs and Wilson that there are no inherent principles of logic or procedure in the law but that law is the outcome of upper-class male beliefs and bias, it will be useful to raise the more general question of the status of beliefs in discussion of law and legal practices. This question has been a major issue in the criticism of scientific and philosophical jurisprudence developed by exponents of realistic jurisprudence or legal realism as it came to be known. The work of Jerome Frank is often cited as the most distinctive contribution to legal realism.

It should be noted that there is no agreed definition of legal realism. Indeed, Frank regrets ever using the term because in his view it suggests a homogeneous doctrine governed by philosophical discourse. He prefers the term 'constructive scepticism', mainly because that identifies the one feature of legal realism that might serve as a definition, namely scepticism towards the conventional theory that legal decisions are the outcomes of legal rules and principles. As we shall see, Frank denies the possibility of extrapolating from the description of legal practices a more general and more internally consistent model of law. In his view, it is bias of one form or another that is the key to the interpretation of legal decisions. We may therefore take Frank's work as being a developed account of the type of assumption made by Sachs and Wilson.

In the Preface to the sixth printing of *Law and the Modern Mind*, Frank summarises his arguments in order to answer the many criticisms made of them up to 1948. He attacks the idea that 'a decision of any lawsuit results from the application of a legal rule or rules to the facts of the suit' (Frank 1949: x). He vehemently opposes a corollary of that idea, namely that it is possible to predict – to prophesy, as he says – the decision, since in his view prediction is impossible because of the fallibility and prejudices of the trial judges. This point is vividly exemplified.

> Those prejudices, when they are racial, religious, political or eco-
> nomic, may sometimes be surmised by others. But there are some
> hidden, unconscious biases of trial judges or jurors – such as, for
> example, plus or minus reactions to women, or unmarried women,
> or red-haired women, or brunettes, or men with deep voices or high-
> pitched voices, or fidgety men, or men who wear thick eyeglasses, or
> those who have pronounced gestures or nervous tics – biases of
> which no one can be aware. Concealed and highly idiosyncratic,
> such biases – peculiar to each individual judge or juror – cannot be
> formulated as uniformities or squeezed into regularised 'behaviour
> patterns'. (1949: x–xi)

If emphasis should be placed on any part of this extraordinary, though in the works associated with legal realism not untypical, statement, it should be on the word 'regularised'. Frank's main argument is against the possibility of prediction based on regularities. For him, such attempts at prediction are a feature of all forms of determinism, including Freudian and Marxist forms. It should be noted that Frank is not opposed to the idea of external, or non-legal, factors having effects on legal practices. What he is opposed to is the claim that legal decisions inexorably follow regular patterns. It is with great fervour, therefore, that he rebuffs Roscoe Pound's criticism of him for being a psychological determinist and retorts that 'nothing in this book, however, faintly intimates a belief in deter-minism' (1949: xxii). But Pound could well return the fire by citing Frank's footnote about political bias in the chapter 'The Language of the Law':

> Many of these powerful biases derive from childish attempts to solve
> childhood problems, that is, problems which properly concerned us
> as children and which, with the limited equipment of children, we
> could not then adequately solve. We do not as adults consciously
> confront these problems but the infantile efforts to solve them
> *continue, buried and concealed, to affect our adult thought and behav-
> iour.* (Frank 1949: 29n, emphasis added)

The similarity of such a view to psychological determinism is hard to deny, particularly when compared with the type of determinism adopted by Sachs and Wilson. There are at least three ways of comparing these authors.

First, one might cite their shared and entirely understandable reluc-tance to specify what really, or uniquely, determines legal outcomes.

Frank has a strategy here.

> The filial relation is clearly indicated as one important unconscious determinant [*sic*] of the ways of man in dealing with all his problems, including the problems of his attitudes towards the law ... We have used the phrases 'one important determinant' and 'an important element' in referring to the father-regarding attitude as an explanation of the basic illusion of complete legal predictability. For it is not pretended that we have isolated the sole cause of a reaction which, like most human reactions, is of course the product of a constellation of several forces. Yet, for the sake of emphasis, we shall in what follows treat a partial explanation as if it were the only one. We shall openly and avowedly take the part for the whole. (1949: 18–20)

Sachs and Wilson have a remarkably similar strategy.

> The implication of the view adopted in this study is that much of the social, and for that matter, sexual, tension that exists between men and women as a group can be explained in terms of clashes of material interests, just as struggles between classes and nations can be explained in those terms. Here again, the emphasis is put rather baldly on the dimension of gender – the sex war as it used to be called – not because gender can never be entirely separated from such factors as class, or race, or nationality, but because it is usually not separated at all. (1978: 12)

Secondly, one might compare the two texts by noting that they are both implicitly opposed to any form of theory according to which eternal truths or values transcending law contrive to intervene in, for example, the criminal courts. One example would be their shared opposition to the alleged intervention of Natural Right into any form of legal debate (Frank 1949: viif; Sachs and Wilson 1978: 11–12).

A still more useful way to compare the two texts, however, is to note that they both identify bias – that is, presumably, the intrusion of extra-legal elements – as having effects on legislation and on legal decisions. They do differ over how far bias could, or indeed should, be eliminated, and they differ over the extent to which the effects of bias can be predicted with certainty. Briefly, Frank denies the possibility of the complete predictability of legal outcomes on the basis of bias, because there cannot be complete predictability on any basis, whereas Sachs and Wilson do claim that bias affords such predictions. But, I argue, they share the general view that the law cannot be understood as a corpus of legislation which is both rigorously (that is, consistently) and scrupulously (that is, fairly and impartially) implemented in the courts by jurists. In this respect, as indicated above, their shared position can be seen as very similar to Engels' attack on the conception of law as a 'harmonious system'.

Far from seeing law as a harmonious system, both Frank and Sachs and Wilson see the law as a corpus of legislation plus the interpretations, decisions and opinions given by members of the legal profession and by legal experts. This view can be summed up by saying that the law always has to be seen as a set of heterogeneous practices, defying organisation into a single coherent unity.

Further, the authors share the view that the law, understood in this way, is a set of practices which can be fully analysed only by reference to certain other sets of elements and practices. Accordingly, a particular piece of legislation or a particular ruling can be understood only if it is seen as at least in part the outcome of certain non-legal elements and practices. In this way, a particular statute or a particular decision might be said to reflect, register, recognise or be read off from non-legal elements and practices of some kind or another. In the case of Frank, the elements and practices which legal practices register or recognise is a pre-legal reality, namely the conditions of childhood, understood in terms of a type of psychoanalytic theory of the filial relation. For Sachs and Wilson, legal practices register bias on the part of men, bias which is variously described as male, upper-class, partial, frequently hidden but knowable, but bias which is always defined as somehow rooted in the non-legal reality of material or economic interests.

It is not clear whether Sachs and Wilson would see legal practices as the *perfect* register of economic interests, and their reluctance to commit themselves on the question of predictability of bias suggests that they consider legal practices to be the perfect register or direct expression of economic interests on some occasions but not on others. Some of the problems of this sort of vacillation will be discussed in the fourth section below. There I draw attention to the fact that Sachs and Wilson explain legal practices normally in terms of upper-class male interests and I note that such explanations pose problems for the explanation of feminist successes in the context of legal practices. Before developing that argument, however, it is important to note some of the difficulties raised by general theories of law as the expression of economic interests.

Law and economy

The problems of theories of law as the direct expression of economic interests can be examined through the complex theoretical-political struggles which occurred between 1919 and 1938 in post-revolutionary Soviet Russia in which the consequences of a socialist economy for the law were contested. In *A General Doctrine of Law*, P. I. Stuchka is concerned to develop the concept of Soviet law through a rejection of bourgeois theories of law and through the adaptation of the Marxist–Leninist revolutionary theory of class struggle to the urgent problems of constraint, persuasion and propaganda characteristic of the transition period. Following his analysis of the variety of meanings of the terms 'law' and 'society', Stuchka raises the problem of how 'social relationships are converted into the form of juridic relationships and are even transmuted into juridic institution' (1951: 41). He pays particular attention to relations of determination:

> the relationships of production and exchange are always primary; *whereas the relationships of appropriation* (that is to say, juridic or legal – as well as moral – relationships – are only derivative relationships – which, however, does not prevent their playing *a predominant part* under certain circumstances and in certain historical phases. (1951: 41–2)

This passage is reminiscent of Engels' analysis. The idea is that since it is economic relations that determine the outcome of class struggles, and since legal relations derive from economic relations, then no matter how important legal relations may be in certain class struggles, they can never be characterised as determinant in them. Stuchka next identifies a corollary of this theoretical-political position:

> he who has understood that the institutions of family, property, inheritance. purchase and sale, and so forth are nothing but *legal relationships* ... will have his eyes open also to the *social relationships latent behind every genuinely legal clause of a statute*. Clear before his eyes will be the outlines of the counterrevolutionary law of the feudal world in its struggle with the social interests of the once revolutionary bourgeoisie, and likewise of the counterrevolutionary bourgeoisie in its struggle with the revolutionary class interest of the proletariat. (1951: 2–8, emphasis added)

Sachs and Wilson also have a conception of the 'social relationship latent behind every genuinely legal clause of a statute', but they do not refer to the theoretical problems of this position, nor to its political consequences. It is exactly the status of this latent social relationship that is addressed by E. B. Pashukanis and by a contemporary Marxist lawyer, Bernard Edelman.

In *The General Theory of Law and Marxism*, Pashukanis criticises first, bourgeois philosophical and, then, sociological and psychological theories of law. The first are rejected because, as Pashukanis says, they turn their back on reality. The second and third are rejected because they necessarily operate with 'concepts extra-juridic' (Pashukanis 1951: 115). By treating law as 'resulting from a struggle of interests, or even as a process in man's psyche', sociological and psychological theories necessarily leave the form of law at any time without theorisation.

It is clear that Pashukanis includes in the above criticism the position taken by his colleague, Stuchka. What is extremely important, however, is that Stuchka later modifies his position in such a way that Pashukanis, noticing the modification, withdraws the criticism. In a crucial footnote, Pashukanis observes that, in the third edition of his work, Stuchka introduces at the outset the proposal that law be analysed as a system of relationships of production and exchange (Pashukanis 1951: 116n). So, with this modification, law is not *the result* of an economic system – it *is* a system of production and exchange relations.

Pashukanis stresses that the modification to Stuchka's position is a great advance on his colleague's part. Instead of the specificity of the form of the law disappearing behind the events of the class struggle, Stuchka's new approach permits the analysis of law as a specific form, so that the particular production and exchange relations characteristic of the law can be given specific and concrete analysis.

Consistently with this approach, Pashukanis argues that 'capitalist society is a society of goods-producers'. He follows Marx's analyses of commodity exchange to argue that in the capitalist mode of production social relations between humans assume a material form in products of their labour and are related to each other as values (1951: 162). He then follows Marx's comment that goods cannot take themselves to market and exchange themselves: 'the social link binding persons in the process of production – materialized in the products of labour and taking on the form of elemental conformity to principle – thus requires for its realization a special relationship of persons as disposers of products'. (ibid.) In this way, Pashukanis contends, human individuals become juridic subjects and the bearers of rights over things (1951: 162–3). Pashukanis proposes that 'every sort of juridic relationship is a relationship between subjects' (1951: 160) where 'subject' is understood as the possessor and disposer of goods. This proposal forms the basis for Pashukanis' investigation of the very specific links between forms of law and forms of commodity relationships within juridical relationships.

For Pashukanis, P. Q. Hirst shows, 'law is the medium in which subjects meet in pursuit of rights', 'right is in essence the recognition of possession', and law is the product of commodity relations. For Pashukanis, law is the formal representation of subjects as possessors of products of labour who enter into the exchange of those products with one another' (Hirst 1979: 8). In this way, law becomes an 'organic outgrowth of commodity relations' and the legal subject is 'a formal representation of the economic subject in commodity society. The subjects the law represents are constituted in social relations prior to it and are its point of origin' (ibid.)

What is instructive here is that although Pashukanis' position differs crucially from Stuchka's original position in terms of the possibility of specifying the form taken by law in a capitalist mode of production, it is similar to Stuchka's later position. Stuchka and Pashukanis in the end share the view that the law registers or recognises elements outside itself, that the legal subject is a recognition of the economic subject.

In contrast to that view, Edelman argues that 'the starting point of bourgeois legal science is man, that is, man constituted as subject in law' (Edelman 1979: 107). To counter this concept, Edelman traces the case history of legal battles in the photographic and cinema industries – what might be called the 'who takes what of the image'. Using Althusser's concept of the interpellation of the subject in the real, Edelman sets up a different view of 'man'.

> Law both sanctions the relations of production within the individual – and here again is the commodity form of the subject – and reveals the imagined relation of individuals to the relations of production. Private property is 'really' the 'historical essence' of man. But this imagined relation in its turn becomes effective in practice itself. The individual lives and acts really as if private property were his 'historical essence', and the courts 'demonstrate' to him that he is right, since he has 'the right' [of private ownership]. (1979: 77)

Hirst gives an apt summary.

> Subjects are not merely recognised but constituted in the form of law. Law is an imaginary representation of an aspect of men's relation to their conditions of existence. It is in the law that men are constituted as subjects in the commodity form. Law interpellates individuals as possessive subjects. Law defines and justifies itself by referring to what it creates as a reality it gives recognition to. (1979: 8–9)

For purposes of this section, the examination of Stuchka, Pashukanis and Edelman is instructive in revealing the problems of any position which characterises law and legal practices as a perfect register, as the reliable (or, as we shall see in the next section, as even only a partly reliable) barometer of extra-legal economic struggles. Such positions are prone to the criticism that they do not explain the law at all. On the contrary, they explain it away: no specifically legal analysis is offered, because the particular form and content of law are systematically attributed not to legal but to economic relations. The form and content of law are reduced to economic determinants. In so far as the basic position adopted by Sachs and Wilson involves representing 'male economic class interests' as determining the law, their position becomes subject to this criticism.

Edelman's analysis of law is a corrective to the reductionist view, because he insists that the subject is constituted in the commodity form not independently of law but *within* it. Similarly instructive is Edelman's analysis of the part played by the courts in the reproduction of the

imagined relation of individuals to the relations of production. This
analysis marks his refusal to appeal not only to economic, extra-legal
elements but also to ideological extra-legal elements in order to explain
law and to make recommendations for changing it. It is of special interest
to the assessment of the position taken by Sachs and Wilson to note that
Edelman's theory of law rules out not only references to economic
determinants of law but also references to moral values, the presence or
absence of which are said to explain the form and content of current law
and the form and content of future law.

In their basic position. Sachs and Wilson make precisely such references to moral values, when they offer a theory of legal and feminist
struggles for a future legal system characterised by an ideology of safe-
guarding non-legal, and abiding, moral values such as equality, fairness,
and impartiality. The question of extra-legal determination and partiality
is further complicated by two considerations. It is complicated first by
what I shall show to be the indeterminate analysis which results from the
emphasis Sachs and Wilson place on *male* bias or on *male* class interest,
and secondly, by the implied claim that the intrusion in law of these
elements is wrong. The following discussion of how Sachs and Wilson use
the notion of impartiality provides an organisation of these issues.

Law and impartiality

As we have seen, a major part of the basic position which Sachs and
Wilson adopt is that legal outcomes, whether in the form of legal decisions, drafting of statutes, or whatever, which discriminate against
women cannot be satisfactorily explained by reference to the internal
principled logic of the body of the law, nor by reference to innate
masculine tendencies, nor by reference to psycho-sexual processes. The
fact that the values of male supremacy have survived so long and so well,
they claim, 'suggests the operation of forces more powerful than the mere
cultural inertia suggested by socialisation theory' (1978: 9). These forces,
Sachs and Wilson hold, are those of the economic interests of upper-
middle-class men, and they maintain it will only be through more and
more campaigns on the part of women and male feminists (out of even-
handedness to Sachs and Wilson, one presumes that such feminists are
not bound by male interests) that the effectivity of these interests will be
reduced, thereby removing gender discrimination and restoring impartiality.

Sachs and Wilson are making two separate claims here. The first is that
two opposed values, partiality and impartiality, are among the determinants of legal phenomena. The second is that partiality, when it determines legal phenomena, makes an unjustifiable appearance in those
phenomena, whereas impartiality, when it determines legal phenomena,

makes a justifiable appearance in them. Both claims are problematic. The first raises the problem of how, that is, by what mechanism, any non-legal mechanism can make an appearance in a legal context and, indeed. override properly legal elements. To complicate the problem, Sachs and Wilson suggest an enormous variety of other determinants to choose from in trying to decide why something does or does not happen in law. The second claim, I shall argue, reproduces precisely the conception of law which the researches into gender discrimination undertaken by Sachs and Wilson themselves could well have been expected to call into question.

To rebut the first claim, take any legal event. A useful example is the passing of the Law Reform (Married Women and Tortfeasors) Act 1935. This gave married women full contractual capacity. If we use the terms of the basic position adopted by Sachs and Wilson, we are faced with a perplexing range of explanations for the passing of the Act. It could be explained by reference to male partiality, though presumably that explanation would have to be supplemented by a comment on how male partiality wrongly identified what is in male interest. It could be explained by reference to the belated appearance of impartiality, gender-free impartiality, in contract law. It could be explained by reference to a rare appearance, historically speaking, on the part of female interest. It could even be explained by reference to male interest which is so efficiently hidden and so heavily, could it be cunningly, disguised that the passing of an Act which appears to be in female interest – a feminist success – is in fact, whether we know it or not, in male interest. Yet another possibility is that it was a clear victory for women, but that the women kept it quiet, so that the men thought they had won. And so on.

It is clear that the basic position adopted by Sachs and Wilson offers no way of choosing between these rival 'explanations'. The result is that the vicissitudes of legal life remain, after all these suppositions, unexplained. To put the point another way, surely the whole point of the first claim – the claim that partiality and impartiality can each appear as determinants of legal phenomena – is that we should be able to recognise their respective appearances? Yet the basic position provides us with no means for distinguishing them.

The second claim – the claim that appearances of partiality are unjustifiable and those of impartiality justifiable – is tied to how Sachs and Wilson conclude in terms of future progress towards gender equality inside and outside the legal system. The reader might well be confused at this point. Are Sachs and Wilson claiming that some moral rule or criterion exists independently of the law, a rule which is to be used for the apportionment of just rewards between parties who are to be seen as equal in law, between equal legal subjects regardless of sex? This is confusing, for to see law as 'in the end', that is, after due struggle, manifesting moral values which are somehow higher than the specific rules of law itself is to reproduce a distinctive kind of legal ideology. This is the legal ideology which claims for law the timeless and hence utopian values of Kantian metaphysical ethics. It is the legal ideology which has been opposed by Marxist positions as different as those developed by Stuchka, Pashukanis and Edelman. It is the legal ideology which has been challenged by the entire positivist legal school. It is the legal ideology which Sachs and Wilson themselves seem to invite us to reject.

What brings a certain irony to my claim that Sachs and Wilson use a concept of law which their own analyses should at least question is their ingenuous remark that the concept of impartiality is not neutral but 'value-laden' (1978: 53). How is this remark squared with their scoffing at the bourgeois values which the interested legal profession would so greedily monopolise?

Now, Sachs and Wilson might rebut this interpretation of their notion of impartiality as utopian bourgeois ideology with the retort that, on the contrary, they are discussing the very real, specific and urgent problems of discrimination between men and women in the present economic and political circumstances. But it should be noted that their claim that the law ought to be impartial as between male and female legal subjects is made at serious cost. It is made only on pain of reproducing precisely the sexist reference which their own notion of impartiality surely suggests should be eliminated from the law.[2] Ironically, a casualty of their emphasis on impartiality is the discussion and implementation of one rather important plank in their platform for the future legal recognition of past legal injustices, namely, the adoption of 'special measures to overcome the shameful discrimination of the past' (1978: 186). For Engels' argument about jurists' consciousness being unable to tolerate the idea of law as the expression of class interest could be adapted to produce the argument that jurists' consciousness is unable to tolerate the idea of the law as partial. It is hardly surprising, then, that, as Sachs and Wilson remark, 'there is at present no basis in British law for requiring affirmative action on the part of employers and educational institutions to remedy past discrimination' (1978: 204). Indeed, it would be astonishing if any such requirement did become law without a tremendous struggle.[3]

To sum up, I argue that there are two unfortunate effects of the fact that Sachs and Wilson retain the notion of the law as (in the end) impartial. First, it undermines what is potentially one of the most useful functions of the book – questioning the limits of bourgeois legal ideology. And, secondly, it presents an obstacle even to raising the issue of positive discrimination, much less implementing any such 'special measures', because the very notion of law as impartial makes it impossible for jurists either to admit to the law's partial past or to make up for it with a partial future.

To conclude, Sachs and Wilson have produced a text of undoubted value as a source book but its pertinence to the enterprise of the development of a socialist feminist analysis of law is limited by their failure to question their basic position. For the authors themselves it is perhaps a more serious criticism that, in taking elements of their basic position to be unproblematic, they have eroded the basis of one of their most serious political proposals.

2

Sexist Bias and Law

Introduction

A considerable variety of claims to the effect that law has a sexist bias can be found, explicitly or implicitly, in radical and feminist literature. This chapter is an attempt to organise the disparate debates and struggles surrounding such claims, on the grounds that some such organisation is an essential part of developing socialist feminist policies and strategies relating to, among other things, campaigns for women's rights, in or out of law. To facilitate this organisation, three models of the claim that law has a sexist bias are outlined together with an examination of some of their theoretical problems and political implications. The three models are as follows:

Model 1   Sexist bias as intervention in law.
Model 2   Sexist bias in law.
Model 3   Sexist bias as effect of law.

Before moving on to discuss these models, two preliminary points need to be made. The first concerns the scope of the claim that law has a sexist bias as examined in this chapter, and the second explains the use of models in this respect.

Bias and discrimination. At least four specific issues might be raised by the claim that law has a sexist bias. The first is the reference to bias which is found in jurisprudential analyses of natural justice. The second is the scope of the Sex Discrimination Act 1975, hereafter SDA. The third is a problem about legal notions of sex as they appear in SDA and in other areas of law. The fourth is the equal treatment of sexes under current legislation. But for the purposes of this chapter the claim that law has a sexist bias is not restricted to any one of these issues.

It is conventionally said that common law operates with a notion of natural justice, not in the sense of an abstract ideal deriving from extra-legal considerations of morality, but in the sense of a number of criteria for the conduct of trials. Alice Ehr-Soon Tay argues, for example, that the rules of natural justice 'enunciate ... the minimum standard that the

Common Law sets for all manner of hearings and tribunals, public or domestic' (1979: 84). She adds that these rules can be 'summarised in the form that no man should be condemned unheard and that every judge must be free from bias' (ibid.). It is true that two examples of sexist bias and law given under the heading of Model 1 are concerned with possible bias in judges, but the claim of Model 1 is that law as a whole has a sexist bias. Its claim is not directed specifically at the operation of the standards for a fair trial, although it might include that question. It is for this reason that no further reference will be made in this chapter to the specific question of natural justice in law.

Secondly, the point of discussing sexist bias rather than discrimination in the context of law is that discrimination too readily suggests SDA. Michael Beloff notes that SDA makes it unlawful to discriminate on grounds of sex in a limited number of fields, for example in employment and education (Beloff 1976: 1). Under the heading of Model 2, some attention is paid to the fact of this limitation, but it is enough here to point out that exclusive concern with SDA and its workings could not do justice to the generality of the claim that law as a whole has a sexist bias.

Thirdly, the claim that law has a sexist bias could suggest the problem of the ways in which SDA and other parts of law treat the notion of sex. In SDA 'woman' includes a female of any kind and 'man' includes a male of any age (Beloff 1976: 97; Oakley 1975). In a short, cryptic and sometimes sensationalist article, Terrence Walton identifies a number of problems and anomalies resulting from the failure of current sex law to recognise relations which may hold between persons who do not fall easily under the headings of female and male (Walton 1974). In failing to recognise unions not between men and women but between males and female transsexuals and between females and male transsexuals (the types of union with which Walton is most concerned), law could be said to have a sexist bias. On the other hand, in his review of current tensions within the law relating to transsexuals, Anthony Bradney notes that 'English law, interpreted literally, now specifies gender not sex; the contracting parties [to marriage] have to be male and female rather than man and woman' (1987: 352). If that argument can be sustained, it would follow that much of the sexist bias against transsexuals would be undermined. This important issue also has implications for the investigation of the law's construction of sexuality, but it remains a specific issue. It therefore receives no further attention in this chapter, which is concerned with the general question of law's sexist bias.

Fourthly, SDA recognises that, in the fields it covers, discrimination on the basis of sex can occur to the disadvantage of men as well as of women. Beloff notes this in his discussion of s. 2, Sex discrimination against men (1976: 1). Accordingly, men have successfully pursued cases under SDA.

Discrimination against men has been alleged in other areas of law too. For example, in the late 1970s, organisations such as Families need Fathers claimed that the law discriminated against unmarried fathers and in favour of unmarried mothers (cf. Campbell 1980: 11). Examples included the fact that there was no legal procedure by which the father could establish the child's paternity without the consent of the child's mother. Responding to this type of criticism, the Law Commission proposed the assimilation of the legal position of the unmarried father to that of his married counterpart (Law Commission 1979). The proposal was in turn opposed, on the grounds that the law now had a bias in favour of men at the expense of women and at the expense of the interests of children (cf. Dewar 1989: 79; Bainham 1989). In this way the claim that law has a sexist bias suggests the specific problem of the equal treatment of sexes in current legislation. Under the headings of Models 1 and 2 there is a brief discussion of what is involved in arguing that law ought to be impartial as between sexes. But, once again, important as that issue is, it is only one aspect of how law's sexist bias might be characterised.

Models. The term 'model' in this chapter does not refer to a norm but to a theoretical construction. The three models outlined here are used to disentangle some of the different theoretical and political positions which inform the claim that law has a sexist bias. I am not claiming either that these models exhaust the variety of claims made about law's sexist bias, or that any one author is exclusively identified with any one of them, or that elements of all three models do not appear in a single work. Rather, the models are intended primarily as means of exhibiting and refining some major themes in these contemporary debates.

But the main import of the claim that law has a sexist bias is certainly that law's sexist bias works to the disadvantage of women. Accordingly, the three models provide materials for the theoretical and political assessment of claims made in the light of that heuristic. They provide materials for an examination of the terms in which campaigns for women's rights are conducted. On the basis of these materials, the chapter affords conclusions about the disadvantages of some traditional ways of conceptualising women's rights and about one type of analysis which is more conducive to successful feminist interventions in law.

Model 1   Sexist bias as intervention in law

The starting point of this model is a distinction which is in fact shared by all the other models. The distinction is between a legal sphere on the one hand and a non-legal sphere on the other. The legal sphere will include the body of statute law, common law, legal practices in courts, the processes of legal education and professionalisation, and the ideologies attendant on and incorporated in those laws, practices and processes.

In contrast with this legal sphere is a non-legal sphere. This will be identified in a number of ways, such as a psychological sphere, a biological sphere, or an economic sphere. These various non-legal spheres have as their content human desires and motives, human physiology, economic interests, political institutions, or whatever.

What is distinctive about Model 1's use of this distinction is that law's sexist bias is conceptualised as the appearance or expression in the legal sphere of elements deriving from one or more non-legal spheres. The usual presumption is that these elements intervene in the legal sphere in ways which are, in some sense, improper or undesirable in that they work to the disadvantage of women.

Model 1 offers a variety of examples. First, Jerome Frank's brand of legal realism posits a non-legal, specifically pre-legal, reality comprising the conditions of childhood as analysed in a semi-psychoanalytic way. Elements of this pre-legal reality are said constantly to affect legal practices (Frank 1949: 29n). On such a view, sexist bias in law would have to be traced to the mental and moral upbringing of judges, court clerks, Law Lords, and so forth.

Secondly, Albie Sachs and Joan Hoff Wilson conceptualise sexist bias in law as the appearance in law of interests which are variously described as male, upper-class and basically economic (Sachs and Wilson 1978: 8-9).

Thirdly, early examples of Marxist theory of law identify laws as the representation of economic struggles, so that, for example, property disputes in law can be read as a map of the class struggle over the means of production and consumption. On such a theory of law, sexist bias in law could be identified as the appearance in law of women's economic status, for example their exploitation in the division of labour (cf. Stuchka 1951). This type of relation between Marxist analyses of capitalism and legal institutions on the one hand and the position of women on the other has received more focused treatment in socialist feminist literature through the use of the concept of patriarchy. So, for example, Annette Kuhn argues that patriarchy is a structure which intervenes in social relations and institutions in ways which are determined by the prevailing mode of production. Contemporary legal institutions can then be characterised as biased against women through their support for the capitalist mode of production, currently through the appropriation of property by men (Kuhn 1978).[1]

To initiate discussion of the theoretical problems and political implications of Model 1, it should be noted that, if sexist bias in law is conceptualised as intervention in this way, the appearance or expression of the intervening elements can be characterised either as inevitable or as something which can be avoided. Further, even where the appearance is seen as inevitable,. it can be characterised as proper or improper, that is, as something to be content with or as something which, even if it cannot be wholly eradicated, should at least be corrected. Frank, for example, sees the intervention of all forms of bias in law as inevitable. But he also sees it as the duty of the judge 'to act in accordance with those basic predilections inhering in our legal system (although, of course, he has the right, at times, to urge that some of them be modified or abandoned)' (Frank 1949: xx). Sachs and Wilson, on the other hand, see the intervention of male, upper-class and economic interests as something which is inevitable under present social conditions but they insist that it can and must be remedied through gender struggle (Sachs and Wilson 1978: x). And Steven Goldberg sees patriarchy as universal in the sense that there has never been a society in which hierarchical authority and leadership have not been associated with men in its political, economic, religious and social systems. He adds, however, that he is uncertain if it makes sense to describe the inevitable as unfair but that it would certainly be utopian to believe that the sort of laws which can prevent occupational discrimination can have much effect on female and male stereotypes (Goldberg 1977: 26, 178).

In fact, the conceptualisation of law's sexist bias as intervention of non-legal elements in law poses general theoretical problems regardless of whether the intervention is seen as proper or improper. Special political problems are posed, however, if the intervention is seen as improper or as a breach of law's impartiality.

The general theoretical problem stems from Model 1's use of the initial distinction between the legal and the non-legal sphere. It seems to involve a conception of law as a social practice independent of, for example, economic or political practices. On this view, it would seem, law operates – or ought to operate – according to its own devices but is subject to interference by economic or political elements. The problem here is not so much the *prima facie* absurdity of conceptualising law as insulated from other social practices. Rather it is the difficulty of identifying the mechanisms whereby the alleged economic or political elements make their appearance. This problem can be illustrated through a brief discussion, first of a legal event which has no obvious feminist interest, and secondly of one which does.

Consider, first, the outcome of appeals made in 1980 by members of the 'Operation Julie' drug gang against forfeiture orders. The five Law Lords unanimously allowed the appeal, in Lord Diplock's words, 'with considerable regret' (*The Guardian* 1980). Lord Scarman pointed out that the forfeiture provision of s. 27 of the Misuse of Drugs Act 1971, hereafter MDA, did not apply to the proceeds of the crime in question. It followed that, while the Director of Public Prosecutions was not to be required to hand back the seized property, the appellants might seek to recover the proceeds of their activities.

On Model 1, it could be argued that here is an obvious case of the intervention of the economic interests of a significant section of the population (villains) to flout the otherwise just course of law. But it could equally well be argued that a different set of economic interests is at work here, namely the economic interests of another significant section of the population – the police, to whom, it would appear, the proceeds might otherwise go. These interests find their expression not, to be sure, in the Law Lords' actual decision, but in their regret at that decision, the implication being that different circumstances could produce the successful appearance of the police interest in the shape of the reverse decision.

The difficulty of deciding between these seemingly plausible alternatives points to at least three problems with the type of analysis offered by Model 1. The first is the difficulty of ascertaining the mechanism whereby either of the rival sets of interests described in the example might manage to gain expression at the cost of the other. Indeed, even with the advantage of hindsight, it is impossible to produce a theoretically determinate account of why, in any particular instance, the one should prevail over the other.

The second problem is the difficulty of reconciling the idea that either set of interests might 'appear' with a quite different sort of explanation, one which need not invoke non-legal elements at all. In this case, for example, it could plausibly be argued that the appeal to non-legal interests is unnecessary. The outcome of the appeal can be entirely, and much less speculatively, explained by reference to the intra-legal debates relating to the confused status of conspiracy under s. 27 of MDA, an important contribution to the decision being the Law Lords' observation that conspiracy was not an offence under the Act.

The third problem is more pertinent to those versions of Model 1 that identify patriarchy as perpetually intervening in legal institutions and practices to produce sexist bias. The difficulty with maintaining this view in the case of the legal event under discussion is that no patriarchal elements, structures or interests seem to have appeared or to have been expressed at all. To salvage this version of Model 1, it would have to be argued that any such patriarchal elements must have been suppressed. But that manoeuvre fails. It fails because no mechanism for that suppression is described. So, if Model 1 is supposed to provide an explanation, a determinate account, of legal events in terms of patriarchy, but if there is no explanation for why patriarchy does not intervene in a particular case, Model 1 collapses into the vacuous claim that patriarchy intervenes in the legal sphere in all those cases but those where it has been suppressed.

Now it might be complained that I have rigged the argument against this version of Model 1 by selecting a legal event into which it is *obvious* that no patriarchal elements would intervene and in which one could hardly imagine what the patriarchal interests might be. In fact, that complaint merely restates the above problem, for the complaint itself presupposes the existence of a mechanism which determines when patriarchal elements will intervene and when they will not, and there is no specification of that mechanism. But to underline the theoretical problems of Model 1 as a model of the claim that law has a sexist bias, it may be more effective to consider a legal event into which patriarchal and gender-partial elements might be more likely to be expressed.

As Sachs and Wilson point out, the passing of the Married Women's Property Act 1882, hereafter MWPA, has been 'held out as a milestone in the march of women to equality' (Sachs and Wilson 1978: 137). Feminists had campaigned for married women to be authorised by statute to hold property separately from their husbands, and their campaign was successful. According to the conception of sexist bias as the intervention in law of male, upper-class and basically economic interests, however, the passing of MWPA must be an anomaly in the otherwise predictable march of male supremacy. Indeed, Sachs and Wilson do go on to argue that the Act did nothing 'in reality' to remove from men the control of women's property. Actually, it is this suggestion that appearances and reality are different that should ring warning theoretical bells.

For suppose that one had not already decided between the view that MWPA was a milestone in progress towards gender equality and the view that it was yet another victory for male, upper-class and economic interests. And suppose too that one retained the conceptual framework according to which such a legal event might plausibly be described in terms of the appearance or suppression of patriarchal and gender-partial elements, such as male, upper-class and economic interests, resulting in sexist bias in law. Consider the range of explanatory options: male partiality momentarily displaced by female partiality; male partiality miscalculating its long-term economic interest; a resounding feminist victory; male dominance in the legal profession briefly overcome by guilt at its history of male partiality; male partiality shrewdly calculating a mere gesture at female equality; the belated appearance of gender-free impartiality; law's timeless bias in favour of marriage over non-marital relationships, and so on. How is one to select an analysis? Sachs and Wilson claim that partiality and impartiality can each be seen as significant determinants of legal institutions and practices. But their claim provides, and can provide, no solution to the theoretical problem of producing analyses which can identify, never mind explain, the appearance either of competing interests or of the conflicting values of gender partiality and gender impartiality.

This criticism of the position adopted by Sachs and Wilson as theoretically indeterminate in the way just described can be extended to all versions of Model 1. But, as indicated in the description of Goldberg's position above, there are also important political implications of Model 1 for purposes of developing policies and strategies for the elimination of sexist bias from law. As we have already seen, the distinction between legal and non-legal spheres characteristic of Model 1 is typically accompanied by the suggestion that law, subject as it is to intervention of economic, political or other elements, ought nonetheless to be free of any such intervention. It should be impartial and disinterested in its laws, rules, procedures and decisions. The notion of sexist bias in law as breach of law's impartiality is in this way set against the notion of law as neutral, impartial and fair, and, by implication, working to the advantage of nobody on the basis of sex.

Legal commentators have often noticed, however, that the notion of law as impartial is very problematic for policies of positive discrimination, since such policies necessarily involve discrimination to the advantage of some people, usually women, on the basis of their sex. Put in this way, any reconciliation of law's official impartiality and policies of positive discrimination seems hopeless. Two attempted solutions, however, are worth mentioning.

First, it might be argued that positive discrimination is desirable as a temporary expedient to restore 'balance' to law and that, just as special measures can be introduced to cope with hitherto sexist bias against women, so those measures can be phased out as and when gender-free impartiality is established. My objection to this attempted solution is not just that it has an air of sexual millenarianism – looking forward to the day when civilisation emerges from its prehistory of sexual injustice. It is rather that the 'temporary expedient solution' for purposes of establishing impartiality 'in the long run' involves the retention of the very conception of law as impartial which Model 1's characterisation of its bias is expressly designed to challenge.

The second attempted solution is more radical. It might be argued, quite consistently with Model 1, that the intervention in law of non-legal, typically economic, political and patriarchal elements working to the disadvantage of women is so extensive that, far from attempting to remedy it through the introduction of positive discrimination – inevitably yet another expression, one way or another, of male dominance in the legal sphere – feminists should not consider law a site of feminist politics. Other feminists have spelled out the political dangers of abstaining from feminist politics in law, for example over access to state-funded abortion

services and over employment entitlements. This issue will not be tackled
directly in this section, but it is addressed in Chapter 3. One point,
however, is worth noting here. Support for the view that law should not be
a site of feminist politics can be found in the observation that, even where
positive discrimination has been allowed in law, it has not been exten-
sively used, and also in the observation that SDA has been used in ways
which positively advantage men as well as women (cf. Lester 1990).
Against the direction of this feminist critique, I would say that there is no
reason why these observations should lead to the conclusion that law
inevitably furthers male interests. They can equally well lead to less
deterministic views about the limitations of law reforms. This point can
be taken up more fully in connection with Model 2.

Model 2   Sexist bias in law

This is perhaps the simplest of the three models seeking to account for
law's sexist bias, since it focuses attention entirely on the legal sphere and
postulates no non-legal elements in terms of which it has to be explained.
Rather, the claim here is that law's sexist bias is to be conceptualised
entirely in terms of law's intrinsic discrimination against people on the
basis of sex, normally to the disadvantage of women. The restriction of
the analysis of law's sexist bias to the claim that law *per se* – in statute law,
for example, in courts, and as Loraine Gelsthorpe (1986) has discussed
the claim, in organisational practices – discriminates against women
suggests the corollary that the elimination of sexist bias from law is simply
a matter of the more or less complex processes of law reform.

On Model 2, attention is likely to be paid to the advances made by the
passing of SDA and the Equal Pay Act 1975, hereafter EQPA. It will be
conceded that SDA has removed a great many examples which could
formerly have been given in support of the claim that law has a sexist bias,
since SDA made it unlawful to discriminate against men or women in a
range of fields: employment; education; the provision of goods, services
and facilities; the disposal of premises, and advertisements. But it will also
be argued that there remains a vast area of law which is sexist. There is an
immense and growing body of cases to test the meaning of the Act (cf.
Rubenstein 1989). Cases frequently have far-reaching financial implications for the provision of services, for example where they have been
related to pensionable age (cf. *James* v. *Eastleigh Borough Council*). Furthermore, the European Court has overridden some of the exceptions in
British equality law, with the result that 'Employers, trade unions, and
public officials will now have to take it [the principle of sex equality]
equally seriously' (Lester 1990). Similarly, SDA did not make it unlawful
to discriminate in another area of private law. Tony Honoré has detailed
the unequal treatment of men and women in sex law, the most notable

and well-known example being the possibility of criminal prosecution in the case of male homosexuality but not in the case of female homosexuality (Honoré 1978: 89–100). Again, SDA did not apply to service in the armed forces. In their pamphlet for the National Council for Civil Liberties (NCCL) Maggie Rae, Patricia Hewitt and Barry Hugill alerted people to the fact that boys could volunteer for the armed services with their parents' consent when they reached the age of 16 but that girls had to wait until 17 for that particular privilege (1979: 105).

By identifying areas of law still exhibiting sexist bias, Model 2 points to the possibilities of eliminating sexist bias in law through law reforms. So, for example, it would be appropriate to investigate Honoré's proposals for the rational reform of law in connection with homosexuality. Among other things, he proposes the substitution of the phrase 'sexual act' for the phrases 'buggery', 'gross indecency', 'unnatural act', 'crime against nature', and so on. He proposes too that the present laws regarding male buggery be changed so that it would be an offence only in the case of a male over 18 with or in the presence of a male under 18. It is interesting that he makes no proposals for the introduction of similar criminal legislation for female homosexuals. He recognises this as offending against the principle of equality between the sexes, but he defends his position in three ways. First, he says people mind less about female homosexuality. Secondly, he claims women are less adventurous than men. And thirdly, he says that in any case it is not a good practice to introduce unnecessary legislation, especially in this case when female homosexuals generally have a much harder time of it than male homosexuals do (Honoré 1978: 110; cf. HMSO 1980).

Whatever reservations might be entertained about Honoré's particular proposals and his defence of them, there seems to be no serious theoretical problem either about the claim that law *per se* discriminates against women or about the status of the claim that legal reforms can remove instances of such bias from law. What is in question is the claim that the elimination of sexist bias from law can be achieved solely through law reforms. That claim can be challenged first at the level of the practical implementation of legal reforms aimed at the elimination of sexist bias from law, and secondly at the more general level of the recognition of rights in law.

With respect to the first challenge, at least four complaints have been made, mainly in connection with SDA. First, even a cursory reading of SDA reveals that it is a morass of exceptions and provisos to exceptions (Beloff 1976; iii; Byrne and Lovenduski 1978 148–65). Secondly, it is not clear how SDA relates to EQPA (Creighton 1979 175; NCC 1980). Thirdly, SDA cases have produced what commentators have taken to be farcical decisions. There is the celebrated case in which an Employment

Appeal Tribunal dismissed a woman's claim that she was sacked from her job because she was pregnant (*Turley* v. *Allders Departmental Stores Ltd*). The Tribunal argued that SDA did not apply because there was no man a pregnant woman could compare herself with as men cannot become pregnant. (As we shall see in Chapter 7, this case also has ramifications for the question of whether to present demands for women's rights in terms of equal rights or in terms of special rights.) Fourthly, although SDA was 'in spirit' aimed to help women, it has been used to the advantage of men (cf. O'Donovan and Szyszczak 1988: 38). The case of *Ministry of Defence* v. *Jeremiah* is relevant here. At the employer's factory, male volunteers for overtime were periodically required to work in certain shops and because of the dirty conditions they were paid extra. Female volunteers for overtime were not required to work in these shops. A male worker successfully claimed discrimination on grounds of sex because under SDA s. 6(2{b}) he was seen to be subject to detriment by the employer's practice. When the employers appealed, his case was upheld on the grounds that if women only had been required to work in these shops it would have been unlawful discrimination against women. It was this case that prompted Lord Denning to offer this critique of the principle of equality: 'Equality is the order of the day. In both directions. For both sexes. What is source for the goose is sauce for the gander' (Denning 1980: 245).

What these four complaints amount to is the problem of whether the attempt to remove sexist bias from law by means of legislation can do more than produce further examples of sexist bias in law, and they therefore reinforce a scepticism about the possibilities of eliminating sexist bias from law solely on the basis of law reform. This scepticism can be transformed into the second challenge to the claim that legal reforms by themselves can eliminate sexist bias from law. The challenge here can be put in the form of rhetorical questions. What grounds are there for supposing that the existence of formal equality in law guarantees non-discriminatory practices in law? What grounds are there for supposing that legal recognition of rights guarantees the enjoyment of those rights by virtue of due process of law?

But the most serious obstacle to acceptance of Model 2 as an account of law's sexist bias is that, by restricting attention to the business of legislation and court practices, it fails to recognise the complexities of social relations which pertain outside the legal sphere. So, even if it were accepted that it is possible to remove all obviously sexist legislation, it by no means follows that there are no sexist implications either of those elements of substantive law which make no reference to treating people differently on the basis of sex, or of legal practices which are not obviously sexist.

To make this point more crudely, legislation and procedures need not be overtly sexist for them to have sexist implications. For example, the Local Government Finance Bill of December 1987, in particular the provisions for poll tax capping enabling the government to set the maximum poll tax level for a local authority, is not drafted in terms which explicitly discriminate against women. But it can be shown that, even though this legislation does not directly specify women as targets, the effects of that legislation does mean that women will be more adversely affected than men by virtue of their greater dependence on benefits and rebates, their greater presence in the category of carers, and their greater presence in the category of workers in residential establishments (Local Government Information Unit 1989). To argue in this way, however, is to look for an alternative model, one which is concerned not so much with the elimination of sexist bias from law through legal reforms alone, as with the capacity of law to have effects reaching beyond the specific area of the legal sphere itself. It is this concern that provides the impetus for Model 3.

Model 3   Sexist bias as effect of law

This model of law's sexist bias identifies it not in terms of prior determinants of law, nor in terms of intra-legal practices, but in terms of law's capacity to have effects which are unfavourable to women in contexts beyond the legal sphere itself. But while the claim that it is law's effects that are the most serious for women may seem intuitively clear, more than one interpretation can be placed on that claim. (O'Donovan and Szyszczak give a useful account of some variants: Sylvia Law's 'impact analysis', Catherine MacKinnon's inequality analysis, the theory of disparate impact, and the general idea of outcome analysis. 1988: 31 47.) In this section, I distinguish two versions of Model 3. They are different with respect to the way that law is supposed to have such effects.

Model 3a claims that law actively perpetuates social conditions and attitudes which differentiate between people on the basis of sex and that it does so in a way which is systematically to the disadvantage of women. So, for example, Sachs and Wilson argue that 'in a modern society it is the law above all that defines social issues and constructs models of appropriate and inappropriate behaviour' (1978: ix, emphasis added). The argument here is that law's sexist bias, both in statute law and in the practices of the legal profession itself, is the prime determinant of social relations which are unfavourable to women. Similarly, within the general theoretical framework of the inevitable relations holding between capitalism, patriarchy and the modern nuclear family, Sheffield Rights of Women (SROW) argue that

> the law plays a role in perpetuating and reproducing patriarchal
> relations within the family (as well as in the public sphere). It does

this by legally enforcing women's economic dependence and sanc-
tioning, in varieties of ways, behaviour that does not fit with the
heterosexual, monogamous nuclear family mould (viz. lesbian
workers and prostitutes). (SROW 1980: 3)

For Model 3a, law is permanently suspect in its inevitably and systematically oppressive effects on the status, legal and general, of women.
Model 3b, however, claims that, while law can and does have unfavourable effects on the legal and general status of women, it can also have
favourable effects on it. So, for example, both the NCCL in its fights for
women's rights and SROW acknowledge that legislation has its place –
that it is worth fighting for the elimination of sexist bias from law by means
of law reform – but they claim that legislation by itself is not enough. What
is urged here is that law can be a help to women, so that attacks on
women's rights (such as the numerous attacks on women's abortion
rights) must be resisted and should not be relegated to the status of
irrelevant or peripheral site of socialist feminist politics. Further, Model
3b pursues the argument that non-sexist legislation can be seen as a
means for the creation of 'an ideological climate that is more receptive to
feminist arguments on a woman's right to choose or on equal pay and
non-discrimination etc.' (SROW 1980: 3). Similarly Tess Gill (1980)
argues the importance of giving SDA cases a public airing. In this
connection, Carol Smart has argued that redressing the balance in favour
of women, in the context of their traditional legal status as comparable to
children and animals, will not be achieved without a transformation of
basic forms of ideology and social practices. This can be done not only
through legal remedies but also through the promotion of women's
studies in criminology. She rejects all analyses which rely on 'a determinate model of female behaviour' and makes a strong plea for specific
analyses of the struggles of women in law, for example in the context of
the Abortion Act 1967 and in the context of 'the impact on women of
having their men put in prison' (Smart 1977: 176, 179). Her position,
then, is that anti-discrimination legislation must be combined with attempts to make existing discrimination obvious and visible if women's
traditional roles can even be questioned.

The strengths and weaknesses of both versions of Model 3 as models of
the claim that law has a sexist bias are varied and complex, but they both
have advantages over Models 1 and 2. They have the advantage over
Model 1 in that they do not require the postulation of non-legal elements
making theoretically incalculable appearances in the legal sphere and they
do not require the retention of the ideology of law as impartial. They have
the advantage over Model 2 in that they point to the limitations of law
reform as the sole means for the elimination of sexist bias from law and in
that they identify that elimination as something more complex than the

simple removal of archaic or 'naturally unjust' legislation. On the other hand, both versions are far from being unproblematic, and this applies particularly to Model 3a.

The weakness of Model 3a derives from the fact that, according to it, the legal sphere is conceptualised as the prime determinant or as a prime determinant of all social relations or as perpetuating a total social structure such as patriarchy. In this way, the effects of law are characterised as the prime determinant or as a prime determinant of the total movement of society. One might say that according to Model 3a there is no stopping law – it is inextricably caught up in its necessary relations with economics, politics and ideology. The problem with Model 3a can be identified by pointing to its strong theoretical similarity to Model 1, since they both conceptualise law in terms of necessary social relations. In terms of patriarchy theories, Model 1 identifies patriarchy as intervening in law, with or without the reinforcing agency of capitalism, so that law becomes the inevitable expression of patriarchy; Model 3a identifies law as inevitably reproducing patriarchy, with or without the reinforcing agency of capitalism. The theoretical difference between them is only that for Model 1 law is necessarily determin*ed* whereas for Model 3a law is necessarily determin*ing*. In that case, all the problems which were identified in connection with Model 1 for purposes of producing specific analyses of legal events and for developing a policy for the elimination of sexist bias from law must also be attributed to Model 3a.

Model 3b, however, challenges Model 3a in that it questions the inevitability of law's systematically unfavourable effects on the position of women. Instead, it emphasises the need for specific analyses of relations holding between prevailing legal and social practices.

A defender of Model 3a might immediately argue that, in denying the systematicity of the relations inevitably holding between law, capitalism and patriarchy, Model 3b is unable to produce any systematic policy or strategy for dealing with sexist bias in law. On this argument, Model 3b is forced into the position of adopting *ad hoc* and even opportunist policies, thereby weakening the force of campaigns for women's rights. Defenders of Model 3b can reply to this objection, however, by questioning both the desirability and the feasibility of developing any such systematic policy and by pointing to the political dangers of ignoring the specific nature of the different issues which are grouped together under the general heading of women's rights.

Model 3b, then, claims the advantage of permitting and encouraging the investigation of the complex relations between, for example, statute law, tribunal practices, and conditions of work. An example here is W. B. Creighton's analysis of whether it is more promising for people in different occupations to bring a case of unfair dismissal under SDA, EQPA, or the Employment Protection Act (EPA) 1975 (Creighton 1979: 175f).

Also, Model 3b allows for a complex analysis of the issues covered by the general phrase 'women's rights'. For example, Creighton gives a useful account of the conflicting views of a Working Party of the National Joint Advisory Council to the Ministry of Labour in its 1969 submission; of the Confederation of British Industry; of the Trades Union Council (TUC), and of the TUC Women's Advisory Committee over whether to retain, abolish, or extend protective legislation for women in connection with restrictions on overtime, night work, etc. (Creighton 1979: 31–7; cf. *Ministry of Defence* v. *Jeremiah*, since it too was concerned with exemption of women from 'dirty work'). Creighton describes the position taken by the TUC Women's Advisory Committee – that special measures protecting women be retained until such time as other safeguards in matters of health and welfare are established.

Creighton's account shows that the defence of 'women's rights' cannot be a universal package deal, not only because of the sheer complexity of particular issues but because the defence of women's rights in one context may well be inseparable from the struggle to improve working conditions for men as well as for women. In this respect it is also worth noting that the removal of a particular right enjoyed by women, or rather by some women, such as the right of married women until 1978 to make reduced insurance contributions, can be seen as a progressive measure because it removed the possibility of married women disequipping themselves for various forms of independence. The removal of one right becomes the assertion of another.

The considerable advantage of Model 3b, then, is that it allows for a complexity of analysis in relation to the effects of law and in relation to decisions about whether or not to fight for the legal recognition of particular rights of women. It is not encumbered with the claim that sexist bias in law must inevitably frustrate those struggles, nor with the claim that sexist bias is a permanent and inescapable feature of contemporary social conditions. In this respect, it is open to Model 3b to claim that, while special measures may be needed to overcome past and present discrimination, it follows neither that such special measures must become a permanent feature of social conditions nor that different special measures might not become desirable in future. In other words, Model 3b is not restricted to claims about the inexorability of female oppression, nor is it committed to a vision of a future non-oppressive society in which there is no need for the regulation of relations between the sexes. Rather, its emphasis on the need for specific analyses must allow the possibility of future social conditions in which regulation and legislation may still be necessary, albeit for the achievement of socialist feminist objectives that are different from those now held.

To argue the advantages of Model 3b in terms of its allowing and encouraging specific analyses of social relations and in terms of its permitting complex analyses of struggles for women's rights is not to argue in an opportunistic way. It is not a matter of starting from an existing commitment to women's issues and casting about for a theoretical analysis to accommodate or embellish that commitment. Instead, it is to argue for Model 3b as a theoretical–political framework with three main advantages.

First, as we have seen, it can escape the theoretical problems of the other models discussed in this chapter. Secondly, it can do justice to the complexity of the relations between women's issues and other socialist concerns, thereby avoiding the segregation of 'women's issues' from other socialist struggles. For example, the publication of the government Green Paper on Family Taxation in December 1980 generated considerable debate about the effects of the prevailing tax allowance system, in particular its bias in favour of married working women. But it also raised questions about how that tax system is related to the general concept of negative taxation, to the Treasury's alleged bias against cash benefits, and to government policy on inflation – three issues which are sites for the development of socialist analyses and strategies irrespective of their particular relevance to feminist politics (cf. *The Observer* 1980). Thirdly, Model 3b points to the need for a reconceptualisation of the notion of 'women's rights' which will facilitate and strengthen feminist struggles under the banner of women's rights. I put forward a candidate for such a reconceptualisation in the next section.

Rights as capabilities, capacities and competences

This chapter has adopted the device of exhibiting three models of the claim that law has a sexist bias in order to clarify the great variety of theoretical and political debates and struggles surrounding that claim. I have also argued for the advantages of Model 3b. To continue the case for Model 3b, I rework these issues by proposing a discourse for the reconceptualisation of women's rights.

I have argued that Model 3b holds out greater hope for a useful characterisation of women's rights in the context of legal institutions and practices than the other models considered. There seems little to be gained, and something to be lost, by Model 1's concept of women's rights as the intervention in law of non-legal elements such as justice or impartiality. There is even less to be gained by explaining the appearance in law of women's rights as the surprisingly successful, indeed apparently anomalous, outcome of the struggle to achieve the non-sexist upbringing and training of legal practitioners. Similarly, there are serious drawbacks to Model 2's conceptualisation of women's rights as entirely a function of their legal rights. Lastly, there is little to be gained, and much confusion, in Model 3a's conception of women's rights as the presumably miraculous effect of struggles against a total and constantly self-regenerating system of non-legal relations necessarily holding between capitalism and patriarchy.

The type of analysis of women's rights required by Model 3b, however, should be one which can satisfy at least two criteria. First, it should resist the temptation to adopt the traditional philosophical conception of rights as axiomatic or inalienable possessions owned by virtue of principles transcending prevailing social and legal conditions. That sort of conception cannot account for at least three important features of debates about rights. First, it manifestly cannot account for the fact that rights certainly can be alienated. Secondly, it cannot account for the fact, noted above, that the loss of a right may be positively desirable. Thirdly, it cannot account for the fact that the gain or loss of rights by persons or groups is a function not of any universal feature of human nature but of the criteria by which persons or groups are identified. Persons or groups have rights by virtue of their age, sex, nationality, income, physical health, or whatever. It is obviously possible to have a right by virtue of being one sort of person or a member of one sort of group, only to lose it through being identified as another sort of person or as a member of another sort of group. An example here is the fact that some women, having won the right not to be discriminated against in employment under SDA, find that their claim is frustrated or subverted by alterations in job descriptions or by practices which discriminate against them in new ways.[2]

The second criterion to be met by a Model 3b type of analysis of women's rights is that it can present an alternative to a particular group of deficiencies of the traditional conception of rights. This is the group that can be summed up simply by pointing out that 'possession' of a right is no guarantee of its enjoyment. The 'all-or-nothing' connotation of the traditional conception of a right must be replaced by an analysis which can accommodate the different and sometimes overlapping ways in which people's rights can be assigned, modified or withdrawn. Now, if it is agreed that an appeal to some abstract or transcendent notion of right is inadequate for the characterisation of women's rights, and if it is also agreed that the phrase 'women's rights' seems to invoke some such notion, then it follows that women's rights must be reconceptualised.

I argue that there are considerable advantages in a discourse which conceptualises women's rights in terms of women's capabilities, capacities and competences, and in terms of the social, including legal, practices whereby those capabilities, capacities and competences are constructed and modified. The nature of this proposal can be indicated through a discussion of three main advantages of this discourse.

First, the terms capabilities, capacities and competences are useful because they are general. They are general not in the sense of describing any sort of basic human attributes constitutive of human nature. They are general in the sense that they are used in a number of areas of law. Take 'capabilities'. Sch. 20 of the Social Security Act 1975, hereafter SSA, defines a person as incapable of self-support 'if, but only if, he is incapable of supporting himself by reason of physical or mental infirmity and is likely to remain so incapable for a prolonged period'. S. 99(I) of SSA also defines a person incapable of work as someone who cannot work 'by reason of some specific disease or bodily or mental disablement, or deemed in accordance with regulations to be so incapable'. Again, under the Trade Union and Labour Relations Act 1974. industrial tribunals have been asked to consider the capabilities of claimants in cases of unfair dismissal. A person can be dismissed if the qualifications on the strength of which that person was appointed can be shown to be dated, incidentally a matter of some interest to women hoping to return to work after a period of leave. Now consider 'capacities' and 'competences'. Legal capacity in general is defined in terms of legal power or competence. For example, the Law Reform (Married Women and Tortfeasors) Act 1935 was explicitly an act to give married women full legal capacity in contract law by repealing certain sections of the Married Women's Property Acts 1882 and 1893. Again, the Aliens Employment Act 1955 enabled aliens to be employed in a civil capacity under the Crown and it removed previous disabilities for employment in any such capacity. Finally, in cases of bigamy the spouse of the accused is a competent, though not a compellable, witness for the prosecution (Metcalfe 1962: 60–5).

Secondly, although the terms capabilities, capacities and competences are general in the sense of being recurrent in different areas of law, they are, at the same time, as the above examples show, defined in very specific ways. This specificity is a valuable corrective to the looseness of the phrase 'women's rights' in two ways. First, for purposes of developing a feminist politics of law, these terms can help to focus attention on the ways in which specific women's struggles can be brought to the legal sphere. They can do this by directing campaigns to the task of formulating desired extensions or modifications of women's capacities or, which may come to the same thing, desired removals of disabilities. It is easy to see how the two types of incapability described in SSA could be modified so as to take account of the specially difficult circumstances of women. Secondly, since the specification of capacities is inseparable from the specification of restrictions and limitations, this vocabulary can help to clarify the ways in which the different criteria by means of which women are defined in law can have the effect of assigning, modifying or withdrawing capacities and competences. A good example here would be the way in which the

MWPA 1882 removed the disability of married women to own property independently of their husband but, in the event of a dispute about domestic support, restricted a wife's capacity to secure a remedy through the magistrate's court until after the couple had separated.

The third advantage of the discourse of capabilities, capacities and competences over the general phrase 'women's rights' relates to the fact that, although these terms are both general and specific legal concepts as illustrated above, they are also central to a number of important contemporary debates about law. For example, the mental and physical capacities deemed necessary for *mens rea* (the mental state which is a necessary condition of criminal responsibility) have been much discussed, in particular with respect to the assessment of legal practices in the light of desirable social consequences (Hart 1968: 218). Smart has shown the importance of those debates to cases of rape and 'delinquent' sexual behaviour, since they draw attention to the grey area between law and morality. These debates are also pertinent to her note about the sex-specific offence of infanticide (Smart 1977: 124, 128, 190n.2).

Misinterpretations

What is the status of the proposal outlined above for the reconceptualisation of women's rights? To clarify its status, I want to reject three possible misinterpretations.

First, theoreticians hostile to the proposal might be tempted to interpret it as the claim that the traditional conception of a right as an abstract and inalienable moral possession owned independently of prevailing social conditions is to be reduced in a strict philosophical sense to statements about social agents' capabilities, capacities and competences. That interpretation would be attractive to opponents of the proposal, because it is so obvious that the reduction is not, and more importantly cannot, be successful. It cannot be successful because the traditional conception of a right as abstract and inalienable typically includes the claim that such a right cannot be reduced to any other sort of analysis, such as the analysis of prevailing economic conditions. The proposed reduction of an entity which is characterised *ab initio* as irreducible is clearly doomed, and it would be absurd to attempt it (cf. Arnold 1978).

The second possible misinterpretation is that the proposal is a programme for the redescription of all clearly defined legal rights, such as right of appeal on a point of law against a decision of an industrial tribunal as provided by s. 88 of EQPA. But if legal rights are clear, there is no point in redescribing them. There might be a political case for changing them, and it might be at that point that the discourse of capabilities, capacities and competences would be useful, just as it might be useful in cases where legal rights turn out not to be clear after all. This point leads into the third possible misinterpretation.

The proposal might be taken as the denial that campaigns for 'women's rights' have political force, and as the instruction that feminists should forthwith abandon the phrase. But I do not deny that such campaigns have political force, although it may not always be the political force for good that feminists want. And even if I thought that my recommendation would have any effect, I would not necessarily argue for abandoning the phrase itself. Rather, I am proposing that the focus of feminists' campaigns under the banner of women's rights must be off the traditional concept of transcending and inalienable rights and on the analysis of prevailing social and legal conditions.

To sum up, if feminist campaigns are to be successful in the broad context of law, either in resisting attacks on existing rights or in establishing new rights within the context of law, they require the formulation of specific objectives which are at least potentially assimilable into law. As I have emphasised, the discourse of capabilities, capacities and competences lends itself very well to these tasks. It can help to focus attention on the complex task of identifying socialist feminist objectives and the strategies which are calculated to achieve them. I do not claim that adopting the discourse of capabilities, capacities, and competences is the only way to reconceptualise women's rights. I do argue that some sort of reconceptualisation is necessary if feminist campaigns under the banner of women's rights are not to be obstructed by the use of traditional concepts of rights. The dangers of these transcendent concepts of rights are illustrated in the next chapter in relation to feminist abortion campaigns.

3

Legal Recognition of a Woman's Right to Choose

This chapter focuses on the question of whether the pursuit of feminist objectives is helped or hindered if feminist demands are expressed in terms of individual rights, such as a woman's right to choose. I begin to answer this question by examining the view that feminist campaigns to defend and improve abortion legislation have been bourgeois and reformist. I argue that this criticism presents an over-simple analysis both of legal struggle in general and of legislation governing the provision of abortion facilities. But I also argue that the attempt to transcend the dichotomy between reform and revolution by invoking 'a woman's right to choose' is equally problematic. This is because the slogan tends to involve an appeal to an absolute right and to give priority to moral values which cannot be translated into legislation. This has the effect of shifting attention away from engagement in legal struggle that is conducive to the realisation of feminist demands. I conclude, therefore, that there is a need for a reassessment of pro-choice campaigners' use of the slogan 'a woman's right to choose'.

Reform, revolution and legal struggle

It is commonplace now to make a comparison between classical Marxist theories of law and certain feminist theories of law. As we saw in Chapter 1, for classical Marxism, the economic interests of the bourgeoisie are formed independently of law but find expression in it. Legislation, legal practices in courts and tribunals, and the attitudes of legal personnel are accordingly seen as the mirror, the representation, of economic class interests, and the legal sphere is seen as a major instrument of the bourgeois state's continuing exploitation of the proletariat. Such theories are increasingly under attack for essentialism, the meaning of essentialism here being the type of reductionism whereby legal relations are said to be reducible to economic relations. Sometimes they are criticised on the grounds that empirical evidence shows that law does not systematically work to the disadvantage of the proletariat. Sometimes they are criticised on the grounds that they are incapable of specifying the mechanism/s by means of which general economic structures can intervene in the specific operations of law.

Feminists have challenged classical Marxist theories for their failure to identify the specific forms of oppression experienced by women. To remedy this deficiency, feminists have developed the concept of patriarchy to explain gender oppression, and this concept has been engaged both to complement that of class and as a substitute for it. Michèle Barrett has noted that 'just as some socialists have argued that the state would "wither away" in the transition to communist society, so some feminists have viewed the state as an instrument of state control that would fall away with the destruction of patriarchy' (1980: 245). Following this type of analysis, law (as a major instrument of state administration) is seen as the expression of state interests and as a key mechanism for the reproduction of patriarchal oppression.

These are complex theoretical debates, and they are typically sustained in academic books and journals. But they are not academic in the abusive sense of the word. This is because reductionist theories of law can result in conflicting views about the way political objectives and strategies ought to be worked out. For example, Bernard Edelman has described the way in which Marxist conceptions of law as the juridical outgrowth of economic relations between classes, as the perfect register of all changes in social relations, leads to the view that class struggle can be transferred to the legal sphere and that revolution can be achieved within the law (1978: 14–15). In contrast, these same Marxist conceptions of law as systematically reproducing non-legal forms of exploitation have been taken to mean that legal activity is necessarily reformist. On this view, law has to be rejected as a site of class struggle because the outcome of legal activity is a foregone conclusion – the further exploitation of the proletariat.

Feminists have been alert to this dilemma. The history of women's struggles for formal legal rights shows that even where women's legal position has been improved there is no corresponding, and certainly no automatic, improvement in their social and economic position (cf. Brophy and Smart 1981: 3). There is little basis, on this view, for the notion that women's struggles can confidently be transferred to the legal sphere. Indeed, some feminists have explicitly rejected those forms of 'liberal feminism' that equate women's struggles with the struggle for women's equality within the law (cf. Eisenstein 1981: 194).

But scepticism about the usefulness of securing formal legal rights for women has also been presented in terms which are reminiscent of the classical Marxist dichotomy between reform and revolution. This is clearly seen in debates which have taken place on abortion legislation. For example, in her description of reactions to the setting up of the National

Abortion Campaign (NAC) in 1975 to fight James White's anti-abortion bill, Lynne Segal notes that many women were suspicious of the national structure of NAC and that they 'objected to its main focus for activities being that of lobbying MPs, seeing this as reformist' (1979: 174). Similarly, Victoria Greenwood and Jock Young attack the reformist policies of the Abortion Law Reform Association (ALRA) in the belief that 'the struggle for a woman's right to control her own fertility is constantly in danger of being co-opted by the state. Legislation even when it embodies progressively increasing concessions is categorized and implemented in such a fashion as to suit ruling class interest' (Greenwood and Young 1976: 129). And Kate Marshall mounts an even more vehement attack with the claim that 'through NAC the WLM [Women's Liberation Movement] made its peace first with Parliament, and then with the Labour Party. NAC allowed the WLM to re-orient itself in a reformist and moderate direction' (1982: 113).

The relegation of legal reforms to the status of political reformism is dependent on a dichotomy between reformist and revolutionary politics. That dichotomy is a feature of reductionist Marxist theories of law. Just as there have been criticisms of classical Marxism for its reduction of law to economic struggles, however, so feminists have drawn attention to the inadequacies of feminist theories that reduce law to a struggle against patriarchy. As I argued in the two preceding chapters, reductionist theories are incapable of specifying the means by which allegedly universal structures such as patriarchy and male economic interest can intervene in the complex workings of the law (cf. Adlam 1979: 88f). Carol Smart has shown that, although legislation governing tax, social security, and divorce can be adduced in support of the view that law overtly and covertly serves the interests of patriarchy, close inspection of the law on custody of children shows that it has been to the advantage of women by removing the power men once had over them through their children (1981: 42). More generally, Barrett abandons the reductionist theory of law, whilst retaining a view which puts the onus of proof on the anti-feminists. She argues that 'the state is not a pre-given instrument of oppression' but that, on the contrary 'political and ideological processes carry considerable weight in the construction of women's oppression' (1980: 246).

It is important to emphasise one corollary of these critiques. Reductionist theories of law involve the consignment of legal reforms to the *general* category of political reformism. It follows that to subsume legal reforms under the general heading of 'what suits the ruling class' or of 'what suits men' is effectively to rule out the possibility that some legal reforms are of greater significance than others to socialists or to feminists: a reform is a reform is a reform. But I would argue that there are reforms and reforms. Moreover, feminists should set aside the conception of legislative measures as necessarily limited by their reformist character. Instead, feminists could benefit from seeing legislative measures as sites of struggle which themselves have the effect of shifting debate and practice on to ground more amenable to the achievement of feminist objectives.[1]

This position requires careful analysis of specific legal issues. To support this position in the next section, I examine three legal issues to do with abortion. But before I analyse those examples, I would emphasise that my position is not exhausted with consideration of a particular topic. Once reductionist theories of law are abandoned, there is no substitute for thoroughgoing analyses of legal and related practices in whatever field has been identified as important for the realisation of objectives. As preceding and subsequent chapters make obvious, my position can be exhibited through an examination of a variety of topics, all of which I think are important for feminists. Sometimes these subjects provoke definite feminist responses, sometimes the feminist interest is difficult to determine. Examples here are where legislation which might at first sight appear to be consistent with long-term feminist objectives, but which constitute a serious threat to significant numbers of women in the short term. A case in point is the Matrimonial and Family Proceedings Act 1984 which reforms the law on the financial consequences of divorce, a reform which may appear to serve the feminist objective of women's financial independence of men but which, with present levels of unemployment and preferences of employers, will mean hardship for many divorced women. The complex calculations necessary to the decision whether or not to resist such a reform have to be based on careful scrutiny not only of current and proposed laws but also of the ways in which the courts have interpreted existing law and would be likely to interpret the proposed reforms. Feminists should resist the accusation that engagement with such legal issues is reformist. That criticism is based on the untenable claim that legislation and legal practices are uniformly oppressive of women, an over-simple view of the significance of elements in the legal sphere for the achievement of feminist objectives. To back up that claim, I can now turn to three legal issues about abortion.

Three legal issues

Contraceptive or abortifacient? Early in 1981, a group of pro-choice campaigners in the medical and legal professions attempted to clarify the question of whether the intra-uterine device (IUD) is a method of contraception or an abortifacient device. They urged the Director of Public Prosecutions (DPP) to prosecute a doctor for inserting a coil into a woman's uterus. Their aim was to get a ruling that the Abortion Act 1967, hereafter AA, is not concerned to protect the developing fetus from the moment of conception. It appears that the DPP has still declined the invitation to prosecute (cf. Clarke 1989: 161).

Participation in medically induced abortions. In 1980, the Royal College of Nursing (RCN) brought a case to establish the duties of nurses and midwives who were asked to assist doctors in inducing abortions by the infusion of the hormone prostaglandin. The Law Lords reversed the Appeal Court ruling that nurses should not be called on to assist with non-surgical abortions; they ruled that, even if the supervising doctor is not present, nurses who take part in medically induced abortions are protected by the Act. Following the Law Lords' decision, the Secretary of State for Social Services lifted the suspension on a department circular. The circular had stated that: 'provided the registered medical practitioner personally decides upon and initiates the process of medical induction and throughout remains responsible for it, it is not necessary for him to perform each and every action which is needed for the treatment to achieve its intended objectives.'

Forms for the notification of termination. In March 1981, the Department of Health and Social Security issued new forms for the notification of termination of pregnancy. These forms were brought into effect by statutory instrument, a measure by which a minister may make subordinate legislation without the matter being discussed in Parliament. The old forms had included space for non-medical grounds to be given for the termination of a pregnancy. The new forms did not. Professor Peter Huntingford and another gynaecologist were referred to the DPP for writing 'none' in the section which in the new form required the main medical reason for the termination. The DPP has not so far prosecuted.

Feminist perspectives

What is the significance of these three legal issues for feminists, especially those feminists who are not prepared to rule out legal activity for the pursuit of feminist objectives?

The importance of the first legal issue has been brought out by Victor Tunkel. He has shown how new developments in medical science in the field of post-conception methods for interrupting pregnancy could have the effect of bringing those methods within the range of criminal law, namely, the Offences against the Person Act 1861, to the extent that these methods are effective after the moment of fertilisation and possibly after implantation too. Tunkel notes that s. 8 of the 1861 Act does not refer to abortion but to attempts to induce miscarriage. Further, although medical literature had frequently contained references to post-fertilisation methods of contraception in the years leading up to 1967, AA makes no mention of them, thereby making it more difficult for family planning to avoid the provisions of s. 58 (Tunkel 1977: 9f).

In fact, the first issue may now be something of a dead letter as far as law is concerned. The absence of prosecution now looks less like indecision than a change in the medico-legal climate. IUDs have been designated 'interceptives' or contragestives', in recognition of the fact that they may not prevent conception but that they may interfere with subsequent implantation; this designation has ensured that they are not prohibited or governed by Criminal Code abortion provisions (Dickens 1985: 259). Against that, Tunkel's point is that mechanical methods may be effective as interference not only with implantation but also with post-implantation.

These developments are important to feminists for at least two reasons. First, the blurring of the distinction between abortion and contraception raises the question of whether the campaign for a woman's right to choose can continue to be a single issue. The Women's Reproductive Rights Campaign (WRRC) has argued that abortion is not an isolated event in women's lives but has to be related to women's experience of policies and practices regarding, for example, sterilisation and the use of controversial forms of contraception such as Depo Provera (WRRC 1983: 26). On this view, abortion is one of a number of interrelated reproductive rights, and whilst an attack on any one of them must be resisted, that resistance must be conducted within a framework which recognises the complexity of women's needs in the sphere of reproduction. If, in the case under discussion, the DPP had decided to prosecute and the prosecution was successful (in the sense that the IUD was deemed an abortifacient device), it would have constituted both a disastrous attack on the availability of contraception and a threat to progressive interpretations of AA.

The second reason for feminist concern over this issue is vividly expressed by Tunkel:

> The spectacle of a hopelessly antiquated law being marched over, unnoticed, by the forces of science and medicine is not an edifying one. It is not made better by the possibility, however remote, of their tripping on it. The fact that the law is seldom, if ever, invoked against Family Planning [FP] is not the point. There is no certainty that it will remain quiescent in all countries [sc. those countries whose abortion law is derived from s. 58], especially when some new method of FP arouses public interest and debate. But anyway, a law which is disregarded, whether from policy, apathy, ignorance or any other cause, remains a law and a potential hindrance. If it is not intended to hinder it should not be couched so as to threaten to. If it is expressed in antiquated terms of uncertain breadth, it should be restated to suit modern needs. (Tunkel 1977: 18)

Tunkel is clearly advocating the drafting of new legislation which is more in keeping with medical advances, but he is also drawing attention to a persistent problem which feminists have to face. That problem is the impossibility of anticipating the ways in which old legislation can be raked up by lawyers and pressure groups to restrict access to contraception and abortion. Further, even where new legislation is drafted and brought into effect, it is impossible to anticipate the outcome of cases which are brought to test the meaning of parts of that legislation. This is brought out clearly in the second of the three legal issues, which concerns participation in non-surgical terminations. Commenting on the 1980 RCN case, Andrew Martin suggests that the RCN 'could only lose', since AA was not designed to deal with abuses of the kind at issue. Unlike Tunkel, Martin believes that the law cannot be made responsive to medical practices and that both lawyers and legislators often make the mistake of trying to compress within a legal framework the complexity of clinical concepts. He believes that 'tampering with the law', as the RCN did, is dangerous (Martin 1980: 9).

Against Martin's opinion, however, it should be said that to many of the people observing the progress of the RCN case, the outcome was by no means obvious – in the end the Law Lords reversed the Appeal Court's ruling by a majority of one. Indeed, the issue was still unresolved in spring 1990, when the Social Services Select Committee finished taking evidence on clause 4 of AA which states that no person shall be under any duty to participate in treatment under the Act to which they have a conscientious objection (WHRRIC 1990: 19).

For feminists, the RCN case was one of considerable importance. This is because it raised the general question of competence to perform abortions. S. 1. of AA makes it clear that medical termination of pregnancy is not unlawful when the pregnancy is terminated by a registered medical practitioner if two registered medical practitioners have authorised the termination in accordance with the specified criteria. Feminists have criticised this aspect of AA on the grounds that it preserves the hegemony of the male-dominated medical profession. Michèle Barrett has noted the complaint that 'because doctors have the technical skills to perform abortions ... they are often held legitimately to control the decision as to whether a woman should have an abortion or not' (1980: 168). Similarly, Victoria Greenwood and Jock Young advocate the breaking of the medical monopoly, not on the ground that medical expertise is irrelevant but on the grounds that 'doctors should be used as technicians not as moral arbiters' (1976: 132-3). Whilst the RCN's case did not directly test the meaning of the term 'registered medical practitioner', Lord Diplock commented, in support of the Law Lords' ruling, that 'the exoneration from guilt is not confined to the registered medical practitioner by whom a pregnancy is terminated ... It extends to any person who takes part in the treatment' *(The Guardian* 1981). Had the Law Lords upheld the Appeal Court's ruling, it would have been a setback to feminists' hopes that trained personnel other than registered medical practitioners might, in the future, lawfully terminate pregnancies.

There is another feature of the RCN's case which is important for feminists assessing such legal issues. When the case came to the Appeal Court, Lord Denning commented that if the Department of Health and Social Security (DHSS) wanted nurses to terminate pregnancies, the proper procedure was to go to Parliament and not to use departmental circulars. In this case, the use of administrative measures was clearly consistent with improved availability of abortion services. But, in the case of the new forms for the notification of termination, the third of the three legal issues under discussion, the use of administrative law was attacked by pro-choice campaigners. Alert to the ways in which relatively inaccessible administrative matters can have momentous effects on medical and legal practices without the parliamentary debate that can be expected to accompany substantial legislative changes, certain Labour MPs and pro-choice groups resisted the introduction of the new forms on the grounds that they went against the spirit (if not the letter[2]) of AA.

Now, it might be argued that the new notification forms left the spirit of the Act untouched, since the forms for the authorisation of terminations remained in use. These allowed doctors to take account of the woman's 'actual or reasonably foreseeable environment' in determining whether the continuance of the pregnancy would involve the mental or physical health risks specified in subsection (l) (a) of s. 1. But pro-choice campaigners were concerned that the absence of reference to the 'environment clause' on the notification forms could influence the willingness of doctors to use that clause when authorising terminations. Resistance to the new forms was situated within a concern that they heralded the removal of the basis for any future campaign for independent social grounds for abortion. Resistance was also situated in a concern at the ever-present tendency of legal and medical practitioners to treat women as legal subjects defined predominantly in terms of medical criteria rather than in terms of their social and economic situation.

This is not to say that medical matters, such as development of new and safer medical techniques, are of no interest to feminists. Rather, it is to draw attention to the way in which medical practices relating to abortion, and the legal controls to which they are subject, are crucial conditions of the achievement of other feminist objectives, such as financial independence from men and improved access to such job opportunities as exist. As Madeleine Simms has argued: 'abortion has come to be seen not only as a crucial issue in preventive medicine, but also as a critical indicator of women's status in society' (1981: 183).

From this perspective, the three legal matters described in this section are not side-issues. They are not about small points of law to be pursued only when more radical struggles permit the release of scarce campaigning resources. The fact that the outcome of such legal struggles can turn on the interpretation of a single phrase in a subsection of an act passed in another century[3] should not be seen as justifying the accusation that vigilance over detail is 'legalistic', reformist, and a substitute for 'real action'. It is ironic, then, and a matter of serious concern, that one of the most successful feminist campaigns – the campaign for a woman's right to choose – should have been criticised for being reformist in this way, and I turn to this issue now.

A woman's right to choose

Recognition of the connection between women's access to abortion and contraceptive services and their unequal economic and social status undoubtedly played a large part in attracting and informing the support for the National Abortion Campaign (NAC) of men and women in unions, in the Labour Party, and in left-wing groups. Since 1975, re-peated attempts to restrict the availability of abortion by legislative means have been resisted on the grounds that, as Simms has put it: 'no true state of equality can exist for women in a society which denies them freedom and privacy in respect of fertility control' (ibid.).

But it is precisely that sort of appeal to the values of freedom and privacy – an appeal which is encapsulated in the campaign slogan 'a woman's right to choose' – that has given rise to misgivings over, and in some cases outright hostility towards, some of the terms in which pro-choice campaigns have been conducted. It has been argued that slogans such as a woman's right to choose, the right to control one's own fertility, and the right to determine one's own sexuality accentuate the notion of a right as inhering in an individual, as the moral entitlement of an individual human being which is possessed independently of prevailing social con-ditions. Jane Marshall and others supporting the establishment of WRRC wrote that 'some of us feel we have become complacent about what "A Woman's Right to Choose" means. "Choice" suggests being able to pick from an ideal set of options' (WRRC 1983: 26). In terms of political philosophy, this means that the concept of free choice is more easily situated in the ideology of liberal individualism, and the right to control one's own body is more easily placed within the ideology of the private citizen resisting the morally illegitimate encroachment of the bourgeois state into private matters, than within the ideology of solidarity and collective decision-making characteristic of much socialist and feminist thinking. Following this sort of argument, Kate Marshall states that the demand for a woman's right to choose implies that what is at issue is an individual problem, not a social one; invoking the rights of the individual is to rely on a concept of rights which is 'at the centre of bourgeois ideology' and is therefore 'a step towards the ruling class' (1982: 113).

A more complex position is advanced by Greenwood and Young. It too is presented in terms of the dichotomy between reform and revolution – between, on the one hand, campaigns for reformist legislation and, on the other, struggle for the transition to a socialist society in which women achieve genuine equality. From this perspective, one might expect them to attack any slogan which appeals to what might appear to be bourgeois rights. In fact, they propose that women's right to control their own fertility be demanded as an absolute right (Greenwood and Young 1976: 112). They suggest, furthermore, that the demand for this absolute right and for genuine freedom of choice can transcend reformism.

To develop this intriguing argument, Greenwood and Young describe the struggles leading up to the 1970 New York State legislation whereby abortion was made legal on the request of the patient, on condition that she was not more than fourteen weeks pregnant and on condition that the operation was performed by a licensed physician. They note the American feminists' complaint that 'despite the liberalization, the medical profession still monopolized the practice of abortion' (Greenwood and Young 1976: 99). They also note, with implied sympathy, the feminists' argument that the only solution to this problem was to decriminalise abortion and to place it in the hands of self-help groups. In discussing the limits of reformism in this country, they indicate support for ALRA's campaign for abortion up to twenty-four weeks, on the grounds that achieving this demand could lead to a situation where there was effectively no time limit at all. In such a situation, they say, it would be relatively easy to call for legal acceptance of no time limits.

In making these points, Greenwood and Young clearly underestimated the tenacity of anti-abortion groups in seeking to reduce the time limits for lawful termination (cf. Clarke 1989: 167f). But optimism is not the most interesting thing about their position. What is striking is the dilemma which their position creates. This is the dilemma that, on the one hand, law is a fundamental threat to women's abortion rights and, on the other, it is correct to campaign within the legal sphere. The dilemma is compounded by the recognition that such legal campaigns can deflect campaigners' attention from the fact that reformist measures undermine the whole basis of women's struggles (Greenwood and Young 1976: 136).

Greenwood and Young attempt to resolve this dilemma in two ways. First, they propose that the abortion debate can be directly related to the limited alternatives open to women in prevailing social conditions and that, by linking the debate to the eleven demands of the Working

Women's Charter (WWC), the debate can be 'widened in terms of general demands put forward from a socialist perspective' (Greenwood and Young 1976: 139). Secondly, in their discussion of the inability of the Society for the Protection of Unborn Children to recognise the fundamental problems faced by all women and by the working class (a criticism which they also make, though less severely, of the pro-choice campaigners), they argue for a welding of free abortion on demand to the full range of social changes necessary for genuine freedom of choice. Only in this way, they claim, is it possible to transcend reformism.

There are at least two problems with this position.[4] In the first place, simply widening the abortion debate in the manner suggested in no way removes the reformist label as Greenwood and Young themselves would attach it. Among other things, the WWC argues for a national minimum wage, compulsory day release for 16- to 19-year-olds in employment, free state-financed child-care facilities, and an increase in child benefits. All these measures would require legislation. But Greenwood and Young argue that legislation, even where it has been to the advantage of the labour movement, is subject to pressures which are 'undeniably shaped by ruling class interests' (Greenwood and Young 1976: 98). Whilst they claim that they reject simplistic analyses according to which significant legislative gains are dismissed by the left as 'the direct expression of ruling class interests', their strategy for coping with the reform/revolution dilemma presupposes precisely the separation of the interests of the working class and those of the ruling powers that is characteristic of that dilemma. This is because, for them, legislative measures, however wide they may be, still have to be viewed with suspicion as shaped by ruling-class interests.

The second problem is that to appeal to a woman's right to choose as an absolute right is indeed to transcend the reform/revolution dichotomy, but that it does so for reasons and with effects which should make the manoeuvre unacceptable to feminists. An absolute right is one which is possessed independently not just of prevailing social conditions but of any social conditions whatsoever. Once a woman's right to choose is situated in the sphere of absolutes, there is a necessary and unbridgeable gap between it and any possible social conditions, including legal practices. It can have no purchase on debates about whether abortion should be lawful up to twenty-four, or twenty-eight, or any number of weeks. Greenwood and Young have replaced the notion of a woman's right to choose as a right which is appropriately demanded only of a bourgeois state with the notion of an absolute right which can be enjoyed in no state at all. So, when Ruth Holley writes that 'nowhere do women have the absolute right to control their own fertility, the absolute right to decide whether or not to have children' (1980: 28), the statement has to be treated not as grounds for initiating a campaign, but as a truism. This is because by definition there is nowhere 'in the real world' that absolute rights can be enjoyed. It is merely a corollary of this general argument to point out that absolute rights cannot be enjoyed in a socialist state.

Certainly, some of the pro-choice campaigners have argued for a shift away from abstract moral debate, such as whether fetuses have rights. Their argument is pitched at the level of strategy – the avoidance of debates which suit the purpose of the anti-abortion pressure groups. Now, there is no denying that to be drawn into a process of pitching claim and counter-claim at the level of absolute rights is to risk defeat in public debate, but the full implications of that observation need to be drawn out. Even if that debate were won, it would indeed be a moral victory. But it would be a moral victory which runs the risk of being only a moral victory. For to continue to claim a woman's right to choose as an absolute right, which is possessed independently of any prevailing or even foreseeable social conditions, is to remove the rationale for the formulation of strategies directed to the improvement of existing social conditions. The sphere of absolute rights by definition transcends that of social and legal rights. Consequently, the absolute right of a woman to choose cannot be reduced to a list of legal rights. The result is that those involved in drafting and interpreting abortion legislation can continue to go about their work secure in the knowledge that the legal sphere is incapable of recognising and giving substantive expression to rights which fall outside not just the legal sphere but also any set of social conditions.

What is the force of this critique? Does it carry any clear message for the strategy of feminist campaigns to improve women's situation in relation to abortion? These questions invite two opposed responses. For convenience I shall call the first the rejectionist response, and the second the retentionist response. Feminists taking the rejectionist position will propose that the appeal to a woman's right to choose should be abandoned and the slogan dropped from the campaign. On this view, feminists should not clutter up their campaigns with abstract philosophical nonsense about rights which can never be given any practical expression. Instead, efforts might be directed to finding campaign slogans which can be related to 'the real world'. But, retentionist pro-choice campaigners might reply, this response leaves out of account the undoubted success of uniting men and women of otherwise disparate political persuasions to resist attacks on the AA and to work for further improvements to facilitate access to abortion facilities. With all its faults, the notion of a woman's absolute right to choose should be retained as an ideological weapon, as a statement of principle the acceptance of which is crucial to the achievement of a moral climate within which feminist objectives can be achieved.

There is much to be said for the rejectionist response. The invocation of an absolute right smacks of utopianism and it is hardly conducive to the precise formulation of politically and legally realisable objectives to improve women's social position. There are, moreover, other slogans – 'free abortion on demand' and 'every child a wanted child' – which have been used in feminist campaigns to improve access to contraceptive and abortion facilities and which do not have the same absolutist connotation.

To justify retention of the slogan, however, feminists might make a number of points about the use of slogans for political purposes. The retentionist position might begin with the observation that it would be foolish to suggest that, to be successful, a campaign has to be governed by ideologically pure slogans which are a perfect match for all of the campaign's short- and long-term aims. On the contrary, when Marshall complains that even anti-abortionists signed the NAC petition for a woman's right to choose because they believed in individual choice (1982: 113–14), NAC activists might well congratulate themselves on having adopted such a politically and ideologically sophisticated slogan and on having understood the complex ways in which the climate of popular opinion could be exploited to yield support for feminist struggles. Clearly, the fact that there can be no legal recognition of a woman's right to choose is no obstacle to people *believing* in the possibility of securing absolute rights. And it would not be the first time that a campaign had the support of people who might well be hostile to it if its longer-term goals were spelled out in detail. Calculation of this sort might make it perfectly sensible to retain the slogan, with all its absolutist connotations, on the understanding that, even if the principle cannot be realised in practice, it nonetheless serves to orientate public opinion towards the reception of those more advanced objectives which pro-choice campaigners have in mind.

The difficulty with this retentionist strategy is not so much that it is vulnerable to the charge of political cynicism as that it presupposes the ability to distinguish between support for pro-choice campaigns which acknowledges the limitations of the notion of a woman's right to choose, and support which is given precisely because that right is presented as an absolute one. There is no reason to suppose that activists in pro-choice campaigns are immune to the undoubted attractions and comforts of belief in absolute rights. Indeed, as noted above, some feminist pro-choice campaigners do appeal to a woman's absolute right to choose, not just when engaged in winning over public opinion, but also when debating with other campaigners.

There are other dangers in the retentionist response. These are serious for those feminists who are not prepared to abstain from legal struggle for the pursuit of their objectives. First, if it is accepted that an absolute right

can have no expression in actual or foreseeable social and legal conditions, then it is a natural, if not a logical, inference that the only social
conditions compatible with that absolute right are ones in which there is
no relevant legislation at all. In the case of abortion, this would mean not
merely the decriminalisation of abortion but also its deregulation. There
would be no regulations governing the organisation and distribution of
abortion services, no controls over the technical competence of persons
performing abortions, and no regulations on safety standards.

But to demand deregulation, effectively the abolition of all restrictions
on the availability of abortion, makes nonsense of the demand made by
almost all pro-choice campaigners, the demand for mandatory provision
of abortion services under the National Health Service. It makes nonsense
of that demand because it is inconceivable that mandatory provision of
this kind could be achieved without legislation and hence without some
forms of restriction, such as rules governing hours of work or follow-up
counselling. Furthermore, if a woman's right to choose is interpreted to
mean deregulation, it immediately follows that women seeking and
getting abortions would have no *legal* rights, and no legal *redress*, since
abortion would be unconnected with questions of legality. Few feminists
would be prepared to countenance such a reactionary situation.

The second danger of the retentionist position, even where it is not
associated with demands for deregulation, is that appeals to a woman's
right to choose are notoriously vague in their meaning. It may well be the
case that appealing to that right is a politically effective way of opening the
attack on existing legislation and related medical practices, and that it is a
politically effective way of resisting a particular set of proposals for reform
which are not strong enough. But, for the reasons given above, an
absolute right cannot be reduced to any set of concrete proposals. Simply
to assert a woman's right to choose is to skate over the complex business
of working out specific proposals and strategies for improving abortion
and related provision. In this way, the slogan 'a woman's right to choose'
can constitute an obstacle to serious engagement with the complex and
detailed legal issues, such as the three I described earlier in this chapter,
which often have direct effects on the chances of achieving feminist
objectives.

Conclusion

I have suggested that feminists should resist attempts to consign feminist
struggles in the sphere of abortion legislation to the category of reformist
politics. But it is also important that feminists should be alert to the
theoretical and practical problems produced by one attempt to avoid the
dichotomy between reform and revolution – the attempt to transcend the
dichotomy by claiming a woman's right to choose as an absolute right. To

adopt that strategy is to be vulnerable to charges not so much of reformism but of utopianism, and dangerous utopianism at that. The dangers of that strategy call for, at the very least, a reassessment of the use of the slogan 'a woman's right to choose' in so far as, claimed as an absolute right, it constitutes an obstacle to working out means of achieving feminist objectives, means which are politically and legally realisable. To engage in that process requires detailed scrutiny of actual and likely legislation and court practices, not as a mere supplement to feminism but as an integral part of feminist struggle.

NOTE TO CHAPTER 3

The Bobigny Case

In 1972, Marie-Claire Chevalier answered a summons to appear before the Bobigny Juvenile Court on a charge of having had an abortion, a felony and misdemeanour punishable under Article 317 of the Penal Code. At the same time, Mmes Bambuck, who caused the abortion, and Mmes Chevalier (Marie-Claire's mother), Duboucheix and Sausset appeared in the *Tribunal de Grande Instance* of Bobigny on the charge of aiding the causation of the abortion, also a felony and misdemeanour under Article 317.[1] Marie-Claire was acquitted, and so were Mmes Duboucheix and Sausset. Mme Bambuck was given a one year's suspended prison sentence. Mme Chevalier was fined 500 francs with suspended sentence. Mmes Bambuck and Chevalier were ordered to pay costs. The cases attracted tremendous publicity. Famous people, like film stars, testified in court that they had had abortions, and an impressive range of public figures launched fierce attacks on anti-abortion arguments when they gave testimony.

Mme Duboucheix's case was particularly interesting. In the hearing, the following exchange took place between Mme Duboucheix, the Judge, and Me Halimi, counsel for the defence.

> *Me Halimi* I don't want to draw Mme Duboucheix into a discussion of precise cases but only wish her to answer me this: 'Who, according to you, decides when it is right to abort?'
> *Mme Duboucheix* The woman, only the woman.
> *Judge* That is not the problem ...
> *Me Halimi* For us it is the problem, indeed the only one.
> *Mme Duboucheix* Could I add a word here? It concerns all women, it is this law; we don't want it to work any longer.
> *Judge* But we're not engaged in the trial of a law. What I would like, Mme Learned Counsel, since we have to face this problem, is that you give the court some guidance as to how it can establish its decision in a case where it adopts your argument and not be in

contradiction of Article 127 of the Penal Code and not expose the magistrates who sit here to prosecution for failure in duty. (Association Choisir 1973: 25-6)

With these remarks the Judge makes it clear that any discussion of the conflict between a woman's right to choose or decide and the law under which abortion was unlawful could not be admitted, without risking the loss of civil rights (the penalty for breach of Article 127) on the part of himself and the magistrates present.[2] For the Judge, the court could only concern itself with whether or not an offence under the Code had been committed.

In fact, Me Halimi ignored the reprimand and continued to refer to a woman's right to choose. In so doing she set in motion a discourse which was later to give her some difficulty. In his speech for the prosecution, the Public Prosecutor took advantage of Me Halimi's appeal to women's rights by countering with the view that the present law was based on 'the respect for life, on respect for oneself and respect for others' (Association Choisir 1973: 96). This in turn put Me Halimi, in her speech for the defence of all the accused, in the predicament of rejecting questions of the right to life as metaphysical and abstract and, at the same time, reasserting the freedom to procreate as 'the liberty among all others, fundamental' and the claim of women to control themselves and their bodies as 'elementary, physical' and a 'birthright' (Association Choisir 1973: 142). For all their materialist appearance, these terms are, of course, just as metaphysical as the ones favoured by the Public Prosecutor.

The Bobigny affair is most instructive for feminists as an indication of the kind of difficulties produced by the attempt to introduce into court proceedings a feminist critique, inspired by the claim that it should be a woman's right to choose, of the French abortion law. The Bobigny case alerts us to the dangers of appealing to rights in the context of law and serves as a reminder that appealing to rights may not be the most reliable tactics for securing feminist objectives through the law. Two observations support this contention.

First, we have seen that, for legal reasons, discussion of a woman's right to choose could not be incorporated into the court's proceedings. But we should also note that both the Defence Counsel and the Public Prosecutor employ appeals to rights which cannot be incorporated into court proceedings for a different sort of reason. For, although they appeal to different rights, they are rights which are typically described as fundamental, absolute, transcendent. This last quality is the critical one. For it means that such rights are, by definition, not a function of prevailing social conditions. In this sense, neither the right to life nor a woman's right to choose *can* find concrete expression in legal proceedings.

The second observation is that the impossibility of transcendent rights appearing in legal proceedings does not mean that their invocation in legal contexts is without effects. As we have seen, Mᵉ Halimi's invocation of a woman's right to choose made it only too easy for the Public Prosecutor to oppose it by invoking other, competing rights. One might call this sort of phenomenon 'the attraction of opposite rights'. There are other examples of this sort of attraction: the right to privacy attracts the right to information, maternal rights attract fetal rights, parents' rights attract children's rights, and in the Government Communications Headquarters affair the right to join a union attracts the right to national security.

There are three important features of such attractions. First, there is no agreed way of ranking competing rights. All attempts to settle competing rights claims themselves become part of the struggle between their proponents. Historically, competing rights claims have been settled by various forms of *force majeure* and by political struggle. Secondly, it follows that, while there is no knowing what the outcome of particular rights fights will be, the balance of political forces at any time may well mean that some invoked rights are more likely than others to be accepted, whatever that may mean in practice. In the Bobigny case, the Public Prosecutor might have been expected to have a better chance of securing victory for the rights he invoked since he was not invoking them in order to change the law but to characterise the current law as embodying those rights. In the event, in terms of the decisions of the two cases, it was the rights invoked by Mᵉ Halimi which 'won'. But it might be argued that they won at a certain price, and this relates to the third feature of the attractions of opposite rights. As we have noted, in placing great emphasis on a woman's right to choose, Mᵉ Halimi made it only too easy for the Public Prosecutor to introduce competing rights. Once embarked on this rights discourse, it was equally easy for the Public Prosecutor to make only fleeting reference to Mᵉ Halimi's frequent criticisms of the disgraceful absence of sex education and of the appalling difficulty of getting contraceptive information. Equally, he did not trouble to refer to the defence's sustained attack on the desperate economic and social conditions of French working-class women. In other words, preoccupation with the attraction of opposite rights facilitates the suppression of wider social issues. Jeff Minson (1981) has brilliantly documented this contention with his analysis of a case concerning the limitations of appealing to personal rights in the context of the sacking of a London homosexual teacher. The next chapter and its accompanying Note develop this theme in relation to sterilisation as a method of contraception.

4

Consent, Coercion and Consortium: the Sexual Politics of Sterilisation

Introduction

Unlike abortion, sterilisation has not been a main target of feminist politics. There are several reasons, however, why it could become a major area of feminist struggle. Again, unlike abortion, sterilisation is not the subject of a specific act in statute law. Cases have been brought under a variety of legal headings, and the most frequently cited cases are characterised by a good deal of uncertainty, not to mention bizarre opinions. In the circumstances, it is perhaps not surprising that social commentators and members of the legal and medical professions should fall back on appeals to rights when debating these controversial cases. But there are good reasons why feminists should not follow that practice. Appeals to rights are notoriously vague and polemical. These qualities may be irresistible in the heat of an adversarial moment. Yet they inevitably frustrate the development of substantive and detailed policies. And in the particular case of sterilisation, uncertainty about which social, legal, and medical policies to adopt seems to invite the invocation of some uncomfortably atavistic rights which should be specially worrying to feminists.

Issues

In this section, I bring together a number of disparate issues relating to sterilisation, issues which are pertinent to the development of a sexual politics of sterilisation. As a preliminary, it will be useful to mention some standard terms which have been used to indicate the purpose of a sterilisation operation. As we shall see, the meaning and implications of these terms can become contentious. 'Therapeutic' sterilisation is performed for medical reasons, for example where the removal of diseased tissue involves an operation which has the effect of making the patient sterile. 'Non-therapeutic' or 'eugenic' sterilisation is performed for social reasons. It may be because the patient is thought likely to produce children with certain undesired characteristics. It may be because the patient, typically a woman, is thought to be vulnerable to sexual attack and/or is thought to be incapable of managing any other form of contra-

ception and/or is thought to be incapable of caring for any offspring. In
the UK, the proposal to sterilise a person for eugenic reasons is made in
the light of the person's individual characteristics and circumstances. In
some other countries the proposal is made, initially at any rate, on the
basis of the individual's membership of one or more specific categories of
persons. These categories are defined in assorted medical, psychological,
or social terms, such as epileptics, the feeble-minded, and the morally
degenerate; the categories feature explicitly in legislation. Sterilisation for
contraceptive purposes is sometimes called 'elective', sometimes sterilisation 'for convenience', and once, in *The Guardian*, 'recreational' sterilisation.

The Brock Report. In 1932, under the minute of the Chairman of the
Board of Control and with the approval of the Minister of Health, a
Committee was appointed under the Chairmanship of L. G. Brock:

> to examine and report on the information already available re-
> garding the hereditary transmission and other causes of mental
> disorder and deficiency; to consider the value of sterilisation as a
> preventive measure having regard to its physical, psychological, and
> social effects and to the experience of legislation in other countries
> permitting it; and to suggest what further enquiries might usefully
> be undertaken in this connection. (Brock 1934: 5)

Appendix VIII summarises legislation on the subject of voluntary and
compulsory legislation in twenty-seven of the United States of America
and nine other countries in which laws existed or in which bills were being
drafted. In the UK, the Committee observed, 'the legal position in regard
to sterilisation is not free from doubt'. The Committee drew a distinction
between eugenic and therapeutic sterilisation, commenting that the legality of therapeutic sterilisation 'is not disputed in principle', but 'that there
is general agreement that sterilisation of mental defectives on eugenic
grounds is illegal'. It added that 'the legal position in regard to the eugenic
sterilisation of persons of normal mentality is less certain, but most
authorities take the view that it is illegal' (Brock 1934: 7).

The Committee recommended the legalisation of voluntary sterilisation in the case of mental defectives or of people who had suffered from
mental disorder, of people who suffered from or who were believed to be
carriers of grave physical disabilities shown to be transmissible, and of
people believed to be likely to transmit mental disorder or defect. Operations for sterilisation were to be performed only under the written
authorisation of the Minister for Health, and in that respect a number of
procedures were to be followed. These included the requirement of the
patient's written consent or, if the patient were deemed incompetent to
give a reasonable consent, the written consent of a parent, guardian or
spouse.

Over twenty years later, Glanville Williams pointed out that the recommendations of the Brock Report were not implemented, although they were supported by a number of public bodies such as the Royal College of Physicians (Williams 1958: 94). He might have added that, interestingly enough, they were also supported in a resolution passed by the Business Conference of Women's Sections at the 36th Annual Conference of the Labour Party (The Labour Party 1936: 69; cf. Weeks 1981: 140 n, 53).

Re *D (a minor) (wardship: sterilisation)*. As in 1934, the legality of therapeutic sterilisation is not in doubt today, but there is still uncertainty and disagreement about the legality of eugenic or non-therapeutic sterilisation. Robert Lee and Derek Morgan (1989) have reviewed and analysed the tendency of recent cases of non-therapeutic sterilisation, but for purposes of this chapter I shall examine one of the most frequently cited cases. D was a girl with Sotos Syndrome. 'When D was a young girl her parents had decided that they should apply to have her sterilised when she was about 18 years of age to prevent her from having children who might be abnormal' (at 326). After discussion with a consultant paediatrician, however, arrangements were made to have D sterilised when she was 10. Among others, an educational psychologist challenged the social and behavioural reasons for sterilising D and applied to have her made a ward of court when the paediatrician refused to defer the operation. The case was heard in the Family Division. Heilbron J. held that:

the operation was one which involved the deprivation of a basic human right, i.e. the right of a woman to reproduce, and therefore, if performed on a woman for non-therapeutic reasons and without her consent, would be a violation of that right. Since D could not give an informed consent, but there was a strong likelihood would understand the implications of the operation when she reached the age of 18, the case was one in which the courts [*sic*] should exercise its protective powers. Her wardship would accordingly be continued ... A decision to carry out a sterilisation operation on a minor for non-therapeutic purposes was not solely within a doctor's clinical judgement. In the circumstances the operation was neither medically indicated nor necessary, and it would not be in D's best interests for it to be performed. (at 327)

The leading article of *New Society*, written before the case was heard, commented that 'the plan to sterilise an eleven year old Sheffield girl has quite rightly given rise to a sense of outrage about human rights' (*New Society* 1975: 634).

What is the significance of this case? Feminists might be tempted to read it as a victory over paternalism in the matter of female reproductive capacities. But it is by no means obvious that it was D's sex that was the key issue. In *Re* D, the court was preoccupied with, and the sense of outrage undoubtedly provoked by, the fact that D was a minor, mentally subnormal[1] and incapable of giving informed consent to sterilisation proposed on non-therapeutic grounds.

This is not to say that there is no feminist interest in this case. Heilbron's decision turned not only on the question of informed consent but also on the distinction between therapeutic and non-therapeutic sterilisation. For Heilbron, there seemed to be no difficulty in distinguishing the two types of sterilisation. Accordingly, and this is important to note, Heilbron's stirring appeal to D's right to reproduce was predicated on the opinion that there were no medical reasons for sterilising her.

Fifteen years later, however, in a not dissimilar case, Lord Hailsham offered this critique of the distinction between therapeutic and non-therapeutic sterilisation:

> for purposes of the present appeal I find the distinction ... between 'therapeutic and non-therapeutic' purposes of this operation in relation to the facts of the present case above as totally meaningless ... To talk of the 'basic right' to reproduce of an individual who is not capable of knowing the causal connection between intercourse and childbirth, the nature of pregnancy, what is involved in delivery, unable to form maternal instincts or to care for a child appears to me wholly to part company with reality. (*Re F (sterilisation: mental patient)* 1989 at 322D)

Now feminists involved in the struggles leading up to the passing of the Abortion Act 1967 will recall that one of the toughest fights was over the inclusion of the so-called 'environment clause'. This made it permissible, if not mandatory, for registered medical practitioners to take account of the woman's actual or reasonably foreseeable environment in determining the risk to her health if she continued the pregnancy. Whilst this clause did not, as some feminists and some opponents of the new Act claimed, provide for independent social grounds for lawful termination, feminists and a good many doctors welcomed its provision in the Act. Doctors were relieved because it legitimated widespread medical practice. And, as we saw in the previous chapter, feminists took the clause to be critical in the struggle to weaken the ever-present tendency of legal and medical practitioners to treat women as legal subjects defined predominantly in terms of medical, specifically gynaecological, criteria rather than in terms of their economic and social status and situation.

In the context both of abortion and of sterilisation, then, the distinction between medical, or therapeutic, criteria and social, or non-therapeutic, criteria is contentious. Accordingly, to return to *Re* D. if that distinction is contentious, and if possession of the right to reproduce is dependent on a judgement about the presence or absence of medical or therapeutic grounds for sterilisation, then at the very least there is no clear basis for ascribing this right to an individual. This problem is intensified by a legal debate about the proper parties to reach a decision in these matters. In *Re D*, Heilbron seemed to argue that the presence of medical grounds for sterilisation was one which came 'solely within a doctor's clinical judgement' and that it was the medical criterion and the medical professional that could override any claim to have a right to reproduce. In contrast, in *Re F*, Butler-Sloss LJ averred that the decision should not be left to the family and to the medical profession alone and that it should always be subject to the supervision of the courts.

These cases are instructive for feminists, because they signal that the right to reproduce is not something which in some sense exists, nor something which belongs to human beings by virtue of their membership of the species, *nem. con.* Rather the ascription of the right to reproduce is just that – an ascription. As with all ascriptions, complex and competing criteria are deployed. It would, of course, be against the theme of this book to make these two cases carry a definitive argument about appeals to rights. In particular, it would be unwise to make generalisations on the basis of these two cases about the right to reproduce, since so much of what was at issue concerned the capacity to give an informed consent, but, as we shall see in the next section, the distinction between medical/ therapeutic and social/non-therapeutic criteria is also an issue where the capacity to give an informed consent is not in doubt.

Bravery v. *Bravery*

The problematic nature of consent, informed or not, and the slippery distinction between therapeutic and non-therapeutic sterilisation were also at issue in another controversial case. Mr and Mrs Bravery had married in 1934 and had their only child in 1936. Two years later, the husband had a vasectomy with the wife's knowledge. The couple continued to live together, sexual intercourse continued, but there were rows about, for example, the husband's dirty habits, his bad language, and his excessive interest in Indian philosophy. The wife left in 1951 and petitioned for divorce on grounds of cruelty, namely, his having had a vasectomy. It was held that:

> the wife had not made out a case of cruelty. As between husband and wife, for a husband to submit himself to an operation of sterilisation, without good medical reason, would, unless his wife were a consenting party, be a grave offence which could, without difficulty, be shown to be a cruel act, if it were found to have injured her health or to have caused reasonable apprehension of such injury. If a husband submitted to such an operation without the wife's

consent, and if the latter desired to have children, the hurt might be
progressive to the nerves and health of the wife. (at 1169)

The case raises important questions. First, was Mrs Bravery a victim of
gender stereotyping, explicit or covert, whereby a woman's capacity to
control her sexuality is deemed less important than a man's? It is not clear
how assiduous the surgeon was in eliciting Mrs Bravery's views on her
husband's proposed vasectomy. In that respect, it is possible that she was
the object of a particular form of discrimination which I discuss below.
But as far as the court's deliberations were concerned, there was a strong
suggestion that, had Mrs Bravery made it sufficiently clear, before the
operation was performed, that she did not want Mr Bravery to be
sterilised, the court would have expressed very different opinions, perhaps
finding that she had made out a case of cruelty.

Now, on Mrs Bravery's own evidence, she knew that her husband was
going to have the operation. What was at issue in cross-examination was
whether she consented to it. As it happened, her husband worked at the
hospital where the operation was performed, and she knew the surgeon
and the nurse in question. She certainly did not give written consent, and
it seems that at no time did she approach the persons concerned to say
that she objected. What appears to have swayed Hodson LJ to the view
that she did consent was, in the end, his finding it difficult to believe 'that
any surgeon, a member of an honourable profession, would perform an
operation of this kind on a young married man unless he was first satisfied
that the wife consented' (at 1173).

But, while there was doubt about whether the wife had consented to
the operation, the court was in no doubt that the husband had given *his*
consent. Denning LJ did not dispute that; he dissented from the court's
decision on altogether different grounds. He argued that an operation of
sterilisation was, in the absence of some just cause or excuse, a criminal
act in itself, an unlawful assault, to which consent gave no answer or defence.
Denning's argument was based on the view that a person cannot effectively
consent to mayhem (the act of maiming) against himself. Denning was
also concerned with a rather different form of assault when he concluded
that 'if a husband undergoes an operation for sterilisation without just cause
or excuse, he strikes at the very root of the marriage relationship' (at 1181).

Denning's remark is clearly predicated on a view of the relation
between marriage and the purpose of sexual intercourse which is at once
familiar and horrifying to feminists. Since that view is discernible in all
manner of legal proceedings and public debate, however, I shall not
pursue the general feminist critique of it. But the possibility that non-
therapeutic sterilisation might be a criminal act has given rise to conflicting legal opinions on the specific question of the legality of non-
therapeutic sterilisation. In examining this legal controversy, I arrive at

the consideration of a legal doctrine of serious concern to feminists, the doctrine of consortium.

The legality of non-therapeutic sterilisation. The reference to mayhem may seem bizarre in the context of sterilisation of a man, not least since mayhem has been defined as an injury to a man so that he is rendered less capable of defending himself (Williams 1958: 102–3). But, whether they merited this attention or not (cf. Dickens 1985: 266), the grounds of Denning's dissent continued to feature in discussions of the legality of sterilisation for some years. A. E. Clark-Kennedy, for example, pointed out that all surgery is an assault on the body, irrespective of the patient's consent, and that it is justified only when a greater evil has been averted. Writing in 1969, he took the view that the sterilisation of a woman merely as a method of birth control and without any medical justification would probably be found to be illegal if the case were brought to court, and he thought the same might be true for sterilisation of a man (Clark-Kennedy 1969: 34). It is interesting to note here that while the National Health Service (Family Planning) Act 1972 allowed local authorities to provide for sterilisation by vasectomy there was no mention of the various methods of female sterilisation. I shall return to this.

Similarly, Bernard Knight has pointed out that no act of Parliament or judicial dictum has reversed the concept of law whereby sterilisation is a maiming operation. In contrast to Clark-Kennedy, however, he subscribes to the view held by the medical defence organisations that there has been a change in the climate of public opinion regarding sterilisation for purposes of birth control and that the courts would take a more liberal line than Denning's about its legality (Knight 1987: 237–8). J. Leahy Taylor confirms this view when he says that a surgeon who performs a sterilisation operation on one of a married couple with the consent of both would not be putting himself at risk (1970: 81; cf. Mason and McCall Smith 1987: Ch. 4).

If, as seems likely, Knight and Taylor are right about the likely attitude of the courts to the legality of sterilisation for birth control purposes, then the question of consent will not be, as Denning thought, an irrelevancy. On the contrary, it becomes one of the central issues.

Consent. In developing his argument about changing attitudes to non-therapeutic sterilisation, Knight cites the opinion of the representative body of the British Medical Association (BMA) in 1967 that 'if the doctor is satisfied that an operation for sterilisation is in the interests of the health of the patient and that the patient has given valid consent and understands the consequences of this operation, there is no ethical reason why the operation should not be performed' (1982: 232).

The wording of the BMA's statement is noteworthy. It suggests that it is the valid consent of the patient alone that is required. In fact, both

Knight and Taylor make a point of stressing the desirability – from the point of view of the surgeon's protection – of obtaining the consent of both husband and wife where the patient is married. Taylor suggests: 'Where sterilisation is being considered purely as an operation of con-venience then, in all probability, no surgeon would be prepared to operate without the consent of both parties' (1970: 81). Again, both Knight and Taylor take the view that a surgeon might proceed with an operation to sterilise a wife without the husband's consent if medical circumstances appeared to necessitate the operation, and Knight seems to countenance a similar possibility where the operation is on the husband.

On the other hand, the views of both Knight and Taylor are called into question on the issue of the spouse's consent by Appendix III of the Birth Control Trust's document *Sterilisation and the National Health Service* (BCT 1978). Written on information supplied by the Medical Defence Union, the Appendix states: 'only the patient can give consent. There is no legal requirement for the spouse's consent. However it is advisable in the interests of marital harmony to obtain the *agreement* of the spouse when the operation is done simply as a means of contraception' (BCT 1978: 104).

The distinction between consent and agreement is not developed, however, and in the absence of precise clarification one imagines that surgeons might well want to cover themselves by getting the consent of the patient and the agreement of the spouse. In fact, the Liverpool Area Health Authority issues a form, to be used in cases of primary (that is, non-therapeutic) sterilisation if the patient is married and living with the spouse. There is provision on this form for the consent of the patient and the agreement of the spouse, and it urges that both parties should sign the form at the same time.

Discrimination and consent. Whatever the legalities of consent to non-therapeutic sterilisation, it would seem that surgeons' practices have not been uniform throughout the country. In 1976 it was reported that the NCCL was collecting evidence of cases where women were being denied intra-uterine devices and sterilisation for contraceptive purposes because they could not, or would not, get the written consent of their husband. 'And, says the NCCL, the same doctors who demand a husband's consent will perform a vasectomy on a man without asking if she consents' (*New Society* 1978: 431; cf. also Dickens 1985: 277f).

There can be no justification for this discrimination against women. The attempt to outlaw it might be made by bringing a test case under or proposing an amendment to the SDA 1975, or through drafting a bill dealing with this issue and others relating to sterilisation.[2] In assessing the measures most likely to eliminate this form of discrimination, however, feminists will also need to investigate the various practices that have supported it. To help with that investigation, I put forward the following points.

Until recently at any rate, vasectomy has been a quicker and safer operation than the various methods of female sterilisation. It is possible, though not defensible, that the male patients and medical personnel have accordingly been inclined to see the decision to operate as unproblematic. On the other hand, as feminists involved in struggles to improve access to abortion facilities will testify, considerations of speed and safety do not appear to have been topmost in the mind of the majority of medical practitioners. It is the non-medical attitudes of those in a position to control access to wanted medical operations that have frequently been decisive (cf. Aitken-Swan 1977).

In the case of doctors' discriminatory practices over consent to non-therapeutic sterilisation, the inference must be that such doctors, consciously or not, attribute a legitimate interest in a spouse's potential fertility to husbands but not to wives. As it happens, that attitude could find support in law, at least until 1982, through the doctrine of consortium. Briefly, this is the ancient notion that a husband has a legitimate proprietary interest in his wife's services (servitium) or society (consortium) (cf. Fleming 1985: 64 n. 6; Blake 1982: 8). Very much in the spirit of this doctrine, it was possible, until 1982, for a husband to bring an action for loss of the services or society of his wife, but not vice-versa. The Administration of Justice Act 1982, however, rectified this anomaly in providing that no person shall be liable in tort to a husband for any such deprivation.

The precise nature of consortium has always been in doubt. In 1977, however, legal advice obtained by the NCCL contained a warning. Whilst consortium probably would not be thought to include the right to a wife's potential fertility, there was still a risk that 'a husband could succeed in an action for damages against a doctor even though the wife had asked for and consented to the operation ... on the ground that the doctor has assisted in procuring damage to the husband's consortium' (NCCL 1972).

The belated removal of the anachronistic doctrine of consortium in this context will rightly be a source of relief to feminists, but there is no reason to suppose that the atavistic rationale of the doctrine will be moribund forthwith. In this respect, it will be interesting to watch the progress of a recent claim for loss of consortium and distress brought by the wife of a haemophiliac who contracted HIV from infected blood. Her lawyer comments that 'interference with a sexual relationship is a recognised claim' (*The Independent* 1990). So, the vestiges of the doctrine of consortium may have to be reckoned with for some time to come, if not through explicit reference to consortium then through ideologically related notions such as conjugal rights or the right to reproduce. I would urge that feminists engaged in the development of a sexual politics of sterilisation should be extremely wary of formulating policies in terms of such rights – for fear of being drawn on to territory long dominated by ideologies and practices inimical to feminist objectives. There is a serious risk that the appeal to a woman's right to reproduce will be appropriated by those who would invoke a general right to reproduce or a human right to reproduce. Appealing to this more general right may in turn be a less than innocent practice, if the alleged general right is identified, covertly or not, with a man's, or worse, a husband's, right to reproduce (cf. Note below, especially n. 1). There are, furthermore, additional and independent reasons for not framing policies in terms of rights, and it is to this issue that the next section is addressed.

Policies

Two recurrent features of the literature on sterilisation provide the impetus for a review of the various policies which feminists might adopt. First, a good deal of research in the last decade or so has shown that there is increasing demand for sterilisation for contraceptive purposes. In 1972 it was found that hospitals which deliberately adopted a favourable attitude to sterilisation experienced a dramatic increase in spontaneous requests for sterilisation (Buckle and Young 1972: 401). Two years later, a survey of 1,079 women in Coventry during their confinement produced the estimate that the potential demand for sterilisation was between sixty and eighty per thousand confinements (Opit and Brennan 1974: 157). Two surveys by M. Bone from the Social Survey Division of the Office of Population Censuses and Surveys on behalf of the Department of Health and Social Security showed a marked increase in favourable attitudes towards sterilisation for contraceptive purposes in the 1970s. Briefly, in 1973, of the total sample of women interviewed:

> only 20% said they would think about it if they had about the number of children they planned to have and most thought it only appropriate in more extreme circumstances, for example if further pregnancies would endanger their health or if they had had several more children than they wanted. (Bone 1973: 20)

The survey was admitted to give only a sketch of women's attitudes but it was surmised that the irrevocability of sterilisation made it 'very much a method of last resort for most women' (ibid.). In 1978, however, the picture had changed. The results of this survey suggested that:

> sterilisation was becoming less of a last resort for the desperate and more of a chosen method for couples who had just achieved the number of children they thought sufficient. ... Sterilisation was therefore not only spreading but increasingly impinging on young

couples who had had few pregnancies and, it seems, quite soon after
they had decided that their second or third baby was to be the last.
(Bone 1978: 62)

Additional evidence for the demand for sterilisation for contraceptive
purposes is collected, and explanations for its increased popularity are
available (Birth Control Trust 1978, Ch. 1).

The second recurrent feature of the literature on sterilisation has not
been so thoroughly researched. It concerns a practice which is generally
frowned on (or at least seen as one which has to be justified) and about
which it is extremely difficult to be precise. It is the practice which has
come to be known as 'the package deal' (cf. Leeson and Gray 1978: 109).
Briefly, a woman's request for an abortion is met on condition that she
agrees to being sterilised at the same time. In 1974, the Lane Report on
the working of the Abortion Act 1967 noted that, although the Committee had been unable to establish the facts in this matter, it was
concerned by comments it had received about the large number of young
unmarried women who had been sterilised as a condition of getting an
abortion. The Report recommended that sterilisation should never be a
condition for terminating an existing pregnancy nor be performed as a
result of any other pressure (Lane 1974: 533-4). In 1981 I. Allen noted
that fears were often expressed about women being pressurised into
sterilisation when they had an abortion, although she was unable to find
evidence to support those fears (1981: 65). On the other hand, a 1971
survey of gynaecologists' attitudes showed:

> respondents to be evenly divided on the question, those in favour
> thinking that the abortion patient should accept sterilisation if there
> were medical or psychiatric indications, if the situation leading to
> abortion was unlikely to change, where there was multiparity, low
> IQ, 'irresponsibility', a previous abortion or other problems.
> (Aitken-Swan 1977: 158)

In spite of the fact that evidence of the package deal is largely anecdotal,
references to it persist, and it would appear that the practice continues
(Roberts 1988).

It is reasonable to suppose that, in responding to these trends, feminists will present their policies in terms of women's rights. Indeed, the
package deal has been described in these terms. K. Greenwood and L.
King connect it to the central demands of the Women's Liberation
Movement for freely available contraception and abortion, observing that
women have no right to abortion (1982: 174). P. Hewitt sees the package
deal as a violation of a woman's right to choose, and she asserts that right
on the basis of its relation to other rights, proposing that 'the freedom of
a woman to control her own fertility is inextricably linked to fundamental
principles of human rights' (1978: 29). In this connection, too, it is worth

recalling that in *Re* D, described above, it was held that the operation proposed was one which involved 'the deprivation of a basic human right, i.e. the right of a woman to reproduce'.

In the previous section, I drew attention to the risks of appealing to rights, such as the right to reproduce, when they are associated with ideologies and practices inimical to feminist objectives. In this section, I show that, even if feminists do present their policies in terms of rights, it is far from obvious that they will on that account be united in their policy preferences. On the contrary, I argue that appealing to women's rights can mask serious differences between feminists and can, in so doing, be an obstacle to the development of detailed policies and strategies in relation to sterilisation. To support this argument, I identify three different ways in which feminists might take up the issue. For convenience, I label them as follows:

Policy A	Deregulation
Policy B	Mandatory provision
Policy C	Safeguards

Policy A   Deregulation. Some feminists might respond to the trends outlined above by demanding the complete deregulation of sterilisation, meaning by this the abolition of all restrictions on it. Only in this way, it might be argued, can a woman enjoy genuine freedom to control her own fertility. That freedom cannot be enjoyed under present social conditions, since the existing legal and medical institutions and practices are necessarily geared to capitalist and patriarchal interests. It is therefore not merely futile or misguided to look to these institutions for recognition of a woman's absolute right to control her own body; it is to advocate reformist measures and, in so doing, to oppose the revolutionary demand for women's rights. The regulation of health care now is oppressive of women, and a socialist society will remove the need for that regulation. In the absence of socialism, but in order to advance towards it, women should concentrate their efforts on demystifying medicine and exploring alternative forms of health care by setting up self-help groups. In the specific matter of sterilisation, a woman's right to choose is both the expression of women's refusal to allow men in general, and doctors and lawyers in particular, to control women's fertility and the expression of their refusal to participate in social practices which support that control.

Clearly, this response has much in common with the way in which some feminists took up the issue of abortion in the USA and in this country, and I have already discussed some of these issues in the previous chapter, in relation to a woman's right to choose. As we have seen, the deregulation response has been forcefully pressed by Victoria Greenwood and Jock Young (1976). It is just as forcefully resisted by Paul Q. Hirst

(1980). Hirst's attack focuses on the absurdity of supposing that socialist states have or will have no need of regulation in the areas of health care, and he demonstrates the problematic politics of arguing for *a* woman's right to choose in the context of forming general social policy. He points out the dangers of demanding the demonopolisation of medical competence: 'Demonopolisation would mean that anyone was free to perform abortions; there would be no limit to personnel, methods or facilities. The possibility created by this *laissez-faire* is of a return to the era of the 'knitting needle', in the guise of alternative medicine and self-help' (Hirst 1980: 102). Hirst concludes that 'socialist states should take the control of medical competence and the determination of means of intervention *more* and not less seriously' (ibid.)

Faced with this sort of criticism, proponents of deregulation might reply that nobody would seriously propose that personnel other than qualified surgeons should perform operations of sterilisation. It is worth noting, however, that there are continuing attempts to find a substitute for surgical sterilisation. One such attempt involves the relatively simple procedure of infusing a solution of quinacrine into the interior of the uterus (cf. Viel and Walls 1976: 148). Informal sources suggest that this sort of procedure could be performed very simply and that the kit could be marketed for a dollar. It would not be surprising if understandable apprehension at the implications of such a development led feminists to adopt an alternative to deregulation, namely mandatory provision.

Policy B   Mandatory provision. Resistance to the argument that law is necessarily oppressive of women, and alarm at the serious effects of deregulation in the sphere of health care in general, and sterilisation in particular, might make feminists adopt a different approach. They may invoke the rhetoric of a woman's right to choose, since it is a potent political slogan. But for these feminists it is not a knowingly unrealisable demand under capitalism and an unnecessary one under socialism. Instead, it is a convenient means of focusing attention on a particular area of health care the provision of which is currently disadvantageous to women, which on that account should not be tolerated now, and which certainly should not be tolerated under a socialist state committed to the removal of obstacles to women's full enjoyment of social benefits.

We have seen that there is a rising demand for female and male sterilisation as a form of birth control. One of the main sources of dissatisfaction with the present NHS sterilisation service, however, has been its uneven availability. In 1981, a survey of thirty Area Health Authorities showed that in only six authorities was the average waiting time for female sterilisation three months or less, that in eight authorities it was two years or more, and that in one authority it could be four years. The average waiting time for vasectomies was just as uneven as between authorities, but generally it was shorter than for female sterilisation (BCT 1978: 6–7).

A major factor in this uneven availability was found to be the manner of its funding. Authorities and district management teams set aside money for item-of-service payments. The discretionary nature of this funding meant that doctors and health authorities were in a position to give priority to other operations and procedures in preference to sterilisation. It also allowed great scope for doctors and gynaecologists to exercise their personal as well as their professional judgements in relation to the moral aspects of sterilisation (Aitken-Swan 1977: 163).

How can this situation be remedied? One obvious strategy would be for feminists to point to the cost-effectiveness of sterilisation in comparison with other forms of contraception, abortion, ante-natal maternity care, and child care. W. A. Laing has estimated that, taking into account failure rates and the cost of unplanned conception, there is a break-even point of a little over a year for vasectomy (Laing 1982: 32). Laing concludes that it seems illogical to restrict NHS sterilisations rather than reversible methods of contraception. It has also been shown that savings in in-patient costs are greatly reduced by the use of modern methods of female sterilisation, such as mini-laparotomy, and that the greatest savings would be effected by setting up special sterilisation units or clinics, perhaps in hospital wards closed as a result of financial cuts (BCT 1978: 8).

The argument for units specialising in sterilisation, contraception and abortion has been put forward by Wendy Savage (cf. WHRRIC 1990: 19). It is a powerful argument, since there is evidence that, for contraceptive and related matters, women would rather go to a specialised clinic than to their GP's surgery (Leathard 1990: 120). But that sort of provision would not by itself solve the problem of uneven availability, since the provision of such clinics would again be a matter of the political will of the relevant authorities to fund them, and there is recent evidence of the reluctance of National Health Service regions to give priority to family planning services and Well Woman Clinics (ibid.)

To ensure even availability, it might be argued that it is necessary to effect a change in national legislation governing the provision of the health services. This would require close and expert scrutiny to identify the most effective legal reforms, and a difficulty here is the typical form of health service legislation. The National Health Service (Family Planning) Act 1972 allowed local health authorities to provide voluntary vasectomy services on the same basis as other contraceptive services. Interestingly, it made no reference to types of female sterilisation, provoking speculation about the role of that Act in the unevenness of sterilisation services as between women and men. But that Act is now repealed, and although it is allowed that male and female sterilisation clinics may be held under the general provisions of family planning (Levitt and Wall 1984: 141), the National Health Service Act 1977 makes no special mention of sterilisation. As in the National Health Service (Scotland) Act 1978, there is just the general requirement that the Secretary of State make such arrangements for contraceptive services as he considers necessary. Feminists might want to look into how it would be possible to rectify this situation, with a view to making this sort of provision mandatory rather than discretionary, in the same way that they have argued for the mandatory provision of abortion facilities, and perhaps to have a minimal level of funding. The formidable obstacles to this sort of feminist intervention are apparent from commentaries on the passage of the National Health Service and Community Care Bill. The Women's Health and Reproductive Rights Information Centre (WHRRIC) has reported that:

> in the early days of the white papers, five core services were mentioned. ... Labour put forward an amendment listing the five core services: accident and emergency, geriatric, psychiatric, public health community-based services and services for the elderly and mentally ill. They also added maternity, gynaecology and family planning which had been left off the original list ... The amendment was defeated, with the Conservatives arguing that market forces would ensure such services were provided! (WHRRIC 1990: 18).

Against this sort of political backdrop, the demand for mandatory provision begins to look utopian. Also, it has to be said that even if mandatory provision could solve the problem of uneven geographical availability of sterilisation services, it would not necessarily deal with the problem of uneven availability as between women and men.

It is clear that the objective of a mandatory and non-discriminatory NHS sterilisation service requires close attention to the most effective means of changing existing legislation and medical practices, whether or not the objective is pursued in the name of a woman's right to choose. But this could hardly be more different from the use of that slogan to advocate deregulation of sterilisation services. A further contrast is that, even if the policy of mandatory provision is fought for in the name of a woman's right to choose, that right will have been converted, as it were, into a number of specific objectives. These objectives raise questions not of the rights of individual women but of general social policy in the sphere of health care, such as priorities in NHS spending. It is in this context that a third feminist response might be developed.

Policy C   Safeguards. Feminists might well be concerned that the setting up of special sterilisation clinics on the grounds of cost-effectiveness would not be in women's (or men's) interests. Local authorities would have strong incentives to ensure that such clinics were not underused and, in consequence, they might be inclined to cut back their funding of existing contraceptive services, thereby restricting the scope of contraceptive choice. Further, the policy of mandatory provision of such clinics might not be implemented in full. Local authorities might be required to offer sterilisation services but not be required to do so through special sterilisation clinics. If, in addition, there were no change in the system of funding through items-of-service payments, there could be greater pressure than now on surgeons to make abortion conditional on sterilisation (cf. Roberts 1988).

To prevent a resurgence or increase in the package deal, feminists might consider a policy which concentrates on strengthening safeguards in present and future provision. At least two such measures would be appropriate. First, a case could be made for mandatory counselling before any decision to sterilise is made, given the mostly irreversible nature of sterilisation and the consequent social and moral questions peculiar to that form of contraception. While it would be difficult to enforce a policy of mandatory counselling, it would certainly be possible for the Department of Health and Social Security to toughen up its guidelines to local authorities on the provision of sterilisation. At present, the guidelines state only that full counselling is 'particularly important' (BCT 1978 Appendix II: 32). Allied to this, close attention should be given to the precise legal and practical meaning of 'consent' and of the distinction between 'consent' and 'agreement' as discussed above. Pressure could be brought on medical practitioners to ensure that consent is genuinely informed, in the sense of giving information both about what is known or believed to be the case regarding the possible effects of sterilisation but also about what is not known. For example, women should be advised about the uncertain state of knowledge concerning the effect of sterilisation on menstruation. Further, great care should be taken to define what counts as pressure or persuasion in the getting of a patient's consent and, where applicable, the agreement of the spouse. Secondly, feminists might consider the introduction of a compulsory period of time which must elapse – a breathing space – between a patient's having an abortion and her having an operation for sterilisation (cf. Roberts 1988). This might be done by pressing for an amendment to the Abortion Act 1967 or by including the provision in a new act concerned with sterilisation.

There are good reasons why feminists who supported these measures would think it inadvisable to campaign under the aegis of the slogan of a woman's right to choose. That slogan is clearly associated with pro-choice abortion campaigns. In so far as abortion is thought not to be a desirable form of contraception, and because the breathing space is intended to dissociate abortion and sterilisation, it would be unfortunate if the two campaigns became identified with each other. Further, pro-choice campaigners have not been predominantly concerned that women would be pressured into having abortions, whereas the main burden of the safe-guards under consideration here is to guard against women (and presumably men) being pressurised into operations of sterilisation by cost-conscious, disturbingly enthusiastic, or just plain busy medical practitioners. To that end, a much more appropriate slogan, if one were needed and if it had to be in terms of rights, would be a woman's right to refuse.

This outline of policy options open to feminists in the sphere of sterilisation provision and practice is obviously not exhaustive, although, under the present attack on the National Health Service and on such contraceptive services as exist at present, it may seem overly optimistic. Even so, the description of Policies A, B and C provides a basis for assessing different types of feminist response, especially where these policies are framed in terms of superficially similar appeals to women's rights.

NOTE TO CHAPTER 4

The Right to Reproduce

Feminists have long been alert to the way that an appeal to a right can be transformed into a general right, and its significance for women lost in the process. If feminists claim that a woman has the right to reproduce, there is no obvious reason why that right should not be claimed for men too, and on traditional liberal grounds of equality it would be difficult to oppose that claim.[1] But, in the light of the materials just presented, there is every reason to suppose that the medical profession and the courts will continue, however subtly, to give priority to a man's right. More particularly, there is also reason to suppose that, whether ascribed to men or to women, the right to reproduce will have its enjoyment restricted to people who can identify themselves as conforming to, or aspiring to, the conventional practices and ideals of marriage and family life. One example here is the Warnock Report's affirmation that 'as a general rule ... it is better for children to be born into a two-parent family, with both father and mother' (Warnock 1985: 11). For those feminists who see in these practices, ideals, and institutions a major source of women's oppression, appealing to the right to reproduce must be a highly questionable means of developing strategies and policies relating to sterilisation and reproductive medicine. In this note, I point to the limitations of appealing to the right to reproduce by reference first to a controversy in population politics and secondly to an issue of public policy concerning a failed sterilisation.

Population policy. In his passionate opposition to 'coercive genetics', that is, the use of society's laws, courts, jails and policemen to practice social therapy through the breeding out of undesirable genes, Amitai

Etzione asserts that 'the basic rights of an individual in a free society
include that of having as many of whatever kind of children as a person is
willing to have' (Etzione 1973: 110).

Further, Etzione would welcome 'the repeal of all genetics-by-legis-
lation, that is, by force of law, which now exist' (ibid.). His examples
include Danish and North Carolinan legislation on compulsory sterilisation. Etzione can see no justification whatsoever for any form of
compulsion in the matter of parenthood and procreation, although he is
not prepared to rule out minimal forms of genetic counselling, such as
advising prospective mothers to have genetic tests. But, whatever the
result of such tests, the decision to have or not to have children must be
that of the parents.

As if replying to Etzione, Gerald Leach suggests that:

> the basic challenge of genetic counselling is, of course, whether the
> parents' decision should be theirs alone, or whether the state should
> have a part in it. At present virtually all medical opinion says that it
> must be the parents' responsibility: the geneticist's job is to present
> the facts and then back out. (Leach 1972: 137)

Leach is alert to the strengths of the arguments about the dangers of
reversing that prioritisation of responsibility. Even so, he urges if not an
automatic reversal of it then certainly a reconsideration of it. He points
out that in many areas of social life, such as drunken driving or atmos-
pheric testing of nuclear weapons, state intervention is accepted as a
legitimate element in the calculation of social benefits. He can see no
good reason for making an exception in cases where there is a risk of
producing children with genetic defects.

Leach does not accept the argument that tolerance of individual
genetic counselling will automatically lead to population genetic counselling and the attendant risk of compulsory sterilisation programmes. He
argues instead that because lethal and severe dominant defects arise
afresh in each generation by mutations, and because mutations cannot be
prevented, compulsory sterilisation programmes for eugenic purposes are
either largely pointless or constitute an almost trivial intrusion on our so-
called rights.

Now, whatever the relation between individual genetic counselling and
population counselling, it is clear that population genetic politics do not
necessarily feature in policies for population control. That the right to
reproduce has been invoked in both contexts is an indication of the
slipperiness of that right. Nevertheless, similar issues arise in the context
of population control in relation to the presumption that individuals have
the right to produce as many children as they want, if necessary in
defiance of a population policy. Leach quotes Kingsley Davis's attack on
this presumption: 'Social reformers who would not hesitate to force all

owners of rented property to rent to anyone who can pay, or to force all workers in an industry to join a union, balk at any suggestion that couples be permitted to have only a certain number of children' (Davis 1967: 737

Davis and Leach are opposed to this 'hands-off' attitude to family rights because it enables governments to dodge the issue of population control in favour of the more politically acceptable but – in terms of curbing population growth – ineffective question of family planning and birth control. The family-planning ethos, argues Leach, tends 'to protect or even boost the traditional image and rights of the family as a unit – a separate unit in charge of its own destiny' (ibid.). For Davis and Leach, then, the invocation of the individual's right to reproduce is an obstacle to the serious confrontation of the main problem of any population policy, the problem of effective, attractive and economically viable controls in the interests of improved standards of nutrition, health, housing and education.

Clearly, the arguments put forward by Davis and Leach are not presented from a feminist point of view. Indeed, there is no reason at all why feminists should argue for the kinds of population controls which Davis and Leach propose, such as bonuses or tax relief for childless couples, not awarding public housing on the basis of numbers of children, not taxing single people more heavily than married people, and so on (Davis 1967: 747). But the arguments put forward by Davis and Leach are instructive in two ways which should interest feminists involved in the formulation of social policy. First, they invite consideration of the way in which appeals to rights in the sphere of population policy typically invoke the ideology of the individual as a free chooser, irrespective of social considerations of resource allocation, and the ideology of the family as the proper social unit in terms of which social policy is debated. Secondly, they invite consideration of the way in which these ideologies can divert attention from, and indeed facilitate the dismissal of, the formulation of social policy in the context of reproductive medicine.

Public policy. A striking feature of the dispute exemplified by the opposed positions of Etzione and Leach is the acceptance of the monolithic categories of 'the state' and 'the individual' characteristic of liberal political philosophy. One may also observe that within such political philosophy the rights and duties of individuals and between individuals, and the rights and duties of the state and of the individual with respect to each other are endlessly debatable. These debates, however, are necessarily inconclusive for purposes of formulating social policy. There are two reasons for this. First, policy decisions have to see individuals as members of groups, however short-lived the definition of any such groups may be. Secondly, however useful polemically such a notion may be, 'the state' cannot plausibly be conceived as a unitary body, acting with a single policy of intervention or non-intervention into an individual's life. To put this point another way, when when S. A. M. McLean and T. D. Campbell claim that 'the point of establishing rights in general, and human rights in particular, is to protect the individual against being used as an instrument of public policy' (McLean and Campbell 1981: 182), I would reply that the effect, if not necessarily the point, of establishing rights in general, and human rights in particular, is to fudge the issue of public policy.

This contention can be supported by reference to the case of *Thake and another* v *Maurice*. In 1975, the plaintiffs, a couple described as living in 'straitened circumstances', consulted the defendant, a surgeon, about arranging for the husband to have a vasectomy. In discussing the nature of the operation with the plaintiffs, the defendant made it clear that vasectomy was final, irreversible, and that the first plaintiff would become permanently sterile. The first plaintiff consented to the operation and the second plaintiff agreed to it. When they signed consent and agreement forms, they also stated in writing that they understood the nature of the operation. On receipt of advice that tests had shown Mr Thake's ejaculate to be sperm free, the couple resumed intercourse without contraceptive precautions. Two years later, Mrs Thake became pregnant but attributed the symptoms to early menopause, and pregnancy was discovered only when it was too late for her to have an abortion. A healthy child was born. The Thakes sued the surgeon, not for negligence in performing the operation, but for breach of contract.

The Thake case raised a number of interesting issues, such as whether the couple was induced into entering into the contract by a false warranty and whether there could be a contract between the defendant and Mrs Thake. The case got a lot of publicity. Not surprisingly, most of it was at the 'miracle baby' level, but there was also thinly-disguised disapproval of what was hinted to be a disproportionate amount of money as damages – £10,000. What was missing from news reports but which was of course included in the law reports was a description of the grounds of the judgement reached by Peter Pain J.

In the circumstances of Mrs Thake's pregnancy, it would be most surprising if any arguments were made in terms of the right to reproduce. If anything, the rights she might claim would be the right to forgo the right to reproduce, not to mention a right to anxiety-free sexual intercourse. In fact, Pain opened his remarks on questions of public policy with a reference to a judgement of the Supreme Court of Minnesota which started with the phrase 'pretermitting all moral and theological considerations ... ' (at 524).

We may reasonably assume that such considerations would include questions of rights. According to the arguments developed in this chapter, setting aside rights discourse should be an advantage in the process of feminist policy formation. The advantage to be gained from the avoidance of rights discourse is not, of course. that one would expect a judgement which was automatically consonant with feminist objectives. Rather, the advantage would lie in the opening up of questions of policy. Since the claiming of rights usually has the effect, deliberate or otherwise, of overriding questions of the wider calculation of the proper distribution of social benefits, the avoidance of rights claims is a strategy which should facilitate discussion of that calculation.

In the Thake case, it can be argued that, by not considering moral or theological questions, the court was able to take a much more progressive line on the birth of Mrs Thake's baby than might have been expected. For in *Udale* v *Bloomsbury Area Health Authority*, Jupp J. had held that it should not be possible to recover damages for the birth of a healthy child 'for a number of policy reasons, including the risk of the child feeling rejected as a result, and the difficulty in setting off the joy of the child against the financial disadvantage to her parents of her birth' (at 1109). In contrast, Pain affirmed:

> In approaching this problem I firmly put sentiment on one side. A healthy baby is so lovely a creature that I can well understand the reaction of one who asks: how could its birth possibly give rise to an action for damages? But every baby has a belly to be filled and a body to be clothed. The law relating to damages is concerned with reparation in money terms and this is what is needed for the maintenance of a baby. (at 526)

Once over that hurdle, Pain had to calculate damages, and it is here that the case is of special interest for a feminist critique of law and for the development of feminist politics. The details of the calculation make fascinating reading. For example, 'the cost of the layette (Mrs Thake having optimistically disposed of all baby clothes) and Samantha's up-keep to her first birthday is agreed at £717' (at 527). But it is the guidelines within which the calculation was made that are most striking. Pain congratulated the Thakes for having claimed damages on a moder-ate basis: 'They have made their calculation on the basis of the supple-mentary benefit scales. This is right. Samantha has been born into a humble household and the defendant should not be expected to do more than to provide her with necessaries' (ibid.). Presumably, if Mr Thake had been a surgeon or a judge, the award would have been quite a lot higher. As it was, the award of £9,677 included £2,000 for Mrs Thake's loss of earnings and £1,000 interest. The rest was meant to cover the costs of rearing Samantha up to her seventeenth birthday. This ludicrous calculation compares atrociously with both intuitive and costed estimates of the money needed to bring up a child (cf. Piachaud 1984).

The reference to supplementary benefit scales and the resulting low award could hardly be a better illustration for the feminist debate on women's dilemma of dependence on the state or dependence on a husband (cf. Smart 1984 passim). Of course, the Thake case can hardly be construed as a feminist victory. But it has always been part of feminist politics that women's economic and social realities should not be glossed by idealised concepts, indeed fantasies, of women's social status, particularly in relation to marriage, childbirth and childrearing. The Thake case and the strategy of avoiding the rhetoric of rights did make it possible for the main policy issues to be exhibited rather than suppressed, as they had been in the Udale case. And to reveal policy issues more clearly is an essential starting point for the identification of policy objectives and strategies.

One final point is by way of brief conclusion. I do not deny that appeals to rights can have the appearance of making an intervention in the sphere of practical politics, and I do not deny that rights discourse has attractions as the discourse of the downtrodden. My argument in this note has been that appealing to a right such as the right to reproduce is a practice which is not only unconducive to engagement with practical policy formation but, deliberately or otherwise, diverts attention from it. Worse still. as was apparent from Chapter 4, the appeal to the right to reproduce can turn out to be something of an ideological Trojan horse, and feminists would be well advised not to rely on its use in campaigns.

5

Cohabitation Contracts: a Socialist Feminist Issue

Introduction

In November 1983, *Cosmopolitan* urged its female readers to engage in all sorts of housework and domestic labour on moving into their lover's household but to refuse such assistance from their live-in lover when welcoming him to their own household (Burgess 1983). What can have prompted this advice from a publication not normally read for its household hints?

It was a reaction to the growing number of 'mistress cases', in particular *Eves* v. *Eves*, in which courts found in favour of rejected or ejected female cohabitants bringing actions to acquire an interest in the cohabitation property when there was no joint ownership. To date, the article warned, there have been no 'male-mistress' cases, but it was only a matter of time, not least since the male cohabitant would usually get around to making some sort of contribution to the household, 'unless' *Cosmo* conceded, 'he's a gigolo'.

There have still been no headline-grabbing male-mistress or gigolo cases in England and Wales, but there have been many more legal actions arising from cohabitation disputes. A variety of positions has developed on what the law's proper or preferable response should be to cohabitation, but in the early 1980s a number of legal commentators expressed dissatisfaction with the uncertain state of the law and advocated the legal recognition of cohabitation contracts as a way of cutting through the increasingly complex, unpredictable, and contradictory development of case law.

In these commentaries there are few references to socialist politics. But the issue of cohabitation should be placed on the agenda of socialist politics for at least two reasons. First, as increasing numbers of people cohabit rather than marry (General Household Survey 1987: 7), socialists can no longer rely on their familiar critiques of marriage to supply the materials for a socialist politics of contemporary living conditions. Secondly, socialists are still subject to the feminist criticism that they have concentrated on inequalities in the public sphere at the expense of inequalities in domestic and sexual arrangements. For these two reasons, cohabitation is a socialist feminist issue.

This chapter is a collection of some of the materials useful for the development of a socialist feminist politics of cohabitation contracts. It does not attempt to cover cohabitation contracts in their broadest application – which would include taxation, inheritance, social security benefits, provisions for children – since that would be a huge project. It is concerned only with the acquisition of property rights. First, some historical examples will be used to show how socialists or feminists have resisted prevailing patterns of the regulation of relations between domestic and sexual partners by the use of contracts. The point of this exercise is not to propose that such contracts have an unbroken radical history. Rather, the debates surrounding these examples serve to direct attention to issues which a contemporary politics of cohabitation will encounter. Secondly, a brief description of current legal issues will be used to show why some commentators have been led to recommend the legal recognition of cohabitation contracts. Relevant items of socialist feminist politics will then be introduced into those legal issues.

The conclusion this chapter reaches is that the legal recognition of cohabitation contracts would increase the variety of options open to people in making their household arrangements and that it should therefore be supported by socialist feminists. This support should be presented as an argument for a policy the outcome of which is diversity, not for a policy which is dictated by the values of fairness, justice, and equal access to social benefits. This is partly because all those values can be and have been invoked in support of arguments against the legal recognition of cohabitation contracts, thus demonstrating their disturbingly promiscuous career in legal–political debates. It is also because emphasis on equality easily results in an unacceptable form of dogmatism, the insistence that contracting parties 'go equal shares'. So the conclusion of the chapter enters a caution against over-enthusiasm for cohabitation contracts by suggesting that socialist feminists should also consider support for other legal devices for the regulation of household arrangements, such as the contractual licence. They might once again take their cue from *Cosmopolitan* and recommend prospective cohabitants to contemplate 'licensing their live-in lover', however distant from the ideals of socialist feminist politics that discourse might seem at first sight.

Historical examples

From classical socialist and feminist criticism of conventional forms of domestic and sexual arrangements, four examples are identified which recommend written contracts as appropriate mechanisms for the regulation of those arrangements.

Revolutionary republicanism and civic rights for women. Olympe de Gouges wrote the Declaration of Rights of Woman and of Citizen in 1791. The main text is given in Chapter 8. Not included in that main text, however, is this part of the Preamble, her 'Model for a Social Contract Between a Man and a Woman':

> We, N & M, of our own free will, unite ourselves for the remainder of our lives and for the duration of our mutual inclinations, according to the following conditions. We intend and desire to pool our fortunes as community property, while nevertheless preserving the right to divide them on behalf of our children and those we might have with someone else ... We obligate ourselves equally, in case of separation, to divide our fortune, and to set apart the portion belonging to our children as indicated by the law; and in the case of perfect union, the first to die would assign half the property to their children; and if one of us should die without children, the survivor would inherit everything, unless the dying party had disposed of his half of the common wealth in favour of someone else he might deem appropriate. (de Gouges, in Bell and Offen 1983: 108–9)

While de Gouges intended such contracts to apply just as strictly to the poor as to the rich, Susan Bell and Karen Offen have argued that the benefit of such contracts could be available only to those parties who could afford substantial legal fees – the wealthy aristocracy and the upper middle classes (1983: 31, n. 3). In this comment, one can discern a basis for some modern commentaries on the use of cohabitation contracts. It has been noted that the accessibility of such contracts may be dependent on the ability of parties to pay considerable sums of money (Kingdom 1990: 297). At a rather different level, there has been criticism of cohabitation contracts on the grounds that, through skilful use of the ideology of equality, cohabitation contracts can be used to legitimate forms of domination and inequality characteristic of the prevailing market (cf. Olsen 1983 and the discussion of Olsen in Kingdom 1990). Certainly, de Gouges' draft contract is expressed in terms of equality: it makes no reference to the origins of the parties' fortunes, nor to the possibility that the parties might want to keep their fortunes, whatever the size of the fortunes, distinct, a preference to which I return in the final section of this chapter. Meanwhile, it has to be said that de Gouges attracted terrific opposition, for all sorts of reasons, not least her temerity in challenging the social justification of the 1789 Declaration of Rights of Man and of Citizen. Some of these issues are examined in Chapter 8. But those feminists who these days are sympathetic to cohabitation contracts as a useful option for the regulation of domestic and sexual relationships can learn from de Gouges. They will learn from her prognostication of the hostility which cohabitation contracts and their proponents can produce.

De Gouges correctly anticipated 'all the hypocrites, clergy, and their gang of diabolic followers' rising up against her. She was guillotined by the Jacobins in 1793.

Utopian socialist feminism. With its emphasis on property, de Gouges' proposal would hardly be consonant with the belief of her Owenite contemporaries that 'the only way finally to end property in women ... was to end property itself' (Taylor 1983: 36). Indeed, when Robert Dale Owen and Mary Jane Robinson drew up a marriage document, he acknowledged that he was unable legally to divest himself of the unjust rights which his marriage gave him over the person and property of another but averred that he could and would divest himself of them morally, along with all the other 'barbarous relics of a feudal, despotic system' (quoted in Bernard 1972: 87). A similar form of protest marriage, as they called it, was enacted by Henry B. Blackwell and Lucy Stone. An interesting feature of their commitment was their stated belief that 'where domestic difficulties arise, no appeal should be made to existing tribunals under existing laws, but that all difficulties should be submitted to the equitable adjustment of arbitrators mutually chosen' (quoted in Bernard 1972: 88). The Owen/Robinson and Blackwell/Stone agreements both display a distrust of bourgeois law, but they were both drafted in the desire that the law should recognise the equality of the contracting partners. As we shall see, this sort of tension is evident in contemporary debates about cohabitation contracts.

Radical feminism. Tackling the moralism of utopian socialism, Shulamith Firestone rejects mere goodwill as the source of a non-exploitative future society. She identifies several lifestyles which might characterise the transitional period between capitalism and the utopia of cybernetic communism (Firestone 1972: 210f). In one lifestyle, 'living together' would become an increasingly common practice. Two or more partners would take out a non-legal sex/companionate contract, the key feature of which would be its flexibility. Another lifestyle, 'the household', would be characterised by a 'limited contract' according to which a group of ten or so consenting adults would apply for a licence to live in the same household for a limited period – long enough to provide a stable structure for children to grow up in. Firestone notes that in the early stages of the household structure people might want to have their arrangements legally recognised. Her hope that a legal structure might eventually prove un-necessary as a safeguard of the domestic basis of the new society is linked to her critique of marriage as restricting choice of domestic and sexual arrangements. She reiterates her belief that socialists and feminists should seek to transfer all the cultural incentives supporting marriage to a much broader range of alternatives. Similar critiques of marriage feature in current feminist arguments for the legal recognition of cohabitation contracts, and Firestone would have been enthusiastic about the current tendency in Sweden to assimilate marriage to cohabitation (Bradley 1989), as in New South Wales (cf. Parker 1987: 189), rather than cohabitation to marriage as implicit in the terms of reference of two Scottish Law Commission discussion papers (SLC 1990a, 1990b). I shall return to this specific issue in the next chapter.

Bolshevik feminism. Whilst the epithet 'utopian' would be welcome to Firestone, it would be a devastating criticism for Alexandra Kollontai. Yet that is precisely the comment made by the modern critic, Alix Holt, in her introduction to Kollontai's 'Marriage and Everyday Life', specifically with reference to Kollontai's proposal for marital economic contracts (Kollontai 1977). This was one of Kollontai's contributions to the debates surrounding marriage law in the Soviet Union. It was a speech made in 1926, the year after the Commissariat of Justice had drafted a new family code. The 1918 family code had abolished the concept of community property of spouses, a proclamation consistent both with the Marxist analysis of the corruptive influence of private wealth and with the belief that women's emancipation could occur only with their entry into social production (Geiger 1970: ch. 4). Under the New Economic Policy, however, female unemployment rose. Many women were unable to work and unable to acquire goods and money themselves. Observing the increasing numbers of divorced and consequently impoverished women, the Commissariat proposed the re-establishment of community property of spouses and, noting the rise in female prostitution, it proposed the legal recognition of *de facto* marriages. This was effectively the proposal that men be required to support past or present common law wives.

Kollontai's objection to the draft code focused on the inadequacy of the alimony provisions designed to protect women. Their inadequacy derived from the problems of identifying, and not infrequently adjudicating between, *de facto* wives. Difficulties also arose when one man had several *de facto* wives as well as a *de jure* wife. Furthermore, registration of *de facto* marriage was a mechanical administrative device which could not solve the problem of a third category, the 'casual wife', typically a poor peasant or working woman new to the towns and who might be unlikely to apply to the courts to prove paternity.

Kollontai's proposed solution was the introduction of marital economic contracts to regulate not the personal but the property norms of household economies. Among the merits of the scheme, she believed, were that contracts could be made flexible enough to suit different household conditions, they permitted easy resolution of disputes, women would have a proper valuation of their household labour, and working women would have the opportunity to establish equality before the government and before the law.

Kollontai thought members of a household would find it in their interests to conclude such contracts. For those women who, either in households or living singly, were not party to contracts, however, there would be a collective fund to which all adult and employed persons in the Soviet Union would make compulsory contributions according to income. In this way, a socialist solution to the protection of motherhood and childhood would be encouraged, until such time as the national economy could afford full social security.

For Holt, Kollontai's proposal was utopian because it was not clearly related either to the connection between women's liberation and industrialisation or to the immediate and critical problem of the Soviet Union's economic development. The criticism is harsh, particularly since, as Holt acknowledges, Kollontai anticipated the likely opposition of the Minister of Finance to the proposed common fund. It is pertinent for the development of a contemporary socialist feminist politics of cohabitation, however, to note three features of Kollontai's case for marital economic contracts.

First, Kollontai supported the notion of clear intent of the parties to a contract, preferring a social system which places confidence in members' capacities to order their own affairs to a social system which imposes a rigid style of living on them. Secondly, in recommending a variety of state forms of contract, Kollontai did not extend her critique of bourgeois capitalist law as the regulation of property to the use of the law for the promotion of socialism and feminism. In this case, she could have argued that the institution of marital economic contracts was a transitional solution to the problem of how to support motherhood and childhood until such time as the complete socialist revolution could consolidate the disappearance of the vestiges of the bourgeois family and its replacement by the community. Thirdly, in recommending that her proposal operate in conjunction with a proper social security scheme, Kollontai did not make the assumption that the institution of marital economic contracts would be adequate to the complete range of circumstances experienced by individuals in the prevailing economy. Of these three points, the first is a regular feature of current arguments for the legal recognition of cohabitation contracts. The second calls attention to current debates about the use of bourgeois law to further socialist feminist objectives. The third should alert socialist feminists to the possibility that, progressive as the legal recognition of cohabitation contracts may be, it is not a universal model for domestic and sexual arrangements.

Current legal issues

Most discussions of the legal implications of cohabitation draw attention to the confused, ambivalent, and occasionally contradictory state of the law's response. The comment is often linked, in the English context, to two very different problems. The first is the difficulty of defining cohabitation, and the second is the influence of Lord Denning.

Attempts at defining cohabitation sometimes refer to the length of time during which the parties have been cohabiting, a somewhat question-begging formula, sometimes to the 'degree of commitment' of the co-habiting parties, and sometimes to comparisons with marriage. In one typically thorough work from the United States, nineteen definitions have been collected (Cole 1977). Some writers, however, refuse to be drawn into such definitional difficulties, on the grounds that cohabitation, unlike marriage, is not self-proving, that it does not have a single legal definition, and that it is not *per se* the object of legal attention (Oliver 1987: viii). Rather, as Martin Parry points out: 'the legal response to cohabitation depends on the qualitative and quantitative nature of cohabitation and the purpose for which it is being claimed, or denied, that a couple are cohabiting' (Parry 1988: 4). Indeed, as we shall see in Chapter 6, different ways of conceptualising cohabitation have significantly different implications for the construction of cohabitation rights.

If cohabitation is a legal chameleon, the situation is at least in part attributable to a number of Denning's judgements. Until the 1970s, practitioners and petitioners could be reasonably sure that, in the case of property disputes, parties to cohabitation would be dealt with according to the following rules. The legal title to property would be distinguished from the beneficial interest in it which allowed a share in the profit from its sale. The beneficial interest would be established in proportion to the contributions made by the parties to its purchase. These contributions, it must be emphasised, related to purchase, and inequalities of purchasing power could make no impact on property law. From 1972, however, the criterion of contribution to purchase, familiar to property law, was challenged by the introduction of other criteria for the establishment of beneficial interest. These new criteria constituted a diffusion of the activities which could count as making a contribution. It no longer had to be direct financial contribution to the purchase of the property. It could be an indirect financial contribution, such as paying household bills, thereby permitting a larger mortgage. It could be a non-financial contri-bution, such as doing domestic labour, particularly if – as in *Eves* v. *Eves* – the female cohabitant undertook major construction work on the property, work which Denning seemed to think remarkable in unmarried women but which he thought in a married woman would create a beneficial interest (at 1342). Other activities which could help towards acquiring a beneficial interest might include having children and making any changes, such as giving up work, which would not have been made if there were not some expectation of the future mingling of property interests. Such an expectation could be formed on the basis of what the various parties had said or had been led to believe. These assorted criteria could be held to support the existence of a trust.

The various types of trust are not easily distinguishable, and the courts often have not distinguished them clearly. More particularly, their failure to distinguish them in the context of property disputes between cohabiting or formerly cohabiting parties has been linked to Denning's judgements in *Cooke* v. *Head*, *Eves* v. *Eves*, and *Hussey* v *Palmer* (Parry 1988: 25–9). His use of trust law has been described as 'creative' in developing what he called a new model of constructive trust, whereby a trust might be imposed by equity, irrespective of the intentions of parties. One advantage of this approach is that it avoids the difficulty of ascertaining intention. Rebecca Bailey-Harris has provided a revealing analysis of these problems in some recent Australian cases, and she proposes that the Australian courts should abandon the criterion of intent in favour of 'the development of a general doctrine of the constructive trust as a remedy imposed, quite irrespective of the parties' intentions, to prevent unconscionable conduct' (1990: 368). But the term 'creative' does not always indicate approval, and Denning's introduction into property law of his chivalrously interpreted principles of equality – ostensibly to protect the interests of vulnerable female cohabitants – has produced both confused case law and almost every type of legal and political response imaginable. Four legal responses are discussed below.

A return to the dictates of property law. There are indications that, since Denning's retirement, the Court of Appeal has retreated from the view that the division of a shared household consequent on the parties' separation should be made in the light of what is just and reasonable (Parker 1987: 136). For some legal practitioners this retreat is clearly a matter for celebration (Sookias et al. 1987: 1309). For other legal commentators, however, the diminished influence of Denning's judgements is a matter of regret and social concern at the plight of the 'informal family'. Diana Parker, for example, argues that the law has a duty to protect the vulnerable, and she makes a preliminary case for the statutory protection of cohabitants on the breakdown of their relationship (1984: 40). The Scottish Law Commission is currently considering law reforms along these lines (1990b).

Extension of statutory protection. Stephen Parker is well aware of the criticism of paternalism if statutes which apply to married couples are extended to cohabiting couples (1987: 189f). He suggests, however, that where judges have been supportive of female cohabitants the more they assume wife-like behaviour, this may be less a matter of conscious policy than the result of the analogical nature of English legal reasoning – in this case, attempting to perceive the justice of a cohabitation case by reference to cases concerning spouses. Conscious policy or not, Parker has contended that 'the law is engaged in reproducing the traditional patriarchal family form by assimilating threats to the marital norm within a slightly wider definition of marriage' (Parker 1981: 222–3). The boundaries are being re-drawn. Gloomily acknowledging this trend, Parker nonetheless supports the extension to cohabiting parties of the procedures presently available only to married people. In particular, he recommends that some sort of adjustive property regime should be available, meaning that by analogy with the provisions of the Matrimonial Causes Act 1973 relating to divorce, the courts would have the power to place formerly cohabiting parties in the financial position they would have enjoyed had their relationship not broken down (Parker 1981: 153).

A single legislative code. Given the foregoing response to the uncertainty of cohabitation law, it is not surprising that one legal commentator, at least, should advocate the introduction of a single legislative code (Johnson 1986: 47). Without a draft code to inspect, it is not possible to assess Johnson's proposal. Two points of interest to socialist feminists might nonetheless be made. First, one might speculate that if the success of such a code were to be judged in terms of how well it removed present anomalies and injustices, it might have to be relatively prescriptive, in the sense of specifying exactly what relationships and causes of breakdown of a relationship would attract the protection and/or intrusion of the courts. An effect of this, intended or not, could be the limitation of the range of domestic and sexual arrangements which people see as open to them. Secondly, there are good reasons for supposing that in England a single legislative code would be more likely to assimilate cohabitation to marriage, rather than, as in Sweden, marriage to cohabitation. In his review of the Swedish Cohabitees (Joint Homes) Act 1987, hereafter SCJH, however, Bradley comments that this major development in the legal status and rights of unmarried cohabitees 'provides an interesting model for the regulation of informal domestic relationships. More fundamentally, it is one indicator in a controversial area of a legal, social and political culture which differs radically from that in the United Kingdom' (Bradley 1989: 324). As I intimate below, socialist feminists should think twice before supporting a single legislative code which, in the legal, social and political culture of the UK, is more likely to strengthen marriage than to undermine it.

The legal recognition of cohabitation contracts. The problems and uncertainties attaching to all three of the above responses to the unsatisfactory state of cohabitation law have led several professional lawyers and legal commentators to advocate the use and the legal recognition of cohabitation contracts. The definitive work in England and Wales is Chris Barton's *Cohabitation Contracts* (1985), in which he scrupulously reviews the present law, including likely obstacles to enforcement of contracts, and sets out arguments for and against the contract approach. In this last task, he acknowledges the fuller work of Lenore Weitzman in *The Marriage Contract* (1981), in which she reviews the case for written contracts, in and outside marriage, in the context of marriage law in the US.

Weitzman argues that 'intimate contracts' have several advantages for the couple, including the promotion of an egalitarian relationship and the enjoyment of privacy and freedom in ordering personal relationships. The reference to privacy is worth noting. As we have seen, the utopian socialists expressed qualms about the intrusion of law in the event of a relationship breaking down, preferring an appeal to a mutually acceptable arbitrator or conciliator. Similar preference might be expressed these days for reliance on non-legal or pre-legal forms of conciliation. On the other hand, the authors of *The Cohabitation Handbook* argue that for the courts not to uphold cohabitation contracts is an unnecessary interference with personal freedom (Bottomley et al. 1981: 181). Furthermore, the possibility of law's intrusion being unwelcome has to be set against the merits of being able to choose the form of one's sexual and domestic arrangements and of not having marriage law imposed on parties who expressly reject it. So, for example, Michael Freeman and Christina Lyon develop their explicitly feminist view that 'women should not be "protected" by having marriage thrust on them willy-nilly', either through the mistaken belief that marriage protects women or through treating cohabitants as spouses (1983: vii). They argue that the assimilation of cohabiting women to the status of spouse and their treatment as dependents provides a way of controlling women and a form of regulation which would properly be eroded by the legal recognition of cohabitation contracts. Together with all other advocates of this legal recognition, they emphasise the desirable outcome of an increased awareness on the part of the cohabiting couple of what their obligations are. This is valuable even if – and perhaps especially if – women are thereby made aware of their inferior social status and financial expectations. To this sort of advantage of the contract approach Weitzman adds the societal advantages of the accommodation of diversity and the reform of antiquated law. These advantages would clearly be acceptable to socialist feminists, even though Weitzman's arguments are presented in terms of 'our pluralist society' rather than in terms of a revolution in or a transformation of existing social conditions.

The previous section identified a number of feminist and socialist positions emphasising the need for flexibility and the importance of finding alternatives to antiquated law in the regulation of domestic and sexual relationships. To those arguments can be added three further analyses by contemporary writers.

First, Jacob Sundberg has drawn attention to the links between early

Bolshevik family law and modern changes in Swedish family life (1976: 34). He points to the shared belief in both contexts that bourgeois church marriage should be replaced by free partnership, a shared belief that legislation should be neutral as between different forms of cohabitation (meaning that there should be no advantages or benefits accruing to people who opt for one form of arrangement rather than another), and a shared dilemma over whether this principle of neutrality could give adequate protection to women who are officially equal but materially unequal to men.

Secondly, Ruth Deech has strongly attacked the notion of the 'weak woman' as a reason for opposing the legal recognition of cohabitation contracts (1980: 496). Whilst recognising that parties to a contract may be in an unequal bargaining position, she sees that as no reason to exempt women from keeping their side of the deal. Her arguments are not presented as either socialist or feminist, but much of her position accords with feminists' and socialists' long-established scepticism about the desirability of extending marriage law – already inadequate to marriage – to cohabitation. It also accords with their belief that the best protection against a court-imposed solution to cohabitation disputes would be for the couple to make a legally enforceable contract.

Thirdly, the strategies for change outlined by Michèle Barrett and Mary McIntosh are predicated on their forceful socialist feminist attack on marriage and the family (1982). Their strategies include advocating greater freedom of choice and greater diversity in the establishment and conduct of households. They do not mention cohabitation contracts, so it is possible that they think the legal recognition of cohabitation contracts would merely extend the arm of the judiciary into previously unregulated relationships. On the other hand, they repeatedly press for experimentation with forms of domestic and sexual arrangements other than marriage and the traditionally constructed family, on the grounds that experimentation can be a constructive part of political commitment to change. So they could well argue that socialist feminists should support the legal recognition of cohabitation contracts on the grounds that this would loosen the grip of traditional – and antiquated – forms of domestic and sexual arrangements.

Furthermore, there is little in Weitzman's discussion of social policy issues with which socialist feminists are likely to disagree. Rather, it is in her discussion of the effects of a contract on an intimate relationship that one of the potentially most serious issues arises for supporters of cohabitation contracts. Weitzman considers the objection to the contract approach that the morals of the marketplace would be wrongly encouraged in the intimate sphere and that neither the conduct nor the rights of intimates should be determined by those morals. She counters this objection in two ways. First, she rejects the over-simple distinction between business and personal morality. Secondly, she denies that negotiation and reciprocity necessarily undermine co-operation, either in business or in personal relationships; she suggests that they may, on the contrary, lead to the achievement of mutually advantageous and agreed objectives.

There is not much to be gained by lodging claim and counter-claim for abstract moral values such as reciprocity and co-operation, but attention must be given to a more sophisticated version of the complaint that women's interests are not best served by reforms which introduce market considerations into the family. Frances Olsen has analysed in detail the history of reform strategies aimed at improving women's lives. She is particularly pessimistic about any strategy which tries to promote equality within the family by making the family more like the market. Her pertinent example here is the importation of contract principles into the family in the form of cohabitation contracts. Where such a strategy succeeds, Olsen argues, it does so because of the success of the market. It introduces greater freedom and equality only to the extent that the market has already done so. Worse, where such a strategy fails, it does so because of the failures of the market. The equality introduced is (merely) juridical equality; it is at best inadequate, at worst a legitimation and reinforcement of the inequalities of the market (Olsen 1983: 1530).

Olsen's critique of the contract approach is not, therefore, that cohabitation contracts bring no benefits. On the contrary, she sees them as progressive in so far as they strengthen the position of individual women, particularly those who manage to negotiate better terms than they might achieve without a contract. She also acknowledges the value of a contract approach as widening people's options and facilitating experiment. Rather, her critique of the contract approach is that it is of necessity presented within the terms of the prevailing but unchallenged dichotomy between market and family, so that – through skilful use of its claimed ideology of equality – its proponents may legitimise substantive forms of inequality and domination, such as unequal earning capacity and emotional inequality.

Olsen's next step is to start a 'conversation' about a new vision: one which transcends the family/market dichotomy characteristic of contemporary thought. To do this she draws on the vision of progress associated with Feuerbach. It has to be said that, from this point on, Olsen's work engages in a debate which can bear no relation to questions of policy or strategy and which cannot connect with current analyses of social conditions. This point has been made tellingly by Nikolas Rose (1987 n. 18) and I have recently made a detailed analysis of the vacuity of Olsen's position in comparison with that of Weitzman (Kingdom 1990).

For immediate purposes, I would merely say that Olsen's work is a perfect example of the dangers of critique catalogued by Paul Hirst and Phil Jones: primarily the danger of issuing 'a challenge to existing institutions and ideas which rejects them wholesale', and in particular the danger of discarding them as irredeemably liberal or bourgeois (1987: 22).

A more useful and usable approach to the question of policy in relation to cohabitation contracts would be to return to the question of whether, currently, socialist feminists should support their legal recognition, at least in relation to the acquisition of property rights. It would be sensible at this point to observe that no realisable social policy is going to bring uniform benefits to all women, or to all men. In this context, for example, it is clear that for some women the notion of a cohabitation contract will never have, or seem to have, any practical value. They may feel adequately protected by the institution of marriage. They may be living singly, from choice or not. They may never, for a variety of reasons, be in a position to purchase property. Here we should recall Bell and Offen's comment on de Gouges' draft social contract, namely that contractual arrangements would be attractive only to those who could afford the legal fees to have them drawn up, never mind enforced. Similarly, we should recall Kollontai's realisation that the institution of marital economic contracts would not help those women whose circumstances could not be covered by such contracts, and that alternative social provision would have to be made for them. Adapted to the immediate question, these points could well amount to the criticism that socialist feminists should concentrate less on strengthening the ideology of private property through advocacy of legally recognisable cohabitation contracts and more on campaigning for improved access to public housing and to better quality public housing (cf. Austerberry and Watson 1981: 49).

There is no doubt that socialist feminists should support the objective of more and better public housing. At the same time, they have had to acknowledge the success of campaigns to encourage people in their aspiration to own private property. To regret the effect of this success on public housing provision is not, however, to justify inattention to the conditions under which private property is bought and sold. It is in this context that the legal recognition of cohabitation contracts should be supported by socialist feminists as one way of increasing the alternatives open to people for the regulation of their household arrangements.

A caution against over-enthusiasm for cohabitation contracts

Materials assembled so far for a socialist feminist politics of cohabitation make an overwhelming case for the legal recognition of cohabitation contracts, at least in respect of the acquisition of property rights. This conclusion is justified primarily in terms of the increased range of options consequently available to people. A caution needs to be lodged, however, against over-enthusiasm for this conclusion. It concerns the spirit of equality said to characterise the use of cohabitation contracts. There are two points to be made here. First, as I have argued elsewhere (Kingdom 1990), the fact that marriage is a site of inequality should not be interpreted to mean that any other form of domestic and sexual arrangement is automatically egalitarian. Secondly, and more pertinently here, it seems to be a common assumption that the use of cohabitation contracts implies a particular type of equality, which for convenience I shall call equalisation.

This second point can be made most easily through scrutiny of two published draft contracts (Bottomley et al. 1981: 191f and n. 26; Gray 1973: 596). Admittedly the drafts are only examples, the content of which could be varied. In both, however, there is constant reference to equal interests in property, joint ownership of assets purchased, equal shares, and the setting up of a common fund to which both parties would be entitled equally. These draft contracts are remarkably similar to the model proposed by de Gouges.

Feminists have long been aware of the dangers of appealing to equality. I argued this in Chapter 4 and its Note and I resume it in Chapter 7 with an examination of one feminist strategy for avoiding the problems of claiming equal rights. In the particular example of cohabitation issues, feminists have argued that formal equality of the contracting parties can conceal substantive inequalities of economic opportunity and purchasing power. This is part of Olsen's argument. Clearly, the assumption in this feminist position is that it is women who suffer these inequalities, and I would agree that for the most part this assumption accurately reflects current social conditions. On the other hand, there is evidence that increasing numbers of women are living in their own property and that the number of female first-time buyers is increasing (National and Provincial Building Society 1987; Nationwide Building Society 1986). There may be several reasons for this phenomenon – alleviation of the problems single women used to experience when trying to get a mortgage, divorced women retaining the matrimonial home, women outliving men. To revert to my opening remarks about the reaction of *Cosmopolitan* to *Eves* v. *Eves*, it is not at all obvious that the interests of women houseowners who are living singly – for whatever reason – are best served, in the event of their beginning a cohabitation relationship, by their drawing up a cohabitation contract which would give the new live-in lover an equal interest in the property and its contents. If the socialist feminist argument in favour of cohabitation contracts on the grounds of diversity of options is to have political credibility, socialist feminists must also take seriously the possibility that some women may not want the equalisation typically assumed to be part of the ideology of cohabitation contracts.

It is interesting in this connection to note that the SCJH recognises that, whilst equality should be a presumption in the event of a cohabitation dispute, it does not follow that equalisation should be a mandatory outcome. Here Bradley's commentary on this aspect of the Swedish law is pertinent.

> The policy of freedom of law and relationships, and the principle of freedom of choice have, to some extent, been preserved. Where unmarried cohabitees give no thought to their property relations, the assumption in the new legislation is that they intend to share the home and household goods which they acquire. If an ideological objection of marriage and freedom to opt out of legal regulation are important in a particular case, contracting out of the right to division of property under this legislation is possible for those who are sufficiently well informed, and who have the inclination to make a contract. (Bradley 1985: 333)

If socialist feminists agree that cohabitation contracts should be legally recognised, and that it should be possible for contracting parties to avoid equalisation, there are good reasons why they should be wary of presenting policies for cohabitation in terms of a demand for 'cohabitants' rights'. As we shall see in Chapter 6, the phrase does have its uses as a convenient pigeon-hole for cohabitation issues. Apart from that, the phrase is dangerously vague, both because it does not invite scrutiny of the very different ways in which cohabitation rights are currently constructed in law, and because, in so far as it has any meaning, it probably does connote equality and equalisation.

If it is allowed that some women may not want the equalisation that is typically presumed to follow from the ideology of egalitarianism claimed by advocates of cohabitation contracts, then Denning's judgement in *Eves* v. *Eves* can be seen in a different light. For, just as some women objected to Denning's chivalry in *Eves* v. *Eves*, so those women would be none too pleased to find some female court of appeal judge solemnly finding a constructive trust – in the interests of equality – in favour of a male live-in lover who, contrary to all expectations of the proper role of men, particularly unmarried men, had done the washing and ironing for a certain period of time. Such women might conclude that their best interests are served by a quite different legal device. They could offer the new live-in lover a contractual licence. Basically, this is a licence to live in and use all or parts of the property, to use items such as a car or television, while the licensor retains legal possession, rights of control and management of the property, and all beneficial proprietary interest in it. The device of the contractual licence might not suit all cohabitants, but it is one of a number of ways they might choose to regulate their domestic and sexual relationships. If socialist feminists are genuinely committed to a politics of diversity in this sphere, considerations of this and any other legal device should supplement their support for the legal recognition of cohabitation contracts as advocated here.

6

Cohabitation Rights: Status, Contract or Dependence?

Introduction

Working from the observation that there is no coherent package of cohabitation rights under English law, this chapter brings together some key questions of social policy for the construction of cohabitation rights.

Martin L. Parry identifies three main ways in which cohabitation rights may be constructed: (1) through the status of the cohabitants (for example, by comparison with married persons), (2) arising from an agreement or a contract (for example, specifying property use and interests), and (3) on the basis of one cohabitant's dependence on the other (for example, in recognition of the unequal economic position of one cohabitant as a result of childcare arrangements). These alternatives are of considerable interest to those specifically concerned with feminist politics. Parry's classification can serve as a clearing-house for the registration of feminist political analyses.

Parry also mentions, though briefly, the possibility of introducing a legislative code of rights. He contrasts this approach with the current practice of judicial discretion. Such contrasting policy options are analysed by Neil MacCormick with respect to inheritance law under the jurisdictions of Scotland, England and Connecticut. He indicates a marginal preference for legal provisions which confer discretionary benefits over those which confer rights. I argue. however, that MacCormick's analysis is flawed and merely restates the problem it addresses. I conclude that the nature of the flaw in MacCormick's analysis gives feminists good grounds for resisting the extension of English law's technique of judicial discretion in the area of cohabitation disputes.

What cohabitation rights are there?

This is not a straightforward question, for the term 'cohabitation rights' is to some extent a bogus one. Indeed, there are a number of reasons for exercising caution in the use of the term. First, in English law, there is no simply and easily identifiable body of legislation dealing exclusively with cohabitation. This is not a distinguishing feature of cohabitation. A. A. S.

Zuckermann points out that 'there is no special law of property or of contract for those who are married' (1980: 251). But most legal practitioners and commentators observe that the courts are working out solutions to cohabitation disputes on a largely *ad hoc* and piecemeal basis, ungoverned by clear policies or principles.

Inevitably, and quite properly, many discussions of the disparate and uncertain nature of the legal position of cohabitants concentrate on specific areas of legal initiatives, responses and practices. For example, there have been what might be called legal-intensive debates about the use of trust devices to support claims to the cohabitation premises, about the removal of succession disabilities of illegitimacy, about the courts' refusal to enforce maintenance agreements between cohabiting couples, and many others. The high degree of legal specificity of these matters is not conducive to the production of a coherent package of cohabitation rights. Further, as one would expect under English law, the courts rarely make explicit mention of rights. Similarly, when legal commentators talk about rights in this context, it is often in a very particular way. A clear example is provided by Zuckerman's analysis.

In his discussion of cases about competing claims over the cohabitation home and about the source of support for children on the collapse, for whatever reason, of informal family arrangements, Zuckerman heads his two main sections 'Rights in the home' and 'Rights of support'. Most of what goes under those headings is not expressed in terms of rights. It is only in his various scene-setting, problem-identifying, winding-up or reflective modes that he explicitly refers to rights. In these modes what emerges very clearly is his terminology of securing rights, creating rights, giving effect to rights, determining rights, acquiring rights, situations giving rise to rights, granting of rights, and conferral of rights.

One might infer from the above reasons for caution in the use of the term 'cohabitation rights' that one might as well recommend the complete abandonment of the term. Removing it from the language could dispel any illusion that there actually existed a coherent package of cohabitation rights. But there is no point in playing Humpty Dumpty. In any case, it is arguable that, although the term has no specific meaning, it does serve as a convenient pigeon-hole for a certain range of relatively new social and legal problems. For that reason, and also because of the seemingly irresistible political–polemical power of rights discourse, the term will persist, even with the vaguest of meanings, both in legal commentaries and in policy debates. If that is so, there is a more judicious inference from the type of rights discourse adopted by Zuckerman (and other legal commentators). This is simply to acknowledge and emphasise that there is no coherent package of cohabitation rights and to stress the need to investigate the various ways in which cohabitation rights are constructed.

An invaluable starting-point for this investigation is Martin L. Parry's classification of the three main ways in which cohabitation rights have been constructed in English law: through status, through contract, and through dependence (Parry 1988: 227f). I now consider these in turn.

Rights through status

Cohabitation rights may be constructed by reference to the status of the parties. Persons would have rights in so far as they met various criteria of cohabitation. Where courts have adopted a status approach, criteria have included: the duration of the relationship; the cohabitants' financial arrangements; the intimate commitment of the cohabitants; the outwardly observable features of the relationship, such as whether or not the cohabitants adopt the same second name.

The status approach is almost renowned for its problems. In the first instance, there are problems of definition. Cohabitation has to be defined because there is no state-imposed cohabitation ceremony and no official cohabitation certificate to prove the relationship. Following the criteria mentioned above, some of the difficulties of definition can be indicated from the following questions. How long would a couple have to cohabit before they acquired the necessary status? What financial arrangements would there have to be for a couple to be described as cohabitants? What is the character of the appropriate intimate commitment? Do they actually have to live together all the time? Do they have to have sexual intercourse? Parry suggests that these definitional problems would produce all the difficulties associated with the operation of a cohabitation rule, such as the invidiousness of detailed enquiry into people's personal lives in order to establish that they merit or must forgo the benefits of a certain status (1988: 228).

In the light of these difficulties, it is hardly surprising that legal practitioners and commentators have relied on comparisons between cohabiting couples and married couples in the resolution of cohabitation disputes (cf. Rights of Women 1979-80: 16). In fact, it is equally unsurprising that this type of analogous reasoning does not solve the problems of definition. In the first place, it is by no means clear what criteria have to be satisfied if a couple is to be said to live together 'as man and wife'. Do they have to make out that they are married? Is it enough if they are thought to be married? More radically, however, legal commentators increasingly point out that there are no compelling reasons why a definition of cohabitation should take its cue from the definition of marriage. David Hodson, for example, notes that 'Cohabitation can be construed in wider terms than two people living together as man and wife' (1990: 28).

No doubt as a result of these definitional problems, arguments for and against the status approach to cohabitation rights have in fact focused on its tendency to assimilate cohabitants to the status of married persons. In favour of this approach, it might be argued that cohabitants should not be excluded from many of the protections and benefits of married couples. Following this line of argument, Zuckerman describes what he calls 'an argument from justice'. He considers the example of the homebound cohabitant who, if the relationship ceases, should be accorded compensation for household and childcare work, just as a spouse would. On this sort of argument, women in particular should not be penalised for making traditional contributions to the household simply because they have not been married to their partner (Zuckerman 1980: 275).

These issues are informed by broader, more sociological controversies and these in turn produce different policy preferences for feminists. Conventional sociological analysis is that the demise of feudal social relations is accompanied by a shift from social relations being governed by status to their being governed by contract. But feminists have questioned the extent to which marriage has followed this pattern. Some argue, for example, that even if marriage, sociologically, is no longer a matter of status, it is still not yet a matter of contract; it is at most a status-contract. This is because the state prohibits certain parties from entering into a marriage and also because the state sets the terms of the marriage 'contract' (Weitzman 1981: 338).

Carole Pateman gives a useful summary of these debates (1988: ch. 6), from which one can construct competing feminist responses to the status approach in connection with cohabitation rights. For some feminists, it is important to secure for unmarried female cohabitants the rights and protections of married women. For other feminists, the assimilation of all women's personal and social relationships to the model of monogamous marriage would be to subject them to one of the worst forms of personal and social life.

A further problem with this assimilation of cohabitation relationships to marriage is that it leaves out of account certain types of relationship which women should be able to choose to have with men without fear of legal discrimination. Here one might note Mary Welstead's analysis of the use of the terms 'mistress' and 'kept woman' in legal discourse. She suggests that the first term refers to an unmarried woman who cohabits with a man, whereas the second refers to a woman who does not cohabit with the man in question but who is in Lord Kilbrandon's words 'installed in a clandestine way, by someone of substance, normally married, for his intermittent sexual enjoyment' (Welstead 1990: 72). Welstead argues that this distinction, with its over-rigid conceptualisation of extramarital relationships, has supported the argument that, if non-marital relationships are to have legal protection, then it should be those that most closely conform to the monogamous ideal, namely cohabitation relationships. Welstead's argument is an intimation of the dangers of the status approach at one remove from the question of comparing female cohabitants with wives. The status approach which compares female cohabitants with wives may be inappropriate not only for female cohabitants but also for those women whose relationships do not approximate even to the norm of female cohabitants.

It would seem that the status approach to the construction of cohabitation rights is beset with problems, mainly through its tendency to assimilate cohabitation to marriage. Unfortunately, it seems more than likely that it is the assimilationist approach which will shape the courts' attitudes to cohabitation disputes in coming years. It already appears to pervade two discussion papers which the Scottish Law Commission (SLC) has produced recently (SLC 1990a, 1990b). The first is on the extant form of irregular marriage in Scotland and the second is on the effects of cohabitation in private law, although it must be said that the assimilationist framework of the second paper has not determined its provisional recommendations. Certainly, the SLC gives scant attention, whilst maintaining an open mind, to another way in which cohabitation rights can be constructed, namely through cohabitation contracts (SLC 1990b: 77).

Rights through contract

Cohabitation rights may be constructed through the existence of an agreement or a contract. Cohabitants agree to a list of rights and obligations which they intend to be legally binding in the event that the relationship ceases, for whatever reason, or in the event of a dispute. Such contracts might cover the use and disposition of property, jointly or singly owned, provision for maintenance and education of offspring and other dependants, and indeed anything else which the parties consider of sufficient importance.

There is a growing literature on the advantages and difficulties of this approach, with Chris Barton's work still definitive in the UK (Barton 1985). One general problem with cohabitation contracts, independently of whether they are seen as desirable or contrary to public policy, is that they have still not been tested in the English courts. Advocates of the contract approach might hazard that, if there have been no court cases featuring a cohabitation contract, it must mean that the various contracts undoubtedly in existence have served one of their purposes, namely to enable couples to settle any dispute without recourse to law. But that is a rather obvious argument *ad ignorantiam*!

Many of the arguments in favour of the contract approach relate to the unsatisfactory nature of the status approach, primarily its outdated conception of cohabitation as the inferior version of marriage. Indeed, resuming the debate described above, some commentators have argued that marriage itself is no longer appropriately characterised as a status relationship and should be regularised through the introduction of a properly contractual approach. A striking example of this argument is given by Moira Wright, who argues that legal intervention in marriage is nowadays justifiable only where the married persons have children. It is children, not married women, who warrant the protection afforded by the attribution of status (Wright 1984: 25f). *A fortiori*, cohabitants should not be saddled with the status approach but their relationship should be governed by a contract to which they themselves consent, perhaps, as Parry suggests, legally enforceable only after each party to the draft contract has taken independent legal advice (1988: 231).

This suggestion is made by Parry as a counter to one of the most frequently expressed objections to the use of cohabitation contracts, namely that one party, typically the woman, is in an unequal economic bargaining position. In this respect, some feminists point to the systematically inferior position of women in social relations. If the marriage contract, if it is a contract, has successfully obscured that social inferiority, that is no reason to allow the cohabitation contract to replicate the deceit. On this argument, the deceit is all the more invidious because it is clothed in the language of equality. The reality, on this type of feminist reasoning, is that the contractarian approach to personal and social relationships reproduces the economic and social oppression of women, their enforced dependence on men (cf. Olsen 1983: *passim*).

The chief problem with this type of argument is that it tends to be deployed less in connection with changing patterns of domestic and sexual relations than on the more general terrain of the ideology and politics of contract. The argument that the contemporary ideology of capitalism, the market and the contract are necessarily interlinked and mutually reinforcing is easily conjoined, through feminism, to the argument that capitalism and patriarchy are also in mutually reinforcing relations. Any element of capitalist ideology easily becomes indistinguishable from patriarchalist ideology. The contractarian approach to the construction of cohabitation rights therefore necessitates the further oppression of women; it does not give women the opportunity to break with oppressive relations, because it reproduces them.

I have argued elsewhere against Frances Olsen's version of this type of feminist argument for purposes of evaluating policy alternatives in the matter of cohabitation (Kingdom 1990). But for purposes of this chapter, which is not concerned exclusively with cohabitation contracts, it is useful to note that it is this type of feminist argument that has won support for the idea that cohabitation rights should be constructed in recognition of the way that contemporary social relations tend to necessitate the dependence of one cohabitant, most often the female partner, on the other.

Rights through dependence

As already noted, feminists have opposed the contractarian approach to the construction of cohabitation rights in recognition of the fact that, outside some idealised utopia, there are systematic forms of social inequality. Even if couples choose not to marry, and even if some couples are more nearly equal, this argument makes a case for ensuring that cohabitants are protected from social arrangements which would reproduce and strengthen those inequalities.

In contemporary British society, despite much rhetoric of equality, this argument continues, women are typically expected to be homebound, performing traditional domestic and childcare tasks, or, if they do work, they will be likely to work for low wages and/or part-time. Either way, they will have had to direct their commitments away from the goal of financial gain to that of child-rearing. Under these conditions, unless they have private money, they will be in an economically inferior position to men and, even if only for specific periods of time, dependent on them.

Justice would certainly seem to dictate that women should not be penalised for social conditions which they are unable to change.[1] Accordingly, cohabitation rights may be constructed by reference to the recognition of dependence of one of the cohabitants, usually the woman, on the other. A test based on dependency, Parry suggests, could be the one in the Inheritance (Provision for Family and Dependents) Act 1975, according to which the deceased has to have been making a substantial contribution in money or money's worth to the reasonable needs of the claimant. In the case of a cohabitation dispute, then, it would have to be shown that the cohabitant, usually the woman, was financially dependent on the other cohabitant, usually the man (cf. Parry 1988: 193-4).

The strength of this line of argument does not mean that there are no problems with this way of constructing cohabitation rights. Feminists will be alert to the way in which the concept of the 'weak woman' can reinforce the courts' sense of chivalry and so lend support to traditional gendered roles. In this respect, one should note Ruth Deech's plea for the protection of law to be reserved, not for former spouses or cohabitants, but for their children (1980: 485). Further, the dependence approach seems morally at odds with the concept of cohabitation as a co-operative and mutually interdependent relationship, the very concept for which it is often preferred over marriage (cf. Parry 1988: 234). The courts should on that score not be encouraged to see domestic labour as the responsibility of women rather than of men. Indeed, feminists should also be concerned that emphasis on the dependence of women on men in typical cohabitation relationships for the construction of cohabitation rights is an approach which has some effects scarcely distinguishable from the status approach, with all its problems of assimilating cohabitation to the unsatisfactory model of marriage. Again, as Deech has intimated, the dependence model may demand that the conduct of the woman be subjected to detailed investigation 'reminiscent of the most offensive traits of the old fault-divorce system' (1980: 487).

Status, contract or dependence?

Parry's work provides a brief but invaluable framework for evaluating the different means for the construction of cohabitation rights, but, even with additional points taken from other sources, there seems to be no overwhelming support for any one of the three approaches he considers. Individual authors continue to argue their respective preferences, nonetheless expressing the hope that there will emerge some serious consideration of the principles, rather than the pragmatics, which should govern legal attitudes towards cohabitation and any rights attaching to such relationships.

Of course, the three alternative approaches evaluated here are not exclusive alternatives. It may be that some combination of them would meet a good many difficulties of any one taken in isolation. For example, a good argument could be made for a policy combining all three approaches to the construction of cohabitation rights. An emphasis on status might well be appropriate for those who have sought to make their cohabitation as much like marriage as possible; there should be legal recognition of cohabitation contracts for those adult cohabitants who favour that approach; and there should be legal recognition of the dependent status of any children of the cohabitants.

Similarly, the three approaches considered here do not exhaust the legal remedies to the presently unsatisfactory state of the law. Parry briefly mentions another pair of alternative policies: the introduction of a legislative code of cohabitation rights and the extension of the practice of judicial discretion. This pair of alternative policies is, obviously, of a rather different order from the first three. Whereas the first three point to ways in which cohabitation rights might be constructed in accordance with legal practices discernible here and there in English law, a legislative code of cohabitation rights would create such rights *de novo*; as such it would be a departure from the usual piecemeal approach of English law and from its traditional hostility to formal declarations of rights. Also, it is clear that none of the first three alternatives rules out the practice of judicial discretion: disputed status, a breach of contract, and a dependence claim can all be subjected to judicial discretion.

The wider importance of Parry's brief juxtaposition of this last pair of alternatives, however, is that it draws attention to a more general and analytic debate, one which has to be addressed as part of the process of evaluating policy options for the formation of law relating to cohabitation. This debate is about the relative merits of legal provisions which confer rights and those which confer discretionary benefits. Neil MacCormick (1989) gives a useful and lucid introduction to that debate.

MacCormick on rights and discretion

To make things plain, MacCormick concentrates on the different answers given by three jurisdictions to this question: 'if a person dies survived by children and a spouse, does the law entitle the survivors to any share in the deceased's estate, or is it entirely for the deceased to decide what testamentary provisions to make, or is there some intermediate possibility [...]?' (1980: 24).

MacCormick describes how Scots law gives surviving children legal rights over one-third of the moveable estate and the surviving spouse another third of it, only the remaining third being subject to freedom of testation. English law allows the provisions of any valid will to govern the whole estate, but a child or a spouse or other dependent may apply to the High Court with the complaint that the will fails to make reasonable provision for the claimant. Connecticut law allows for the complete disinheritance of the surviving children, with no recourse to judicial remedy, but the will can be defeated *pro tanto* by the surviving spouse.

To open up the debate about the respective merits of the direct conferral of rights and the technique of judicial discretion, MacCormick employs a concept of 'operative facts' to propose a distinction between, on the one hand, non-judgemental or judgement-independent or non-discretionary aspects of a case and, on the other hand, its judgemental or judgement-dependent or discretionary aspects. 'Operative facts' refer to the simple occurrence of acts, events or states of affairs which obtain independently of anyone's judgement about them. In terms of inheritance law, an operative fact might be that the deceased has a child. The establishment of these operative facts is non-judgemental, judgement-independent, and non-discretionary. One might add to MacCormick's account here by saying that, at this point in MacCormick's analysis, operative facts are the type of facts which are popularly referred to as the facts of the case.

MacCormick proceeds by saying that operative facts might have what he calls 'normative consequence'. An example here is that under Scots law, if the child is the sole surviving child, then that child has a legal right over one-third of the deceased's estate. A further quality of operative facts is that their establishment may include the requirement that some judgement be made by a person with some special competence, office, or qualification. An example here would be the requirement that a High Court judge decide if the deceased's will has made reasonable provision for the surviving child. At this point in MacCormick's analysis, the distinction between non-judgemental, judgement-independent and non-discretionary issues and issues which are judgemental, judgement-dependent and discretionary is completed.

In the light of MacCormick's distinction: Scots law confers clear and non-judgemental or non-discretionary legal rights on the deceased's children and surviving spouse; English law accords no such rights to the deceased's children and surviving spouse but it does accord them the privilege and power to apply to the courts to consider 'reasonable provision'; and, in allowing no recourse in the courts against total disinheritance of the children, Connecticut law rules out the conferral of judgement-dependent and discretionary right or remedy.

The critique of discretion

At first blush, the production of MacCormick's distinction appears to be unproblematic and intuitively acceptable: one starts with the facts and moves on to the tricky bits. There are, however, some obstacles to accepting this otherwise reassuring proposal. There are three interconnected obstacles, all of which, directly or indirectly, MacCormick acknowledges but to which his replies compound the original difficulty.

The first problem with MacCormick's distinction arises from an example of an operative fact which he himself supplies. In his examples he includes: '*a*'s act causes '*b*'s death, and '*a*' intended this, or that '*a*' offers goods for sale and '*b*' accepts the offer' (1989: 27). The really tricky one here is the example of the operative fact of intention. In what sense does an intention exist independently of anyone's judgement that it does obtain? MacCormick might anticipate the example of the importance of intention in rape cases by saying that the establishment of the operative fact requires that a certain sort of person establish the existence of the intention. Even so, there seems to be a difference between, for example, establishing that someone was electrocuted and establishing intention to commit a criminal act.

The second problem is that, if the proposed boundary between the non-judgemental and the discretionary is problematic in one case, then in keeping with epistemological rigour, the boundary has to be suspect in all cases. MacCormick faces up to this objection to his distinction with a section referring to 'omnipresent discretion?'. In this section, MacCormick agrees that there may be discretion in establishing – in terms of his inheritance example – just how many surviving children (or even spouses?) there are and just how much the moveable estate amounts to. Is there nothing, then, which is non-judgemental? Here MacCormick's analysis is disappointing, because he seeks to evade this problem by saying that 'all this seems *much less* judgemental than deciding, e.g., how much financial provision it would have been reasonable for the deceased to have made ... ' (1989: 30, MacCormick's emphasis). For MacCormick, then, some judgements are more judgemental than others!

MacCormick does acknowledge that it is a matter of degree, but in so doing he raises suspicions about why, if the distinction is one of degree, whatever the scale, he seemed to raise the question of the relation between rights and discretion as one of legal principle. He explicitly agrees that the discovery of mere breadth and depth in the difference between legal remedial provisions is neither surprising nor embarrassing.

At the same time, MacCormick's candour is disquieting, given the seemingly intractable difference between the three jurisdictions he has chosen. One reading of his article is that, despite its initial analytic intention, he has from the start set his argument against formal declarations of rights. He describes the US Bill of Rights and the Canadian Charter of Rights as examples of 'the grandest legal rights'. ('Grand' here is presumably a relation of the usually derogatory term 'grand theory', rather than of the Lancastrian term of approbation!) MacCormick clearly thinks he has achieved a *reductio ad absurdum* of the 'omnipresent discretion' thesis with his suggestion that these formal declarations of rights cannot in all politically informed or proper thinking be thought to be reducible to judicial discretion. Yet there is ample literature to support precisely that type of interpretation. In the next chapter, we shall see a fragment of the considerable corpus of commentary on the vicissitudes and vagaries of the Equal Rights Amendment (ERA) to the US Bill of Rights. We shall see how ERA fared at the hands of the judiciary, leaving out for the moment the various state interpretations of the likely effect of the Bill on their patch. Here is a real example of the exercise of discretion in the interpretation of the Bill of Rights. And, as we shall also see in Chapter 8, there is a growing literature on the reservations of feminists over courts' interpretation of the Canadian Charter. Furthermore, there has been a continuous feminist critique of the supposition that formal declarations of rights, whether or not they contain references to equal rights, can address substantive or 'real' social questions (cf. Arnaud and Kingdom 1990, *passim*).

As if anticipating this body of critical analysis, MacCormick attempts what seems to be his last-ditch argument against the 'omnipresent discretion' thesis. This is the third obstacle to accepting MacCormick's analysis of the difference between rights and discretion. For MacCormick invites us to scrutinise the 'surface structure of primary legal provisions'. He hopes by doing this we can 'draw a simple differentiation between those which categorically impose duties or confer rights under judgement-independent conditions, and those which make no judgement-independent provisions of any sort'. He is confident that the latter are 'through and through discretionary' (1989: 32).

So MacCormick distinguishes between a surface structure of a primary legal provision, the scrutiny of which will reveal clear rights and duties, all non-judgemental, and some other structure in which everything is a matter of discretion. But the distinction reads less like a solution to the problem which MacCormick seems to have thought neglected than a restatement of it. For in the same paragraph, MacCormick wonders about the other side of his started distinction between primary legal provisions and secondary ones. At this point, MacCormick seems genuinely undecided about the strengths and weaknesses of the discretionary technique. On the one hand, MacCormick argues to the effect that, whatever the strengths of clarity and certainty in Scots and Connecticut law, the legal rights approach as he describes it can be a very blunt instrument, incapable of the morally sensitive reasoning which individual cases require. In contrast, MacCormick suggests, the advantage of the English legal provisions is that, in permitting the use of discretion, they make for just that sort of moral sensitivity and for morally nuanced law. For MacCormick, 'morality and discretion are inevitable bedfellows' (1989: 35).

On the other hand, MacCormick seems troubled by his own distinction between judgements at the primary level and those at the secondary level:

> 'the absence of a primary discretion should not blind us to the presence of what may be an alarmingly broad discretion at the secondary level. Resort to the technique and of rights at the primary level can be rather a sham if at the secondary level any enforcement of the right in question is broadly judgement-dependent, that is, broadly discretionary.' (1989: 32)

This broadside on the use of discretion is reminiscent of P. S. Atiyah's warning over the proliferation of discretions and guidelines in modern law:

> they appear to encourage a flexible approach to legal practice which may be useful and even necessary in certain cases, but can easily degenerate into complete 'ad hockery', a casuistical methodology which eventually supplants the need for rigorous legal analysis and thought and replaces it with gut feeling and sentiment. (1987: 129)

If Atiyah's critique of discretion and guidelines is converted from being expressed in epistemological terms to being a social analysis, it serves as a warning to all those who are apprehensive about the scope allowed to the technique of judicial discretion. Zenon Bankowski and David Nelken have observed that 'those groups who are concerned about discretion construct the problem in the light of their material and ideal interests' (1981: 247). Feminists will be no exception to this observation, and they will point to the accumulating legal research which demonstrates how the traditional use of discretion results not merely in specific examples of unfairness but also in the systematic reliance on gender stereotypes which are damaging to women. Two obvious examples are the work of Susan Edwards (1981) and Katherine O'Donovan (1985). Their findings show that the defence of the discretionary technique is the defence of a legal space in which women can expect to be treated in accordance with outdated and risible conceptions of properly feminine conduct.

Conclusion

I have assembled certain legal and jurisprudential materials, the consideration of which is necessary to the formation of policy for the construction of cohabitation rights. There is no easy answer to the question of which approach to choose. The construction of cohabitation rights through status, contract and dependence each has its problems. What is beginning to emerge from the contrast between rights and discretion, however, is that the time-honoured claims for the sensitivity and flexibility of the use of discretion are difficult to sustain. It may be that discretion works better in areas of law which are reasonably well established but that in undeveloped areas of law, such as the law relating to cohabitation, the use of discretion is particularly problematic. For if there are no reasonably clear principles and rules, there is no clearly defined framework within which discretion can be exercised

If that surmise is correct, then it may well be the case that, in the context of cohabitation law, feminists and other progressive thinkers should pursue policies which minimise the scope for discretion. It does not follow that they have no alternative but to argue for the direct conferral of cohabitation rights. Similarly, it does not follow that they must argue for the construction of cohabitation rights through status or dependence. In the previous chapter I argued for the legal recognition of cohabitation contracts, not only as a way of adding to the range of options open to people in the organisation of their living arrangements, but also as a way of minimising judicial intervention. That argument can be expressed as a preference for the construction of cohabitation rights through agreement or contract.

7

Birthrights: Equal or Special?

Introduction

Both in the United States and in the United Kingdom, feminists have
been concerned at the inability of the concept of equal rights to address
the realities of women's unequal treatment.[1] In general, their concern has
not been to attack the achievements of equal rights campaigners. Rather,
what is involved is a well-documented awareness that the ideology of
equal rights has severe limitations for feminist politics, limitations stem-
ming from its failure to recognise the implications of significant differences and divisions between females and males, between men and
women. This line of argument can be, and has been, pursued in a variety
of legal contexts, but it has peculiar appeal where reproduction in general
and childbirth in particular are at issue. Here, the argument continues, is
an obvious case where the differences between men and women, notably
but not exclusively in relation to the capacity to give birth, point to the
need for legislation which accords special rights to women.

In this chapter, I first present examples of the equal rights strategy.
Through that presentation, three concepts of equality are identified.
Explicitly or implicitly, these different concepts are employed both by
supporters of the equal rights strategy and by those feminists who, for one
reason or another, have doubts about equal rights legislation.

Secondly, I describe an alternative strategy. It is introduced by its
supporters as a solution to the problem of equality and it emphasises the
justice of special rights for women. I criticise this strategy on two main
grounds. First, in so far as the shift from an equal rights strategy involves
an appeal to biological sex differences, it has some familiar and some new
risks for women.[2] It should on that account be treated with caution by
feminists. The second criticism starts from the observation that supporters of the shift to the special rights strategy themselves acknowledge
that there is no criterion for the identification of a difference between men
and women which is sufficient for the constitution of a special right for
women. My criticism is that this acknowledgement is far from innocent.
On the contrary, it is typically informed by a battery of references to 'real'

sex differences, to 'the human family', to the fact that the human species is 'sexed', to 'our wonder at the talents and perspectives of the other sex', and so on.[3]

My objection here is not that conventional values are being asserted. (Who, at the end of the day, has not wondered at the talents and perspectives of the opposite sex?) My objection is that these conventional values are asserted at precisely the point in the special rights strategy where what is called for is a reappraisal not just of the equal rights strategy, nor just of the special rights strategy, but of the use of either strategy. Briefly, if it can be shown that the equal rights strategy poses serious problems for feminist politics, and if it can also be shown that the special rights strategy, far from solving those problems, merely redescribes them, then a strong case can be made for avoiding both strategies. In practice, it may not always be possible to avoid them, because the terms of political discourse and dispute are not always a matter of choice. For example, there are periodic calls for the introduction of a Bill of Rights in this country. If such a campaign started to gain political ground, feminists would almost certainly have to engage in some sort of equal rights/special rights debate. As we shall see in the next chapter, formal declarations of rights present special problems for feminists, but experiences in other jurisdictions suggest that putting claim and counter-claim for rights is a less useful activity than scrutinising small print and calculating the likely effects of such a bill on existing legislation, legislative practices, and social institutions in general. It would be more useful to argue for statutory provisions, exclusionary requirements, codes of practice, exemptions, appeals procedures, and monitoring organisations, their standards and functions, than to get caught up in irresolvable wrangles about rights.

The equal rights strategy

In encounters between feminist politics and legislation in the USA and in the UK over the last twenty years or so, the concepts of equality and equal rights have had a complex public life. In the first part of this section, I present arguments which have been typically the support of women's struggles for equal rights through the courts. In the second part, I outline the main reasons why that strategy has met with scepticism, disillusion and even hostility from politically experienced individuals and organisations forming part of the women's movement, whether or not they would describe themselves as feminist.

In 1972, the century-old history of women's struggles in the USA for equality before the law came to a head when Congress sent the Equal Rights Amendment (ERA) to the states for ratification. Whereas the Fourteenth Amendment included an equal protection clause under which the Supreme Court had designated race and nationality 'suspect

classifications' for discriminatory practices, no court had unanimously
declared sex an impermissible classification. To remedy this, the ERA
was to eliminate differential legal treatment of the sexes. If ratified, the
ERA would apply not to purely private action but to governmental and
state action, for example in the areas of employment and family law and
in statutory control over education, prostitution, and jury service.[4]

Writing in 1973, Karen DeCrow, then president of the National
Organization for Women (NOW), had reason for optimism when thirty of
the necessary thirty-eight states had ratified the amendment, including
California where victory had not been seen as likely. Significantly, she
uses the active future tense to point out that although debate about the
ERA frequently turns on the matter of public bathrooms (cf. *Evening
News* 1990) it is on women's employment that the ERA will have most
effect. She cites two major objections frequently made to the ERA in this
context, first, that women will be forced to work overtime or lose their
jobs and, second, that women will lose some significant existing advantages, such as being allowed to retire earlier than men. She replies that
state protective laws should apply not only to women but to all workers.
She uses a similar appeal to equality in her discussion of the effect of the
ERA on domestic relations law. While opponents of the ERA argue that
it will deprive women of rights of support from husbands, DeCrow argues
that it could be used to require that the spouses in divided families
contribute equally *within their means* to the support of children. She
suggests that a corollary of this would be the requirement that the spouse
with custody of the children, typically the woman, should be no worse off
than the other spouse and that, in consequence, the position of divorced
women with children will improve overall.

Immediately after that discussion, and of particular interest in any
discussion of rights surrounding childbirth, DeCrow tackles the question
of the ERA's effect on maternity benefits. She mentions that special
maternity benefit laws are virtually non-existent and she also claims that
the ERA will not prohibit such laws. These assertions are clearly designed
to fend off any objections that the ERA would itself have the effect of
permitting discrimination on grounds of sex, either through state legislation proposing special maternity benefits where none exists or through
state legislation making them unlawful where they do exist. She recognises, however, that whichever way a state might try to legislate, a further
argument is needed to deal with the view that there is something unique
about pregnancy and childbirth which justifies making an exception to the
general principle of equal treatment for men and women in all areas of
social life.

DeCrow's argument, briefly, is that 'Since men do not bear children, a
law which applies to pregnancy and childbirth and which refers only to

women is not making a sex classification' (1975: 312). The implication would seem to be that a law is not discriminatory in an unlawful way, in the sense of contravening the amended Constitution, if it seeks to allocate benefits to a category of persons which, as a matter of fact, can be filled by women only or by men only. Similarly a law is discriminatory in an unlawful way if it refers to a category of persons which can be filled by men or by women and if it seeks to allocate benefits to men only or to women only. To develop these points, DeCrow cites Mary Eastwood's claim that:

> singling out childbirth for special treatment does not discriminate on the basis of sex even though the law refers only to women because men cannot give birth. But if in referring to childbirth the law goes beyond to spheres other than the reproductive differences between men and women (e.g. employment), the law must treat women who give birth the same as men are treated in respect to the area of regulated employment (e.g. absence from work for temporary disability). ... Similarly, women and girls could not be discriminated against in pursuing education because of childbirth. The expulsion or segregation of girls in public schools who have become mothers, but not the boys who have become fathers, would be inconsistent with the Equal Rights Amendment. Just as laws prohibiting women from working certain periods before (or after) childbirth regulate women's employment, not the childbirth, exclusion of pregnant girls from public schools regulates their education, not their pregnancy. (cited in DeCrow 1975: 313)

The precise legal implications of this type of reasoning would clearly depend on how the distinction between the law's treatment of 'the reproductive difference' and the law's 'going beyond' that were to be drawn. In the event, it was not possible to test the effect of the ERA on state legislation in these respects, because the ERA was not ratified but defeated in 1982.

For UK readers, Eastwood's reasoning is instructive as evidence of the commitment to project the principle of equality into as many areas of social life as possible. It is also instructive as an argument against the widely-held view that a law is itself discriminatory on grounds of sex if it allocated benefits to a category of persons which can be filled by men only or by women only. To be more precise, Eastwood's reasoning can be used in defence of the provision of Equal Pay Act 1975, hereafter EQPA, s. 6(1)(b) that a woman can be given 'special treatment' in relation to birth or expected birth of a child. Perhaps even more usefully, it can be used as an example of reasoning which is committed to the concept of equality and which is unencumbered with the ideology of comparability that has been such a problem for women who engage with British equality legislation. One of the most frequently cited examples of that ideology is

Turley v *Allders Department Stores Ltd* in which the Employment Appeal Tribunal decided that Ms Turley could be lawfully dismissed for pregnancy. It argued that, since she was no longer simply a woman but a woman carrying a child and since there could be no comparison with a masculine equivalent, there could be no less favourable treatment (at 299; cf. *Brown* v *Stockton-on-Tees B.C.* at 935). As a result of the Turley decision, among others, Catherine Scorer and Ann Sedley argued for an amendment to the Act, namely that the words 'special treatment' be replaced by 'more favourable treatment' (1983: 14). It is clear that this proposed amendment raises the whole question of the relationship between equal and special rights, between equal treatment and special treatment. Before moving on to the discussion of that issue, however, one or two comments are necessary about the type of reaction there has been to the equal rights strategy in the USA and the UK.

Whether informed by optimism or apprehension, much of the literature surrounding the ERA in the 1970s was necessarily speculative and all of it in the mid-1980s is retrospective. A useful account is given by Hester Eisenstein. She suggests that the second-wave feminism of the 1970s aimed at the minimising of gender differences, that the defeat of the ERA symbolised how far women were from achieving parity with men in respect of rights, and that recent feminist theory has moved to a celebration of female difference. In some versions of this woman-centred programme, she suggests, 'the concept of the social construction of gender was replaced by a claim to the intrinsic moral superiority of women' (Eisenstein 1984: 140–1).

In the UK there has been some support for the ideology of female superiority, but reaction to UK equality legislation has for the most part concentrated on the shortcomings of the legislation itself. The two Acts – EQPA and the Sex Discrimination Act 1975 – have come under sustained scrutiny and criticism. For example, soon after the EQPA became effective, even its supporters in the women's movement argued that the concept of equal pay for equal work could make no impact on women's average-earnings so long as successful awards depended on demonstrating comparability between men's work and women's work, often in industries where employers and unions have been adept at segregating work according to sex, either historically or in deliberate response to the new Act. Again, the NCCL Rights for Women Unit argued for substantial amendments to the two Acts in 1977 and 1983. The burden of this argument has been the need for the amalgamation of the two Acts (Scorer and Sedley 1983: 7f). The need for this rationalisation has had further support from the Equal Opportunities Commission (EOC 1986). Its case is in turn supported by the recent passing of the Sex Discrimination Act 1986, dealing with matters such as overtime restriction and night work

which have obvious implications for equal pay and contractual matters in
the area of employment (EOR 1987). And another example of tension
and conflict was noted by Albie Sachs and Joan Hoff Wilson. They make
the point that while the principle of gender equality is expressed in the
anti-discrimination legislation it is denied in much social security legislation. They also refer to the position taken by the NCCL Rights for
Women Unit on protective legislation:

> They favour the use of exemptions to cover cases of women without
> family responsibilities, urge the extension to men of protection
> against special hazards, and generally call for the creation of a
> comprehensive system of social support for parents and genuine
> equality at work as a pre-condition for repeal of the laws. The Unit
> concedes that there are strong arguments the other way, in par-
> ticular that differentiation in one area of the law leads to inequality
> in another. (Sachs and Wilson 1978: 205)

In much the same spirit, Jean Coussins argued that 'rather than to
promote and enforce equal pay, the Act ... was designed, and has been
used to, control and delay it' (1980: 8). More recently, Katherine
Donovan and Erica Szyszczak have argued that, although it is always
difficult to evaluate the impact of legislation on female-male pay differentials, there is little grounds for optimism that the Equal Pay (Amendment)
regulations 1983 (S.I. 1983 No. 1794) introducing the concept of equal
pay for work of equal value, will improve the differentials (1988: 151–2).
Women will not achieve pay equity, they argue, so long as legal discussion
conceptualises equal pay without reference to the specificity of women's
wider social position and of their participation in the labour market. Alert
to the danger of male dominance being continued through recognition of
women's different position, O'Donovan and Szyszczak nonetheless argue
for proclaiming that difference as the first step towards enlarging the
concept of equality to accommodate diversity (1988: 235).

Explicitly or implicitly, all these commentaries make use of three
concepts of equality:

- the moral principle of gender equality
- formal legal equality, as it might be defined in Acts
- substantive equality, as found in domestic, economic, financial,
  political or other relations between men and women

A characteristic way of relating all these concepts can be found in the
writing of Susan Atkins and Brenda Hoggett as they discuss, first, the
removal of married women's legal disabilities and, secondly, the attempt
of the 1970s legislation to prevent discrimination on grounds of sex,
marital status, or pregnancy:

> But behind the thin veneer of formal equality lay the structural

inequality produced by the relegation of most married women to
their separate sphere. ... But the process [sc. of anti-discrimination]
is far from complete. Nor do we find that the values underlying
modern legislation are inevitably translated into action by the courts
and other agencies. (Atkins and Hoggett 1984: 4)

But, in terms of these three concepts of equality, four different responses
to the problem of equality and equality legislation can be identified.

The first response is that, no matter how deep the scepticism and
disillusion with equality legislation, the equal rights strategy must be
sustained. The moral principle of gender equality, so it could be argued,
has been badly served, whether by poorly drafted legislation, whether by
that enacted legislation's weakness in comparison with other areas of law,
whether through the sexism of the judiciary, or through lack of political
will on the part of employers and unions. What is needed, on this
argument, is continued pressure for legislative reform, better funding of
agencies such as the EOC to improve enforcement, and constant publicity for the potential of the laws in making society more just.

The second response is from those feminists who have opted for
analyses and strategies which they see as more radical. These feminists, as
Carol Smart and Julia Brophy point out, are not concerned 'to achieve
formal legal equality. This is primarily because much of the work has been
done, but it is also because there is now little faith that formal equality will
provide substantive equality' (1984: 15). Such feminists prefer to put
their political energies in struggles outside the sphere of law, for example
in setting up rape crisis centres, rather than engaging directly with what
they see as bastions of male power and privilege.

The third response is the one from Smart and Brophy themselves.
They acknowledge the discrepancy between formal legal equality and
substantive equality, but what distinguishes their position from the second is that they resist the notion of law as a unified bastion of male power
and privilege. On the other hand, they insist that the law must not be
'read' as gender-neutral and that 'it is important to distinguish between
the law and the *effects* of law and legal processes in order to identify the
contradictions which allow space for change' (Smart and Brophy 1984:
17). I argued for a version of this position in the chapters on abortion,
sterilisation, and cohabitation contracts.

These three responses all emphasise the gap between formal legal
equality and substantive equality and they propose remedies through a
variety of legal or extra-legal strategies. In contrast, and this is the fourth
response, supporters of the special rights strategy see the problem of
equality as a problem with the prevailing analyses of the moral principle of
gender equality. The remedy, it is argued, lies in the redefinition of that
moral principle in terms of a combination of equal rights and special

rights, a combination which must find expression in legislation.

The special rights strategy

In the first part of this section, I summarise arguments presented in support of a shift away from the equal rights strategy to a special rights strategy. In the second part, I point to a danger which this shift holds for feminist politics and also to its supporters' failure to pursue the logic of the shift. I suggest that, if the logic of the shift is pursued, it is apparent that feminists should seriously think about abandoning not only the equal rights strategy but the special rights strategy too.

Since the special rights strategy typically emanates from dissatisfaction with prevailing analyses of the moral principle of gender equality, it is not surprising that it is moral philosophers who have given most attention so far to the need to redefine the principle. The clearest and best-known position is that of the American philosopher, Elizabeth Wolgast, in *Equality and the Rights of Women* (1980), and I shall treat her work as representative of the special rights strategy. Of special interest to this chapter is the way in which Wolgast pursues her philosophical arguments on to the terrain of law. British readers might find the framework of the American Constitution too obtrusive for Wolgast's analysis to be instructive in this country. On the other hand, Section 1 of the ERA was drafted in very abstract terms, just as abstract as the moral values of equality and anti-discrimination which heralded the British equality legislation and which it is supposed to embody. Both in the USA and in the UK, then, legal and peri-legal struggles and disputes have been about the precise legal meanings to be attributed to 'equality', either by the courts or by any interested parties.

Wolgast's opening remarks throw down a challenge to the assumption that equal treatment is a remedy for injustice. Her view is that men and women are not the same in all respects: they have natural sex differences and naturally different sex roles. She identifies two unacceptable results of ignoring these facts and of continuing to argue for women's rights on the basis of their equality with men. First, women are encouraged to stress the qualities which they share with men rather than to develop women's different natures, concerns and perspectives. Secondly, the model of equality 'does not give a credible place to such a basic social form as the human family' (Wolgast 1980: 155).

Wolgast does not reject the concept of equality. Indeed, she acknowledges that 'some rights should obviously be equal'. She cites as an example the case where an Idaho law was challenged in the Supreme Court because 'it provided that when two persons of different sexes had comparable claims to be appointed administrator of an estate, the male candidate should be chosen over the female' (*Reed* v *Reed* 1971, cited in

Wolgast 1980: 49). The Supreme Court ruled that the appellant, a woman, should be entitled to the same treatment as a man and that her qualification as administrator should not include her sex. Wolgast supports this ruling on the grounds that nothing intrinsic to being a woman entails that women are unqualified to administer an estate.

For Wolgast, the Idaho law is a clear example of sex discrimination in a context where 'justice should be blind' (1980: 49). She means that, in the case of equal rights, no attention should be paid to the distinguishing characteristics of individuals; rather, people have these rights anonymously, as a presumption, and as if individuals were substitutable for each other. In contrast, Wolgast proposes, special rights depend on individual differences, on accidents or fortune, or on other features that distinguish people. Examples she gives include the right of a blind person to use a white cane, the right of a veteran to burial at public expense, and the right of a fatherless child to public support. A key example she gives is the special right of women to maternity benefits. It is worth noting that at this point Wolgast briefly considers the possibility that the distinction she wants to make could be expressed in terms of a contrast between equal rights, on the one hand, and benefits or privileges on the other. But she cursorily rejects this alternative to the discourse of special rights. Her grounds are, first, that when people use the phrase 'women's rights' they commonly mean to include benefits such as maternity leave, and, secondly, that her terminology of special rights merely follows that established practice (Wolgast 1980: 48).

Armed with the distinction between equal and special rights, Wolgast turns to law to see how the two types of rights and their respective justifications are related. The section in which she discusses the ERA opens with this remark: 'Where the differences of sex is [sic] relevant to a right, say, in the case of a right to maternity leave or medical coverage for pregnancy, claims to equal rights can interfere with rational ways of arguing' (Wolgast 1980: 87–8). She gives as examples the types of reasoning described earlier in this chapter. Here are two of Wolgast's quotations from the Senate Hearings on the ERA. The first is from a response by Myra Harmon, then President of the National Federation of Business and Professional Women's Clubs, to Senator Bayh's question about laws governing maternity benefits and criminal assault against women. The second is from the response by Aileen Hernandez, then president of NOW, to a similar question from the Senator:

> It seems to me that these are special aspects of our life and would require special laws. For instance, the maternity laws are provided to help the extension of the human race and not [just women] ... If a man could bear children he would be under the same law as a woman is.

> Maternity benefits are not a sex benefit. They are medical benefits
> for some women who are about to become mothers, and mother-
> hood, it seems to me, is a different kind of concept and a legitimate
> benefit. (cited in Wolgast 1980: 92)

Faced with what she calls comical reasoning, Wolgast replies that the
more women are encouraged to make their case in terms of equality the
less they can make sense of a great deal of their everyday life. The use of
the concept of special rights restores meaning to women's, especially
married women's, ordinary experiences by permitting women's differences from men to be properly acknowledged, both in laws and in
institutions.

Clearly, the identification of these differences is crucial to Wolgast's
argument and, to that end, in her chapter devoted to arguing that humans
belong to a two-sexed species, she develops the concept of women as
'primary parents'. This means that they are the ones who bear children
and who, it is reasonable to argue, should learn something about child
care. The concept of primary parenthood is used to combat feminist
ideals of androgyny and feminist distinctions between mere biology and
sexual reproduction on the one hand and the social construction of
gender on the other. Wolgast cites evidence from research into the sex and
social roles of other species and from psychological researches of Eleanor
Maccoby and C. N. Jacklin to support her claim that 'concrete differences
exist between the sexes besides the reproductive ones' (1980: 126).
Precisely what these differences are is a complicated matter, opines
Wolgast, and in order to avoid stereotyping she advocates a piecemeal
approach to the matter of choosing sex roles. I shall return to this point
later.

In presenting these arguments, Wolgast is most sympathetic to the
position adopted by British moral philosopher, Mary Midgley, in her
work *Beast and Man: the roots of human nature* (1978). Returning the
compliment, Midgley and Judith Hughes give strong support to
Wolgast's attack on the ERA and its supporters. Like Wolgast, Midgley
and Hughes believe that 'starting from a total commitment to an equality
principle can lead us into silly situations like talking about pregnant men'
(1983: 162). They can, however, follow the reasoning behind why feminists have used the equality principle – to curb the time-honoured elision
between women's being different because of their biology and their being
deviant because of it. Their considered assessment, on the other hand, is
that it is no longer necessary to combat that hierarchical view of the world
which gives pride of place to the human male, since nobody who wishes to
be taken seriously would nowadays dare to advance such a theory.

All feminists would like to think that this historical judgement is sound;
scarcely any think it is. Even so, feminists would agree with Midgley and

Hughes that women have been disadvantageously defined in terms of their biological sex differences from men. Again, while a few feminists might politely assent to their proposition that 'some differences are real' (Midgley and Hughes 1983: 164), the majority of feminists would be likely to voice strong scepticism about the intellectual advances intimated by that proposition. For the difficulty with the type of position taken by Wolgast and by Midgley and Hughes is not that they are unsympathetic to a number of feminist views. There is, in any case, no convergence of feminist opinion in these matters. Rather, the difficulty is with these authors' attempt to reclaim biology – and in Wolgast's case, it would seem, sociobiology too – for the characterisation of relations between men and women. The difficulty is with their attempt to rescue biology from its bad reputation of supporting and colluding in a concept of women as inferior to men and to reinvest it with the moral values of the stable and caring relationship to be found between men, women and children in the human family.

Two points are pertinent here. First, this endeavour is identical in structure with radical feminists' and political-lesbian feminists' reclamation of biology for the celebration of female superiority; as for content, the difference between them is only the matter of which moral values are to be reinvested in biology. It would be worth making this point if only to give the lie to these authors' persistent claim that feminists invariably favour an androgynous society geared to the needs and interests of men. But the comparison produces a more important point. Despite the structural similarity, there is a further difference of content. Radical feminists have never thought that the biological sciences are an uncontested academic discipline in which the pursuit of truth and the facts could be immune from ideological constructions of what it is to be a mother/wife/woman, a father/husband/man, a boy child/girl child sibling, or whatever. They have been specially resistant to this conceptualisation of biology where such biological/ideological analyses are incorporated, however variously, indirectly, or subtly into the practices of medicine or law. In contrast, and this is the second point, Wolgast and Midgley and Hughes appear to think that their appeal to the biological sciences is both a matter of common sense and an inquiry capable of yielding 'the facts' about 'the sex difference' (1980: 125f; 1983: 187). Further, Midgley and Hughes insist that just because some areas of knowledge, such as genetics, have 'been put to bad use', that is no excuse for ignoring them. 'If certain facts are dangerous, the remedy is, as usual, not suppression but more facts' (ibid.).

What is immediately striking about this confidence in the capacity of biological sciences to deliver undisputed truths about the commonsense categories of men and women is that it is made in the contexts first of sexual reproduction and secondly of appropriate legislation. Yet it is in precisely these contexts that, at least since 1978, the date when the first child was born as a result of *in vitro* fertilisation, there have had to be the most radical reappraisals of what exactly is meant by terms such as 'mother', 'offspring', 'parenthood', 'family', and so on. There is no shortage of examples, either of the extent to which current research in the sphere of human reproductive technology is forcing new concepts of the limits of human biology, or of the ensuing uncertainties produced by unprecedented legal actions. Even so, it is worth mentioning three of the issues that have been given media prominence.

First, in the light of remarks by Wolgast, Midgley and Hughes, it has to be said that talk about pregnant men will not go away simply because they have described it as comical or silly (a not uncommon philosopher's fancy). One serious weekly magazine, two television programmes and a popular magazine gave coverage in 1986 to the views of various consultants and scientists about a woman who conceived a few days before having a hysterectomy and whose child, now seven years old, was delivered from her abdomen by Caesarean section (WRRIC 1986). This phenomenon raises the possibility, bruited by consultants and scientists, that a man could carry a baby, and there is no doubt that the possibility of male pregnancy is taken very seriously, at least by some men. However repugnant or incomprehensible the idea may be to most people, the 'successful' outcome of any such experimentation would give curious substance to Harmon's position on maternity benefits as described above. Whatever the shock-value of male pregnancy, the effect, in terms of the ERA debate, would be quite simply to admit new members to the category of those who can give birth.

More familiar in the field of new reproductive technology is the practice of surrogate parenting where a child is carried by one woman on the understanding that it be transferred to another after birth. It is clear from the opening paragraph on surrogacy in the Warnock Report that the practices making surrogate pregnancy possible – artificial insemination and *in vitro* fertilisation – have to be matched by new terminology: the carrying mother, the commissioning mother, the genetic mother, the commissioning father, the genetic father, the male partner of the carrying mother, and so on (1985: 4). The legal implications of these various relationships and statuses are far from clear. As the Report points out, questions of inheritance, citizenship, claims for wrongful death and, I would add, claims for wrongful life, are all likely to be affected by any decision as to whether the commissioning mother or the carrying mother should have custody of the child in the event of a dispute. In the UK, the High Court rejected the claim of a commissioning father in a disputed custody case (*Re P custody* 1987, at 314). The Supreme Court of New

Jersey, in an important American test case, reversed in part the decision of the lower court judge. The Supreme Court held a surrogacy contract between Mary Beth Whitehead and William Stern contrary to public policy. They refused to overturn the lower court's order in favour of the father's claim to custody but they did award the child's carrying mother visiting rights. The case had been brought against the carrying mother for refusing to give up the nine-month-old baby girl. John Naughton probably spoke for many when he wrote: 'Thus a sensible solution which could have been thought up in a nanosecond by a tennis umpire took umpteen months and several million dollars in legal fees' (1990). But, whatever the attractions of this commonsense approach, and whatever people's shared suspicions of the invocation of 'the tawdry majesty of the law to sort out the question of when is a Deal not a Deal' (ibid.), it has to be said that there were many important legal complications to the case – not only whether the contract was invalid through violation of a New Jersey law banning baby-selling, but also whether the commissioning parents were guilty of fraud in claiming the commissioning mother to be infertile, and whether adoption principles can govern surrogacy arrangements (in *Re Baby M* 1987 at 1128, 1988 at 1227). Whatever the outcome of this and similar cases, it is clear that concepts such as 'the real mother' and 'parental rights' are in suspense.

While those concepts are in suspense, a new concept is proposed in another debate surrounding artificial insemination and surrogacy: the 'right to genetic information' and the 'right to control genetic inheritance'. In September 1975 Andrew Veitch reported that the Infertility Services Ethical Committee of a District Health Authority refused to give a widow an operation of artificial insemination using the deep-frozen sperm of her dead husband (1985; cf. Smith 1985: 27). This was in spite of the fact that before he died the husband had been warned that his treatment for cancer might leave him infertile and in spite of the fact that he had left both a written and a videotaped request for artificial insemination for his widow. The hospital committee said that the husband had no legal dominion over his genes and that the wife had no legal right to receive them.[5] Consistent with that view, the hospital also refused the treatment to the widow's sister, who subsequently volunteered to be a surrogate mother. In contrast, Veitch refers to the views of Robert Jansen, an Australian gynaecologist. Jansen has argued that although society has no obligation to use reproductive technology to fulfil the desires of dying patients to preserve their genetic potential, nonetheless, 'because the implied motive in leaving stored semen behind after death is the wish for it to be used to secure offspring, an explicit or testamentary wish for passage of inheritance rights during the reproductive life of the wife should, if she wants it that way, be allowed'. This view is then redescribed by Veitch in terms of the widow's right to the genetic information contained in her dead husband's sperm and the husband's right to control his genetic inheritance. He concludes that for the sake of future generations, it may be that we need a Genetic Protection Bill.

Cases such as Veitch describes have not yet come to court in the UK, although Douglas Cuisine (1977: 163–5) has identified some of the issues for medical ethics. If comparable cases were to be the subject of legal action, feminists would find themselves faced with an increasingly familiar sort of dilemma. On the one hand, there is sympathy for the childless widow (or, indeed, the widow who wants more children) and for the helpless sister-in-law. On the other hand, the notion of a right to control genetic inheritance has to be seen as an alarming extension – beyond death – of rights based on biological relations between fathers and children. In this respect, feminists should recall the remarks of the Rights of Women, Family Law Subgroup (ROW, FLS) in their discussion of the liberal-sounding proposal that the status of illegitimacy should be removed from law and that any child should be linked to a father as if that child were the child of a married father:

> We felt that the drift of this legislation ... was, in fact, very anti-women because it was suggesting that a child could only have a proper status if it was linked to a man. ... We also felt it was important in some cases to acknowledge and formalise the relationship between non-parents and children, and to take more seriously social relations rather than always putting such a high premium on biological relations. (ROW, FLS 1984: 194–5)

The phrase 'in some cases' is significant. Alert to the complex ways in which the biological sciences and current law are making the concept of parenthood problematic, feminists involved in legal studies and in legal struggles are increasingly taking the position that there is no single principle from which to derive feminist politics (cf. Smart and Brophy 1984: 16f). Indeed, this is the main theme of this book.

At this point, one might expect moral philosophers to complain about such unprincipled opportunism, especially a moral philosopher like Wolgast who has gone to the trouble of producing a distinction between equal rights and special rights to tackle just these sort of social complexities. It comes as a surprise, then, to find Wolgast herself advocating a case-by-case approach. She arrives at this position in the crucial chapter on Gender and the Law. As already noted, she grants that there are cases where men and women should have equal rights, such as those connected with jobs and promotions. What she also argues, however, is that there is no general principle of equality from which such cases can be derived, since their various justifications are not all the same. Quite consistently with this position, Wolgast goes on to make the point that there is no one rationale either for equal rights or for special rights. And in case the reader is in any doubt, she stresses that: 'For some issues the biological and reproductive differences of the sexes play a crucial part, but in others they have to be carefully ignored' (Wolgast 1980: 87). In other words, rights ought to be equal when they ought to be equal, and rights ought to be special when they ought to be special.

The vacuity of the distinction between equal rights and special rights could, of course, be surmised from any attempt to apply the distinction. In the Baby M case in New Jersey, for example, the adult parties would not be eligible for equal treatment on Wolgast's analysis and the two women could not have equal rights as between each other, because although they are both women their circumstances are crucially different. Further, even if a case could be made for giving each category – carrying mothers and commissioning mothers – special rights, appeal would still have to be made to some independent principle in order to arrive at a decision as to which category of special rights should have priority over the other. Wolgast herself might appeal to her concept of primary parenting, but, since she herself wants to blur the distinction between childbirth and child care (cf. Morgan 1989), both carrying mothers and commissioning mothers could claim to be primary parents and therefore to have identical and conflicting special rights. Wolgast offers no other independent principle an appeal to which could settle that conflict. Indeed, to identify any such independent principle would present a *prima facie* contradiction of Wolgast's claim that there is no general principle for settling rights disputes.

What remains to be considered is why, having pushed her analysis to the point where she rules out the possibility of general criteria for the settling of the equal rights/special rights question, Wolgast should not have realised that the concept of special rights, far from being a solution to the problem of equal rights, is no more than a redescription of it: people ought to be treated equally except in those cases where they ought to be treated specially, but there is no criterion for determining the exceptions. One answer to this question may be that Wolgast's continued use of the distinction between equal and special rights is a function of the nature of jurisprudence, of philosophy. In those areas of enquiry, there is no pressing need to produce draft legislation or to engage in analysis of the social effects of legislation. If that explanation is plausible, then feminists could quite reasonably conclude that they can safely leave such debates to the philosophers. But feminists do need to be aware of philosophers' characterisations of these issues, not least since such characterisations can provide smart barristers with useful bits of rhetoric. More importantly, as I have argued elsewhere (Kingdom 1987: 9), even apparently feminist philosophy can have detrimental effects on the development of feminist policy recommendations. This is because it effectively reduces policy to questions of moral values and in so doing deflects attention from the analysis of material social conditions.

But these observations still leave unexplained the continued use of the distinction between equal and special rights when it is demonstrably vacuous. It is all the more puzzling for the fact that within philosophy and jurisprudence there is a strong utilitarian tradition of dismissing rights discourse as being incapable of determining policy and legislation. Faced with the inadequacy of the equal rights/special rights distinction to the determination of legislation, feminists must wonder why the whole discourse of rights has not been seen as suspect and, moreover, as a discourse which might sensibly be abandoned.

This proposition can be phrased in terms of the vocabulary which I used in Chapter 3 in connection with a woman's right to choose. There I described the rejectionist and the retentionist position on the appeal to rights. There, as here, I think there is less to be gained from retention than from rejection, but it is not in the general spirit of my argument to think that rejection should be automatic. Accordingly, the case for rejection and retention must be examined. In the context of the birthrights issues covered in this chapter, the rejectionist position in relation to the discourse of rights is unlikely to meet with easy assent from feminists. There are at least three *prima facie* persuasive grounds for retention, all pragmatic. The first is that feminists will make no inroads into the politics of birthrights unless they utilise the discourse of rights. The second is that there are dangers in walking down from the high ground of moral rights and on to the slopes of what they, and more importantly their opponents, are inclined to see as *ad hoc* and unprincipled struggle. The third is that an alternative vocabulary has not been developed.

I shall take these retentionist views in reverse order. Against the third, I would point to the existence of the discourse of capabilities, capacities and competences which I referred to in Chapter 2. This is a developed discourse, indeed more developed than its description there suggests. Terms which might be added to that discourse include exemptions, status definitions, qualifying conditions, favourable treatment, removal of disabilities, and so on. This is the discourse used by Scorer and Sedley to make their numerous recommendations for amending the equality laws, without once having recourse to the discourse of rights. It is, of course, the discourse explicitly rejected by Wolgast. But it would be naive to suppose that this discourse could function as a straight alternative to rights discourse. This is because, as I have shown in Chapter 2, the discourse of moral rights can never be reduced to that of prevailing social conditions. A more promising way of relating rights discourse to the discourse of capabilities, capacities and competences is in terms of the reconceptualisation of the term 'women's rights'. With this in mind, in Chapter 3, I suggested that the discourse of capabilities, capacities and competences could serve as a corrective to the loose meaning of the term 'women's rights . The point is that there is and can be no exact logical or philosophical or theoretical equivalent of rights discourse, and that in so far as it still exercises a hold over feminist politics, it has to be examined in terms of its ideological attractions and repellants. This leads into my reaction to the second of the retentionist claims.

Rights discourse always occupies the moral high ground. That is the point of rights discourse. It is a recurrent theme of this book, however. that occupants of that high ground are constantly under siege. The specific disputes described in this chapter are witness to how proponents of rights, equal or special, have gained, lost and elbowed for the high ground of birthrights. These disputes are typically presented in terms of moral rights, but because there can be no agreed ranking of these competing rights – the ranking is precisely what is at issue – these ostensibly moral disputes can be settled only in political arenas. That is why I have constantly argued for the importance of much more worldly, politically realistic calculations. This argument must now address the first of the three retentionist positions, namely, that no progress will be made unless the feminist case is presented in the terms of rights discourse.

A defender of this retentionist stance could make the point here that I have been less than realistic myself in speculating on why Wolgast continues to use the equal rights/special rights discourse which she herself comes close to acknowledging is pretty well worthless. As we have seen, Wolgast explicitly retains that rights discourse in preference to the discourse of capabilities, capacities and competences, on the grounds that people understand what she means by it, seeming to make it a philosophical point about language and thought. A defender of the first retentionist position can argue that Wolgast should have retained the rights discourse not on the grounds she gives but for the simple reason that the discourse is part and parcel of US constitutional politics. On this view, Wolgast would have as much and as little scope for rejecting rights discourse as any other American feminist.

I have considerable sympathy for this first retentionist position. The point in its favour is not so much any philosophical or linguistic felicity, but that the decision whether or not to invoke rights, equal or special, is one that must be based on calculations of likely success or failure of the campaigns so presented. As I remarked at the start of this chapter, it is not always possible to choose the terrain of feminist politics, and it is not always possible to choose the terms in which those politics are conducted. Further, political arenas are never identical. The political climate of the US is not the same as that of the UK, both because in the UK there is no written constitution expressed in terms of rights, and also because, as we saw in the previous chapter, the English legal system is more at home with judicial discretion than with direct conferral of rights. For these reasons, it would easier for UK feminists than for US feminists to abandon the discourse of rights. It is possible, of course, that at some stage in the future, a UK government will introduce a Bill of Rights or incorporate the European Convention on Human Rights into UK domestic law. In that event, the political debates surrounding any such decision may well drive feminists to engage with rights discourse of the type characteristic of US constitutional politics, whatever their misgivings about its usefulness to feminist struggles. Even so, I would still make a case for reconceptualising 'women's rights' in terms of capabilities, capacities and competences, as a political working habit to help with the identification of the benefits and drawbacks for feminists which a formal declaration of rights may carry. I turn to some of these issues in the following chapter.

8

Formal Declarations of Rights

Introduction

In the disputes surrounding the periodic resurgence of proposals for a Bill of Rights in the UK, references to women's rights are scarce. It may be that disputants take it for granted that, although it is typically in terms of the claimed rights of man or men that bills of rights are expressed, this time-honoured legal terminology also refers to the rights of women. On the other hand, contemporary feminist writers on law and jurisprudence have seldom been persuaded of the innocence of the generic use of the singular or plural masculine pronouns. It may be, then, that the absence of a discernible feminist politics of a UK Bill of Rights is better explained by a different feminist critique. This is the critique of the discrepancy between formal and ostensibly gender-neutral rights and the adverse substantive or material social conditions experienced by women. With this critique translated into a heuristic applied to the Bill of Rights debate, feminists might well expect the formal rights of a Bill of Rights to be gendered, to the disadvantage of women.

Support for this heuristic can be drawn from the analysis of a remarkable eighteenth-century text. In 1791, Olympe de Gouges published *Déclaration des Droits de la Femme et de la Citoyenne.* Her purpose was to draw the attention of her co-revolutionaries, of women in general, and of Marie-Antoinette in particular, to whom she addressed the document, to what she saw as the 'lost rights' of women in prerevolutionary and revolutionary France. The document takes the same formal structure as the *Déclaration des Droits de l'Homme et du Citoyen* of 1789. Section 1 of this chapter charts the significant differences between the two documents and gives brief explanations for them. The exercise is not, however, antiquarianist. Charting the differences between the two documents is most instructive for the development of a contemporary feminist critique of a proposed UK Bill of Rights. It is instructive both by exhibiting the complexity of the claim that formal rights are gendered to the disadvantage of women and by identifying various strategies which feminists could adopt when faced with a formal declaration of rights which they may suspect of being gendered to the disadvantage of women.

From this starting point, I examine available grounds for what appears to be feminist abstention from the current UK Bill of Rights debate and some arguments which undercut the bases of that abstention. I conclude that there are no general reasons why feminists should be hostile to the idea of a UK Bill of Rights but that they have to pay attention to a number of well-established ideological and political positions which might be detrimental to feminist objectives.

'Especially resistance to oppression'

With the inclusion of 'especially' in the above phrase in her 1791 Declaration of the Rights of Woman and Citizen, Olympe de Gouges gave a new twist to the natural and imprescriptible rights which appeared in Article 2 of the 1789 Declaration of the Rights of Man and Citizen: life, liberty, property and resistance to oppression. De Gouges was referring not merely to the oppression of all people under the *ancien régime* but, as the Preamble makes clear, primarily to the oppression of women by men, before and in the early years of the Revolution.

De Gouges was by all accounts an extraordinary woman who survived an inauspicious youth to flout the conventional apolitical role of women and to become one of the most outspoken and hence notorious women publicists of the French Revolution (cf. Groult 1986; Kelly 1989). Her literary and political writings were passionate and fearless, if not always stylish or sensible. They drew a predictable range of reactions from men and women: indifference, derision, and hostility.

The 1791 Declaration met with little interest. Indeed, of the various categories of people excluded from the vote, only the category of women was not the subject of debate among the constitution-makers of the Constituent Assembly; a woman was not deemed politically competent (Hufton 1989: 26). Even so, it is useful today to observe the discrepancies between the two Declarations, juxtaposed in the Appendix to this chapter,[1] as an early illustration of the problems facing any attempt to incorporate women's rights into a formal declaration of citizens' rights. Working from a similar juxtaposition, Joan Wallach Scott (1989) has given a useful account of what she sees as the ambiguity of de Gouges' feminism, but for purposes of this chapter I shall restrict my analysis to the identification of ways in which de Gouges' Declaration differs from the 1789 Declaration with respect to the gendering of rights.

There are three different ways in which de Gouges' document departs from the earlier Declaration. First, there are places where she was happy with the simple addition of phrases such as 'woman and', 'female and', or 'to both sexes'. Examples are in Articles 1, 14, 17. These additions, of course, were neither cosmetic nor purely formal. Only a few women had or could hope to have property rights, and women had no liability to public functions (Hufton 1975: *passim*; Kelly 1989: 33f; Levy et al. 1979: 6). Similarly, when de Gouges proposed a voluntary tax to ease the national debt, a tax to which women would be subject, she was proposing a measure which would introduce women into public life as never before (de Gouges, *Lettre* 1788, in Groult 1986: 69-72). The proposals in Articles 14 and 15 would be seen as similarly provocative. One might say that, with these additions, de Gouges identifies the covert gendering of the formally declared rights and makes these rights explicitly gendered so as to achieve exactly equal rights.

Secondly, there are places where de Gouges replaces references to the domination and tyranny of the *ancien régime* with references to the domi-nation and tyranny of women by all men, whether of the *ancien régime* or of the Revolution. The most prominent example is her Preamble and Article 4. What is curious about these examples is the tension they create between on the one hand the attempt to raise women's social position to the level of men's and on the other hand the terminology which hints at a picture of a society in which women had rights over men – as if to shock men into envisaging what life would be like if women were in positions of power over them. Here it might be said that, whilst de Gouges is usually content to note the gendered nature of formal rights to the disadvantage of women, and then to gender rights so as to achieve equal rights, with these examples she adopts the strategy of re-gendering rights, to women's advantage.

Thirdly, there are examples where de Gouges introduces elements for which there is no parallel in the 1789 document. One example is, again, the Preamble. Her last paragraph audaciously replaces the reference to the National Assembly as the author of the 1789 Declaration. Instead, it is women who are the authors of the 1793 Declaration but they are its authors because they are superior both in beauty and by virtue of their courage in maternal suffering. Another example is Article 11. Here she makes a special case of the general right of free thought by drawing attention to a particular injustice of her day. As she notes in the Postamble:

> A married woman can, with impunity, present bastards to her husband and the bastards with the fortune that does not belong to them. An unmarried woman has merely a slim right: ancient and inhuman laws have refused her the right to the name and property of the father of her children, and no new laws on this matter have been passed. (de Gouges, Postamble in Bell and Offen 1983: 108)

With these two examples, de Gouges is content neither to note the gendering of a right to the disadvantage of women, nor to gender such a right in order to achieve equal rights, nor to re-gender such a right in such a way that women would have that right over men. Her strategy here is to introduce a special right, to be claimed only by women.

De Gouges' exploit was, of course, in vain. Jane Abray has chronicled the various reasons for the failure of French feminism in this period. In her estimate, it was a 'minority interest', the feminists made a number of strategic and tactical errors, and their demands were, if anything, even more radical than those of their male revolutionary counter-parts (Abray 1975: 56f). As Norman Hampson remarks drily, 'feminism was equally suspect to Jacobins and *sans-culottes*' (Hampson 1979: 114). Indeed, the position of women deteriorated rapidly after 1791. For example, Article XIII of the Police Code, proposed to the National Assembly in 1791, accorded men only the right to file a formal complaint against an unfaithful spouse. Bell and Offen note that 'It also stipulated a two-year prison term for the wife, as well as giving husbands the opportunity to dispossess their wives of dowries or other property brought into the marriage' (1983: 98). And from October 1793, the women's clubs which had been one of the main vehicles for women's political involvement were prohibited by the Jacobins, forcing women back into an apolitical private existence (Groult 1986: 44; Kelly 1987: 127; Levy et al. 1979: 5). A chosen few only were offered a symbolic public role as goddesses of reason to preside over religious festivals (Kelly 1987: 128).

It is a moot point whether this reaction was provoked by the political activities of women such as Olympe de Gouges or whether it represented merely the continuation of forms of oppression in practice before 1789. What is certain is that de Gouges' 1791 Declaration illustrates a range of strategies for contemporary feminists to consider in forming their response to proposals for a UK Bill of Rights. For convenience, I describe these strategies in terms of gendering and re-gendering rights, and creating special rights.

'Especially with respect to the rights of women'

Why have feminists not been more prominent in debates about a UK Bill of Rights? If eighteenth-century French women's contribution to the Revolution, in particular Olympe de Gouges' idiosyncratic, rights-based emphasis on the oppression of women by men, had so little effect in improving women's position after 1791, indeed, might even have contributed to making it worse, should contemporary feminists question the value of a UK Bill of Rights which emphasises women's rights? In the context of Charter 88, should they be wary of a proposal for a Bill of Rights supported by a platform advocating the extension of the concept of liberty 'especially with respect to the rights of women' (Charter 88 1988: 11)? Again, if they suspect that the rights in formal declarations are gendered to the disadvantage of women, should feminists attempt to

136   *What's Wrong With Rights?*

gender those rights, with a view to making them equal rights; should they attempt to re-gender them so as to create rights over men; or should they seek to create special rights which only women can claim? What follows is a review of some of the strategies which are open to contemporary feminists in the debate on a UK Bill of Rights.

Several prominent feminists were among the original signatories of Charter 88, and its launch included an albeit oblique welcome on behalf of 'Citizen Cain's silenced sisters' from Sarah Benton (1988). Otherwise, there has been a marked absence of feminist analysis in public debates about a UK Bill of Rights. This apparent lack of interest can no longer be attributed to feminists' indifference or fastidiousness over the the use of law for the achievement of feminist objectives, as the following three examples show. First, there has been some feminist, academic and media coverage of feminists' attempt and failure to pass the Equal Rights Amendment in the United States. As we saw in Chapter 7, feminist debate has been conducted not in terms of whether women's rights should be defended in the legal arena but in terms of whether they should be defended through appeals to equal rights or through appeals to special rights. Secondly. there has been considerable interest in the attempts of some American feminists to use the Constitution to ban pornography (cf. *Harvard Law Review* 1984). Because of their ability to appeal to the Constitution, their attempts clearly had greater chance of success than Clare Short's Bill 'to make illegal the display of pictures of naked or partially naked women in sexually provocative poses in newspapers' (Indecent Displays [Newspapers] Bill 140). Thirdly, Canadian feminists celebrated a notable victory in securing the constitutional entrenchment of sex equality rights, with no legislative override of the equality guarantees, in the Canadian Charter of Rights and Freedoms in 1982.

A case of feminist disillusion with a formal declaration of rights. In fact, it is the Canadian experience that provides, if not an explanation for there being no strong feminist line on the issue of a UK Bill of Rights, then at least a good case for feminists not to get carried away by enthusiasms for formal declarations of women's rights. In her scrupulous review of the possibilities and limits of the Canadian Charter for the furtherance of feminist struggles, Judy Fudge comments: 'whilst the struggle around the issue of sexual equality was both a mobilizing and radicalizing process for many Canadian feminists, the same cannot be said about the outcomes of the implementation of that political victory' (1978: 486). The examples which Fudge provides are presented through the perspective of the distinction between the public and the private realms. This is because the distinction has been used by the Canadian courts to determine the scope of the rights and the freedoms guaranteed in the Charter in such a way that women's material and substantive inequalities are not addressed.

One example is the courts' view that collective agreements and trade union constitutions are private and therefore beyond Charter review. As Fudge notes:

> Consequently, seniority, productivity, overtime and premium shift provisions cannot be challenged on the ground that they violate equality protection in the *Charter*, even though research has indicated that such provisions frequently result in large wage differentials between male and female employees. ... Because the courts have opted for a liberal approach to the scope of rights and freedoms guaranteed by the *Charter*, the coercion of privacy remains intact in the employment relation. (1978: 493-4)

One criterion used for the applicability of the Charter, however, is where state action, either through legislation or through administrative action, is involved. Fudge identifies three such areas which raise equality issues: protective or remedial labour legislation, the legal recognition and regulation of a specific type of family, and legislation designed to protect women from sexual violence or victimisation. In each of these areas, Fudge argues that the courts have adopted a liberal approach, emphasising formal equality, in preference to a contextualised approach to equality which would require the courts to go beyond abstract rights and formal guarantees and to consider the socio-historic roots of current inequalities (Fudge 1984: 497).

Fudge gives several illustrations of this argument. For example, she cites *Bliss* v. *A. G. of Canada*, in which the Supreme Court ruled that the denial of various social benefits on grounds of pregnancy did not constitute discrimination on the basis of sex nor a denial of women's equality before the law (Fudge 1984: 505). Similarly, Fudge cites cases to show that appeals to formal legal equality under the guarantees of the Charter have been used with very mixed results for women. One group of cases was successful in allowing a married woman to use a name other than her husband's name and to pass her own name, not her husband's, on to her children (Fudge 1984: 513). In another group of cases, the courts withdrew state benefits from single mothers with dependent children on the ground that the relevant Act did not provide similar benefits for single fathers with dependent children, even though many more women than men are in need of such benefits (Fudge 1984: 519).

Fudge's conclusion is that the formal rights of the Charter are gendered not exclusively but overwhelmingly to the disadvantage of women, both in the courts' interpretation of the equality guarantees, and in the very process of constitutional entrenchment. 'Once translated into legal rights, the demand for substantive equality for women has become truncated and divorced from broader political demands' (Fudge 1978: 486).

Accordingly, she concludes that the Charter has a limited capacity to further feminist struggles but that it also has the capacity to undermine them. So long as the Charter incorporates only formal equality and because the courts refuse to address women's substantive inequalities, feminists involved in the struggle for social transformation are advised to approach Charter litigation 'with great trepidation, if at all' (Fudge 1984: 554).

More reasons why feminists should hesitate before supporting a UK Bill of Rights. To counter this apprehensive conclusion, it might be argued that, like most Canadian feminists, and on her own analysis, Fudge was overoptimistic about the potential of the Charter for the transformation of women's social position, or that they were mistaken about the very nature of such a charter. In the context of the UK, a comparable point is made by Nicola Lacey in her reply to opponents of a Bill of Rights:

> although we cannot expect the Bill of Rights itself to resolve funda-
> mental political, moral and economic conflicts – for example,
> between the principle of free expression and that of freedom from
> discrimination, which can arise from the publication of racist
> propaganda – ... we can expect a bill to focus judicial, political and
> public attention on the fact that these cases really are about such
> fundamental conflicts. (Lacey 1986: 242)

Lacey's comment adumbrates a distinction which is a recurring feature of arguments about a UK Bill of Rights, namely, the distinction between civil and political rights on the one hand and social and economic rights on the other. Peter Wallington and Jeremy McBride give a fuller exposition of the distinction:

> Human rights are broadly divisible into two kinds – civil and
> political, and social and economic. ... Civil and political rights cover
> the right to vote and to free elections, protection of individual liberty
> from violence or detention, the equal protection of the law, ...
> freedom of speech, freedom of political association and assembly,
> freedom of movement, freedom of religion and conscience, and the
> protection of privacy. As we move across the borderline towards the
> social and economic rights we pass, straddling the line, rights such
> as the right to form trade unions, and to strike, and the right to
> adequate legal services. More firmly in the field of social and
> economic rights we find the right to housing and employment, and
> to a living wage; rights to a safe and healthy environment and
> adequate medical services; rights to education; and dominating all
> the others equality, or equality of opportunity. (1976: 11)

What is crucial, next, is the authors' remark that the rights which a Bill of Rights can create and safeguard are primarily towards the civil and political end of the spectrum. They emphasise that they are not hostile to the social and economic rights which they identify; rather they see no practical possibility of legislating to protect economic interests. 'An Act of Parliament proclaiming a right to be housed is a nonsense, if there are not enough houses' (ibid.). Similar, though less even-tempered, arguments have been made by Maurice Cranston. He urges that all reference to social and economic rights be removed from the text of the Universal Declaration of Human Rights, on the grounds that they are so vacuous as to be incapable of realisable legislation (Cranston 1973: 68f). Joseph Jaconelli's invocation of the spectre of the planned economy creates the impression that any argument for economic rights necessarily emanates from sinister Marxist quarters (1980: 8–9). And Margaret Thatcher has subscribed to a similar position, though expressed in less theoretical terms, in relation to the European Social Charter (Usborne 1990).

At this point, feminists might take heed of Fudge's observations on the Canadian courts' typical response to the equality guarantees of the Charter: through the use of the public/private distinction, ostensibly gender-neutral formal rights of the civil and political kind have regularly been interpreted in such a way that women's social and economic inequalities cannot be addressed and are, to that extent, reinforced by the legislation. The supposedly gender-neutral formal rights turn out to be gendered, overwhelmingly to the disadvantage of women. In so far as the distinction between civil/political rights and social/economic rights is sustained in the various draft Bills, feminists can reasonably predict much the same outcome were a UK Bill of Rights to be enacted. Support for that prediction might be found in the view of Wallington and McBride that equality does not fall neatly into the category of civil and political rights. This uncertainty could open up the possibility of equivocation as to whether it should be covered by a Bill of Rights or not, equivocation comparable to the Canadian courts' reluctance to let the Charter apply in the sphere of 'private' employment. Lastly, feminists might note that Wallington and McBride are prepared to resist the prevailing view that a Bill of Rights should not give a favoured status to any ideological position. They argue that there is one ideology the expression of which should be curtailed by a Bill of Rights. This is the ideology of the racist right. No such argument is advanced in relation to the sexist right. In this respect, feminists might well be reminded of Carole Pateman's (1988) analysis of classical contract theory, showing how it has left a legacy of problems about women's incorporation into civil society through its misrepresentation of the social contract, the employment contract and, most of all, the marriage contract. On this sort of analysis, one might say that the rights referred to in the classical contract theory are gendered, to the disadvantage of women. And feminists might well ask themselves if the ostensibly gender-neutral language typical of civil and political rights as identified above would effectively constitute a covertly gendered Bill of Rights.

Why feminists should not withdraw support for the idea of a UK Bill of Rights. In the light of the above considerations, it would hardly be surprising if contemporary feminists shied away from any proposal for a UK Bill of Rights and from any similar constitutional device. But before they vacate that political arena, feminists might consider two arguments which weaken the impact of the growing case for withdrawing their support for a UK Bill of Rights.

The first argument refers to the view that it is not possible to legislate for social and economic rights. David Trubek has supplied the materials for a counter-argument in his analysis of what he calls 'social welfare rights' in the Third World. He notes that whilst much academic work has been done on the concept of civil and political rights, there is relatively little on the field of economic, social and cultural rights (Trubek 1984: 207). He also notes that, following the Universal Declaration of Human Rights, it was decided that its principles required greater specificity. The United Nations accordingly developed a Covenant on Human Rights, but in the course of its drafting it was decided that two separate instruments were required. The first covered civil and political rights: the Political Covenant. The second covered economic, social and cultural rights: the Economic Covenant. Part of the reasoning for the decision appears to be that civil and political rights could be enacted into law immediately, whereas economic, social and cultural rights would require programmes of action over time (Trubek 1984: 210–11). Because the implementation of such programmes could not be uniform in all different countries, it was recognised that specialised agencies (such as the International Labour Organisation, the World Health Organisation, and the United Nations Educational, Scientific, and Cultural Organisation) should take responsibility for the development, implementation and monitoring of concrete programmes to foster specific rights.

Trubek's analysis can be used to rebut the arguments, described above, that it is not possible to legislate for social and economic rights. It may be true that, if there are no houses, then an Act of Parliament proclaiming the right to be housed is worthless. Certainly an Act of Parliament by itself cannot put pressure on an administration to adopt measures requiring new houses to be built or old ones refurbished. What is needed is some independent body to develop practical programmes and guidelines for their realisation, and to establish mechanisms for monitoring and reviewing progress.

This sort of approach might provide a way in which women's social and economic rights in any one country could be protected under the aegis of a broader declaration of rights. Indeed, many feminists today look to the

European political and legislative structures for amelioration of the UK's poor record on women's social and economic rights. This might make a case for the incorporation into UK legislation of the European Convention on Human Rights. On a broader scale, however, it is worth noting that the 1950 European Convention on Human Rights has been supplemented with the adoption in 1981 of the Convention on the Elimination of all Forms of Discrimination against Women, on the grounds that, unlike racial discrimination, sexual discrimination had not been the focus for concerted international action. It is clear that both the ideologies and the mechanisms supporting this Covenant have been the subject of strong disagreement, not least for the fact that the Covenant extends the field of application of the Convention into private and interpersonal relations. For example, Meron is concerned that this extension might result in unacceptable state regulation of interpersonal conduct and conflict with rights in the sphere of opinion and religion (1986: 62). Clearly, there will be further argument in this context, but for immediate purposes one might note that the approach described by Trubek is relevant to the themes of this chapter in four ways.

First, it shows that, even if formal declarations or conventions are typically gendered to the disadvantage of women, in the sense that they cannot be relied on to address women's social and economic rights, there are existing models of mechanisms to remedy that deficiency. In particular, secondly, it shows that, contrary to what sometimes seems to be no more than the received wisdom of western commentators, it is not impossible to legislate for social and economic rights. Thirdly, if taken in conjunction with Fudge's analysis of the Canadian Charter, it shows there is no general or *a priori* answer to the question of what the use of the public/private distinction will produce in the context of a formal declaration of rights, and, therefore, no *a priori* answer to the question of whether it is used disadvantageously to women. Fourthly, it shows that the question of women's rights can be approached not just through the devices of gendering or regendering rights but also through the introduction of special rights. Bearing in mind the argument of the previous chapter, these special rights would not be presented as moral rights, of course, but they could be presented in the form of a separate document, declaration or convention in which specific provisions were identified.

The second reason why feminists should not abandon involvement in any campaign for a UK Bill of Rights relates to the second half of the quotation above from Lacey's article and to what Fudge calls symbolic victories (cf. Fudge 1987: 523). A UK Bill of Rights which explicitly accorded women the same rights as men could well provide ammunition for feminist campaigns. For example, it could be the peg on which to hang feminist campaigns to remedy the weaknesses of the Sex Discrimination

Act, to secure equal protection for women and children in non-conventional sexual and domestic relationships, and to protect women from sexual harassment and violence.

Neither of the above two arguments constitutes decisive grounds for feminists to campaign for a UK Bill of Rights. They do constitute grounds, however, for not taking as given two recurring features of the contemporary debate: first, the division between civil and political rights on the one hand and social and economic rights on the other, and secondly, the assumption that the declaration of formal rights, even when gendered by making explicit reference to women's rights, or supplemented by the introduction of special rights, can have no value for feminist politics.

Conclusion

There is a volume of analysis, both historical and contemporary, which feminists could use to advocate rejection of a UK Bill of Rights. The analyses I have presented, however, suggest that, powerful and persuasive as these arguments are against a Bill of Rights, this rejection would be premature and feminists should sustain an interest in, if not actively supporting a UK Bill of Rights, then at least developing political responses to such proposals. A further argument is that, whatever the limitations of a UK Bill of Rights for feminist struggles, feminists might judge that it should be supported on other political grounds, such as grounds elaborated by Michael Zander (1985: 27f). Zander identifies the main argument for supporting a Bill of Rights as the restraint of excesses or abuse of power by public authorities, and he identifies a number of subsidiary arguments, such as the slowness of the procedure for the enforcement of human rights in Strasburg. This is a point of some interest to feminists watching the progress of the European Court in the period from 1976 to 1990 as it debated the meaning of 'direct and overt' discrimination and 'indirect and disguised' discrimination (O'Donovan and Szyszczak 1988: 129; Lester 1990) or the socialist considerations outlined by Charter 88. Alternatively, feminists might judge that they should support the case for a UK Bill of Rights on the sort of grounds appealed to in Charter 88. The document avers that we are currently witnessing the government-initiated erosion of 'important civil freedoms: for example, the universal rights to habeas corpus, to peaceful assembly, to freedom of expression, to membership of a trade union, to local government, to freedom of movement, even to the birth-right itself' (Charter 88 *New Society* 1988: 10). These freedoms are not usually included under the heading of women's rights, but it does not follow that they are of no concern to feminists.

Appendix: The Two Declarations

Declaration of the Rights of Man and Citizen	*Declaration of the Rights of Woman and Citizen*
	To be decreed by the National Assembly in its last meetings or at the last meeting of the next legislature.

Preamble

The representatives of the French people, organised as a national assembly, considering that ignorance and neglect of, and contempt for, the rights of man are the sole causes of public misfortunes and of corruption of governments, have resolved to display in a solemn declaration the natural, inalienable and sacred rights of man, to the end that this declaration, constantly in the presence of all members of society, will continually remind them of their rights and duties, to the end that the acts of the legislative power and those of the executive power, being constantly measurable against the goal of all political institutions, will be better respected, so that the demands of citizens, based henceforth on simple and incontestable principles, will always contribute to the maintenance of the constitution and the happiness of all.

Consequently, the National Assembly recognizes and declares, in the presence and under the auspices of the Supreme Being, the following rights of man and citizen.

Preamble

The mothers, daughters, and sisters, representatives of the nation, demand to be constituted a national assembly. Considering that ignorance, disregard of or contempt for the rights of women are the sole causes of public misfortunes and of corruption of governments, women have resolved to display in a solemn declaration the natural, inalienable and sacred rights of woman, to the end that this declaration, constantly in the presence of all members of society, will continually remind them of their rights and duties, to the end that the acts based on women's power and those based on men's power, being constantly measurable against the goal of all political institutions, will be better respected, so that the demands of female citizens, based henceforth on simple and incontestable principles, will always contribute to the maintenance of the constitution and of good morals, and may contribute to the happiness of all.

Consequently, the sex that is superior in beauty as well as in courage of maternal suffering, recognizes and declares, in the presence and

Article One. Men are born and remain free and equal in rights; social distinctions can be established only for the common benefit.

II. The goal of every political association is the conservation of the natural and imprescriptible rights of man; these rights are liberty, security, and resistance to oppression.

III. The source of all sovereignty is located in essence in the Nation; no body, no individual can exercise authority which does not emanate from it expressly.

IV. Liberty consists in being able to do anything that does not harm another person. Thus the exercise of the natural rights of each man has no limits except those which assure to the other members of society the enjoyment of these same rights; these limits can be determined only by law.

V. The law prohibits all acts harmful to society. There can be no hindrance to what is not forbidden, and no one can be forced to do what it does not order.

VI. The law is the expression of the general will; all citizens must participate in its expression personally or through their representatives; it should be the same for all, whether it protects or punishes. All citizens being equal in its eyes

under the auspices of the Supreme Being, the following rights of women and citizen.

Article One. Woman is born free and remains equal in rights to man; social distinctions can be established only for the common benefit.

2. The goal of every political association is the preservation of the irrevocable rights of Woman and Man; these rights are liberty, property, security, and especially resistance to oppression.

3. The principle of all sovereignty is located in essence in the Nation, which is none other than the union of Woman and Man; no group, no individual can exercise authority which does not emanate from it expressly.

4. Liberty and Justice consists of rendering to persons those things that belong to them; thus, the exercise of women's natural rights is limited only by the perpetual tyranny with which man opposes her; these limits must be changed according to the laws of nature and reason.

5. The laws of nature and of reason prohibit all acts harmful to society; there can be no hindrance to what is not forbidden, and no one can be forced to do what the law does not command.

6. The law should be the expression of the general will; all female and male citizens must participate in its expression personally or through their representatives. It should be the same for all; female and male citizens, being equal in are equally admissible to all public honours, positions, and employments, according to their capacities and with no distinctions other than those of their virtues and talents.

VII. No man can be accused, arrested, or detained except in cases determined by the law, and according to the forms which it has prescribed. Those who solicit, draw up, execute, or have executed arbitrary orders must be punished; but any citizen summoned or seized by virtue of the law must obey instantly; through resistance, the citizen renders himself culpable.

VIII. The law should establish only punishments that are strictly and clearly necessary, and no one can be punished except under a law established and promulgated prior to the offence and legally applied.

IX. Every man is presumed innocent until he has been declared guilty, if it is judged indispensable to arrest him, all severity that is not necessary for making sure of his person must be severely repressed by law.

X. No one should be threatened for their opinions, even religious opinions, provided that their public demonstration does not disturb the public order established by the law.

XI. The free communication of thoughts and opinions is one of the

the eyes of the law, should be equally admissible to all public honours, positions, and employments, according to their capacities and with no distinctions other than those of their virtues and talents.

7. No woman is exempt; she can be accused, arrested, and detained in such cases as determined by law. Women, like men, must obey these rigorous laws.

8. The law should establish only punishments that are strictly and clearly necessary. No one may be punished except under a law established and promulgated prior to the offence and which is legally applicable to women.

9. Since it is possible for a woman to be declared guilty, then, in that event, the law must be enforced rigorously.

10. No one should be threatened for their opinions, however fundamental. Woman has the right to mount the scaffold; she should likewise have the right to speak in public, provided that her demonstrations do not disrupt public order as established by law.

11. The free communication of thoughts and opinions is one of the most precious rights of man: every citizen can therefore freely speak, write and print; he is answerable for abuses of this liberty in cases determined by the law.

most precious rights of woman, since this liberty assures the legitimate paternity of fathers with regard to their children. Every female citizen can therefore freely say: 'I am the mother of a child that belongs to you,' without a barbaric prejudice forcing her to conceal the truth; she is also answerable for abuses of this liberty in cases determined by law.

XII. The guarantee of the rights of man and citizen necessitates a public utility; this guarantee should be established for the advantage of everyone, and not for the personal benefit of those entrusted with this utility.

12. The guarantee of the rights of woman and female citizen necessitates a public utility. This guarantee should be established for the advantage of everyone, not for the personal benefit of those entrusted with this utility.

XIII. For the maintenance of the public utility and for administrative expenses, a tax, supported in common is indispensable; it must be assessed on all citizens in proportion to their capacities to pay.

13. For the maintenance of the public utility and administrative expenses, the contributions of women and men shall be equal; the woman shares in all forced labour and all painful tasks, therefore she should have the same share in the distribution of positions, tasks, assignments, honours, and industry.

XIV. Citizens have the right to determine the need for public taxes, either by themselves or through their representatives, to consent to it freely, to investigate its use, and to determine its rate, basis, collection, and duration.

14. Female and male citizens have the right to determine the need for public taxes, either by themselves or through their representatives. Female citizens can consent to this only if they are admitted to an equal share not only in wealth but also in public administration, and in their right to determine the proportion and extent of tax collection.

XV. Society has the right to demand an accounting of their administration from every public agent.

15. The mass of women, allied for tax purposes to the mass of men, has the right to hold every public official accountable for their administration.

XVI. Any society in which the guarantee of rights is not assured, or the separation powers not determined, has no constitution.

16. Any society in which the guarantee of rights is not assured, or the separation powers not determined, has no constitution; the constitution is nullified if the majority of individuals who compose the Nation have not co-operated in writing it.

XVII. The right of property is inviolable and sacred; no one may be deprived of it except when public necessity, certified by law, clearly requires it, subject to just and prior compensation.

17. The right of property is inviolable and sacred to both sexes, jointly or separately; no one can be deprived of it, since it is a true inheritance of nature, except when public necessity, certified by law, clearly requires it, subject to just and prior compensation.

Conclusion

What are the implications of the preceding chapters for feminist politics of law?

First, this book makes it apparent that I have little time for principled abstention from legal politics. Feminists should, of course, note Carol Smart's warning about playing into the law's hands, according it the very power that it claims (Smart 1989: 5), but her warning does not mean that law is a no-go area for feminists. My view is that, just as analysis and activism with regard to economic struggles do not automatically accord economy the privileged status which monetarists claim for it, so writing about and participating in legal struggle is not automatically to cede the legal ground to antifeminist institutions and practices. On the contrary, as I argued in Chapter 3, it is *not* becoming involved in feminist politics of law that cedes legal ground to the antifeminists. Rather, the main implication of this book is that feminists have to make decisions about whether or how to intervene in legal issues, and that the decisions are a matter of deliberation and calculation, paying attention to the specifics of the legal–political issue to hand, not appealing to essentialist theories of law and of rights.

Consistently with that argument, I advocate neither the simple rejectionist position in relation to appeals to rights, as I described it in Chapters 2 and 7, nor its simple retentionist counterpart. So, although it is true that I have recommended 'abandoning the concept of rights as a means of pressing feminist claims in law' (Smart 1986: 121), that recommendation is specific to the appeal to a woman's right to choose and the right to reproduce, as analysed in this book in Chapters 3 and 4 and the Note to Chapter 4. Certainly, I argue that those instances of rights discourse are impediments to the formulation of feminist policy. But I resist any extrapolation from that argument to a kind of policy essentialism to the effect that every and any mention of rights must be expunged from the feminist dictionary of legal politics. A much more defensible argument is that rights discourse needs to be reconceptualised, and I have made a viable suggestion for how this can be done. I resist the policy essentialism over rights, partly because there are some legal–political contexts in which it is simply not possible to avoid engagements with rights discourse, and also because I want to emphasise the fact that there can be no single principle in relation to feminist politics of law and the appeal to rights. Instead, I reiterate that there has to be a calculation of specific issues, strategies, tactics and possible outcomes which are important to feminists. There is no single principle, then, in terms of which it is possible to know in advance, in each and every case, whether feminist politics of law should make an appeal to rights. There has to be calculation of specific issues, strategies, tactics and possible outcomes which are important to feminists.

One of the reasons why there is no single political principle, beyond the advocacy of cautious calculation, to be recommended to feminists, is the fact that 'rights' do not form a homogeneous group. First, as is evident from the chapters on abortion, sterilisation and cohabitation, there are many and varied substantive contexts in which rights have been invoked, each with its distinctive political history of ideologies, campaigns and outcomes. This will not surprise feminists involved in so-called single issue politics. Nor is it surprising, then, that specific rights differ in the ways in which they are excluded from prevailing legal–political agendas, jostle for position once on them, get turned into different agenda items, or for reasons which nobody can remember just never get discussed. Secondly, rights do not form a homogeneous group even when they have been grouped together in a formal declaration of rights. Indeed, the complexity of the analysis demanded by the invocation of specific rights, such as a woman's right to choose and the right to reproduce, is compounded in the debates surrounding campaigns for formal declaration of rights, both on the question of whether feminists should support such campaigns at all and, if they should, on the question of what rights feminists should seek to have inserted into any such declaration.

With more and more frequency, there are public debates about the promotion of a UK Bill of Rights, the incorporation into English law of the civil rights in the European Convention on Human Rights, the European Social Charter (notably with respect to the UK government's hostility towards it on the grounds – analysed in Chapter 8 – that economic rights must be opposed at all costs) and the Campaign for a Scottish Assembly's 'Claim of Right'. It looks increasingly as though feminists are going to have to address the politics of formal declarations of rights, and I shall conclude with a few observations on this type of politics.

There is no doubt that a formal declaration of rights can have considerable appeal to feminists. Such declarations appear to hold out hope of the incorporation into constitutional law of a good many of the rights for which feminists have fought, and there is something strangely comforting in the thought that such rights might become *entrenched*. But the above examples of formal declarations of rights make the point that feminist politics in this sort of arena is almost certain to be a matter of responding to calls for formal declarations of rights which are made initially from non-feminist quarters, even if feminists prefer to use the vocabulary of intervention to characterise their responses. They can be under no illusion about their being able to dictate the terms of reference of these legal–political struggles. As we saw in Chapter 7, the attempt to introduce the Equal Rights Amendment was a response to well-established American constitutional politics and, whatever some Canadian feminists' claims, the enacting of the Charter was less to do with feminist mobilisation than with the federal government's response to nationalism in Quebec (Fudge 1989: 446). Could she have heard this point about reactive feminist legal politics, and had she been less of an enthusiast for her 1791 Declaration, Olympe de Gouges might have stifled a yawn.

To resume one of the themes of this book, the issue for feminists, then, is less whether to initiate a campaign for a formal declaration of rights than whether, and if so how, to respond to legal–political structures which are ineluctably characterised in terms of rights. These constitute formidable problems for feminist politics of law, and I will finish with a brief reference to two indispensable source materials for the production of a feminist politics in this area of legal–political struggle. The first is Judy Fudge's development of her sophisticated analysis of the Canadian Charter discussed in Chapter 8. Any comfort which feminists might derive from thoughts of entrenched rights will be quickly dispelled by her account of the disadvantageous effects for feminists of the entrenchment of the Charter (Fudge 1989). Her argument focuses on the dangers of invoking abstract legal rights, in particular the way in which that invocation allows a superficial agreement between feminists at the cost of working out policy differences and at the cost of being unprepared for the anti-feminist backlash occasioned by the enactment of the Charter: 'Any positive evaluation of abstract legal rights which rests on the ability of feminist and other social movements to exploit abstract rights as political symbols can be exploited by groups with opposing political agendas' (Fudge 1989: 449). There was a further effect:

> What the *Charter* does is detach form from substance. ... Instead of directly addressing the question of how best to promote women's sexual autonomy under social relations which result in women's sexual subordination, feminists who invoke the *Charter* must couch their arguments in terms of the rhetoric of equality rights. Whilst it is true that social conditions will figure in their argument, they will figure only indirectly and to the extent that it is necessary to

establish the rights claim. In this way the feminist discourse about power is translated into a discourse of rights. (Fudge 1989: 458)

Fudge's analysis is pessimistic and persuasive, certainly as far as Canadian feminist politics are concerned. With its detailed exploration of how rights discourse is actually operating within Charter politics, concentrating on the specific question of the courts' attitudes towards sexual violence against women and children, it is very much the type of analysis which any feminist exercised by issues of rights discourse, especially the strengths and weaknesses of formal declarations of rights, should treat as exemplary. In fact, Fudge's position confirms many of the arguments developed in this book. In that respect, I have only one qualm about Fudge's article, and it concerns the final sentence in the last quotation above. As I indicated in the Preface and Introduction, there is little point in adverting to the limitations of rights discourse, on the grounds that it is essentialist, if it is immediately replaced with a different form of essentialism, such as the discourse of power. It would, of course, be absurd to take Fudge's brief reference to 'the feminist discourse of power' as symptomatic of a fully-fledged essentialist theory of power, particularly since she is so obviously hostile to the effects of standard forms of essentialist rights discourse. Even so, the phrase can serve as a reminder of the importance of keeping the anti-essentialist antennae in good working order and of the need to take further in the UK the debate about alternative constructions of feminist politics in the context of formal declarations of rights.

This point brings me to the second example of a text which is indispensable reading for feminists in the UK who are formulating a feminist politics of formal declarations of rights, whether in relation to a campaign such as Charter 88 or in relation to the opportunities afforded by European legislation for feminist politics. It is an unpretentious text, not expressed in high theoretical terms. The document is *A Woman's Claim of Right in Scotland* (WCoRS 1989), the impeccably feminist submission of the campaign of that title to the Scottish Constitutional Convention. Its opening outline of principal barriers to greater participation by women in politics is followed by an eleven-point programme of recommendations for the improvement of Scottish women's political status. The recommendations include the requirement that parties participating in Scottish elections should provide an 'equality audit', itemising their record on the involvement of women, for example as sitting members of the Scottish Assembly. The document also proposes that there should be positive discrimination in the higher levels of the Scottish Civil Service, so that there is a better gender distribution among the officials preparing and implementing policies. In addition, the recommendations suggest measures to ease the practical problems which women and men would experience in combining a full-time job in a national legislature with domestic responsibilities.

There are a number of interesting features of the WCoRS campaign and the document, but for purposes of concluding this book I would point to just a few. First, as noted above, WCoRS is explicitly a response to a call for a formal declaration of right, the 1988 Document of *A Claim of Right for Scotland* (a pamphlet given more substantial form in Edwards 1989, but see also WCoRG 1991). There appears to be no reference in that claim of right to the need to involve more women in Scottish politics, despite the fact that only 4 per cent of Scottish MPs and 13·5 per cent of regional councillors are women (Wilson and Fletcher 1990: 136). Very appropriately, then, the title of the WCoRS submission is a deliberate echo of the 1988 document's title – just as de Gouges' Declaration was an echo of the 1789 Declaration. Thereafter, the WCoRS invokes no rights at all. It may be that this is a deliberate decision not to employ a discourse which feminists have identified as bound up with adversarial styles of politics. Whether or not that is the case, the WCoRS document bears out one of the claims which I have made in this book, namely that it is possible to construct the materials of feminist politics of law without using rights discourse. Whatever the loss, if it is a loss, in terms of high rhetoric, the gain is that it becomes easier to identify realisable feminist social policies and objectives.

Notes

Chapter 1

1 One rather obvious question which might be raised immediately is the justification of concentrating on male beliefs when, however few they may be, there are some women legal practitioners, and some of these may be just as sexist as the men. To make that point, of course, would be to question the authors' claim that 'while there are clearly no barriers of intellect to prevent women writing about men's consciousness ... there are limitations of experience' and that 'men are therefore in a position to make a special contribution to a debate that involves both sexes, by drawing on their special experience as males living in a male-dominated society' (Sachs and Wilson 1978: 6). But to become involved in the pros and cons of that issue could obscure the more general issue of the status of belief, female or male, in accounts of legal phenomena.

2 The authors' discussion of legal manners and work-style illustrates perhaps better than anything else how close they sometimes sail to the sexist wind. They make a connection between the exclusion of ordinary people from competence in legal matters and the organisation of offices. They suggest that male and female lawyers have been investigating the possibilities of law centres being more responsive to clients' needs, and they comment that it is women lawyers who are most instrumental in this movement. They resist the idea that this is because 'they as women in some mystical way are more tender or motherly than men' but they allow that it is because they have more experience of struggling against oppression than men and are on that account more likely to be able to develop 'more direct, friendly, spontaneous and egalitarian relationships with clients' (Sachs and Wilson 1978: 182–4). But it is just as 'sexist' to attribute acquired character traits on the basis of sex as it is to attribute innate character traits on that basis. And, of course, either form of sexism must be arbitrary in its selection of sexually-based character traits. It is indeed mystical to suppose that women are innately tender or, for that matter, innately vexatious, but it is just as mystical to suppose that the experience of struggle is more likely to produce the qualities of friendliness and egalitarianism than it is to produce the qualities of deviousness, suspicion and aggressiveness towards possible competitors, or, for that matter, undifferentiated apathy.

3   In this respect, however, Edelman's warning of the de-politicising effect of legal recognition of the right to strike, with its implied warning about legal recognition of other rights, is pertinent.

Chapter 2

1   The best critique of works on the relation between patriarchy and capitalism is still the one by Diana Adlam (1979).
2   The case of Shirley Boyle is pertinent. Her medical report, detailing backache, was used against her, not at the time when she was refused a job as a hospital porter but only later when she complained to an industrial tribunal (Gill 1980). It is also important to note that the Sex Discrimination Act 1975 does acknowledge the existence of indirect discrimination and discrimination by victimisation (Beloff 1976: 1). There is evidence, however, that neither SDA nor EQPA has been adequate to the problems of women in part-time employment (NCCL 1980, 4/5 May/June). Since the 1980s, too, there has much interest in the proceedings of the European Court on the matter of 'whether it is contrary to European Community Law to pay a lower hourly rate to female part-time workers than to full-time male workers, although the women do the same work and have the same productivity' (Beloff 1980; O'Donovan and Szyszczak 1988: 175-6).

Chapter 3

1   Adrian Howe has exemplified this type of approach with her theorisation of 'social injury' and her proposal that privileging gender-specific social injuries within feminist legal theory, and ultimately legal discourse, can advance feminist struggles (1987: 432).
2   S. 1 (2) of the Abortion Act 1967 provides that 'in determining whether the continuance of a pregnancy would involve such risk of injury to health as is mentioned in paragraph (a) of Subsection (I) of this section, account may be taken of the pregnant woman's actual or reasonably foreseeable environment'. Whatever the spirit or intention of the law, strictly speaking the so-called environment clause does not constitute independent grounds for lawful termination.
3   It is worth noting in this respect that two important applications heard in the Patent Office in the mid 1970s – one for a method of inducing abortion and the other for a method of contraception – were decided by reference to, among other things, the meaning of 'invention' as defined in section 6 of the Statute of Monopolies Act 1623!
4   For a full critique of this position from the point of view of socialist legality. including a discussion of the famous *Paton* v. *British Pregnancy Advisory Service Trustees* on the matter of the existence, or to be exact, the non-existence, of rights in law, see Hirst 1980.

Note to Chapter 3

1   A transcript, in English, of these cases was published, in breach of the French censorship laws, in Association Choisir (1973). For the text of Article 317 of the French Penal Code, see Mueller 1960:

109-11. Briefly, it is a felony or misdemeanour to cause or attempt to cause an abortion, by whatever means, and regardless of the pregnant, or putatively pregnant, women.

2 For the full text of Article 127, see Mueller 1960: 127. Briefly, the Article states that any judge or prosecuting attorney of a Felony or Misdemeanour Court shall be deemed guilty of breach of duty and sentenced to loss of civil rights if, among other things, he makes rules involving legislative dispositions, questions whether a law should be promulgated or executed, or in any way acts beyond his powers.

Chapter 4

1 Cf. in this respect the substitution of 'mental impairment' for subnormality in the Mental Health (Amendment) Act 1982.

2 Cf. in this respect the parallel situation in the USA and the way the inequality would have been removed by the passing of the Equal Rights Amendment; cf. Switzer 1976: 104.

Note to Chapter 4

1 In a spoken introduction to a conference version of this Note, I also warned feminists against claiming rights, such as a woman's right to choose, in the belief that to claim the right necessitates a corresponding duty of the state to provide suitable abortion and contraception facilities. This warning was based on my recollection that some philosophers have a liking for symmetry between rights and duties: where there is a right, so must there be a duty. Then, following delivery of my paper, one contributor to the discussion put up a defence of the right to reproduce as a fundamental human right, claiming that the right was inseparable from the duty of a wife to reproduce. The desired symmetry of rights and duties was manifest, and so was the asymmetry between the *human* right and the duty of a *wife*. This was a perfect, if unnervingly clear, illustration of the arguments in this Note in particular and the thesis of the whole book about the dangers for feminists in appealing to rights.

Chapter 6

1 Pertinent to this point, Regina Graycar has documented a tough public debate on feminist interventions in Australian matrimonial property law (Graycar 1990: 163). On the one hand, there is the argument that, on divorce, a fifty/fifty split of property would leave women disadvantaged, because they did not have the same earning capacity as men. On the other hand, there is the argument that inequality of earnings should not be remedied through individual property adjustments but through government training programmes.

Chapter 7

1 The emphasis in this chapter is initially more on American than on UK sources. This is because the existence of the American Constitution and the politics of the ERA put into sharp focus the debate

about equal rights and special rights. This is not to say that the
debate is predominantly American. At the European Conference
on Critical Legal Studies in April 1986 in London, the special
theme was Feminist Perspectives on Law. Speaker after speaker,
both in formal papers and in the discussion following them, expressed doubts about using the discourse of equal rights for feminist
politics. Occasionally the question of an alternative to it was posed
in terms of the discourse of special rights. That debate was the
impetus for this chapter. The chapter developed out of remarks
which I made as Recorder for a session in which M. L. P. Loenen
commented on Wolgast's book. In her as yet unpublished paper,
Loenen sought to defend the principle of equality against what she
saw as Wolgast's misinterpretation of it. My remarks were to the
effect that, whether or not Loenen made her case, the debate is
pitched at a philosophical level which permits neither its own
solution nor the formulation of precise feminist policy in relation to
legal issues.

2 Selma Sevenhuijsen (1986) has spelled out these risks with chilling
clarity. Similarly, although she does not conduct the argument in
terms of rights, Zillah R. Eisenstein (1988) has used the phrase
'reconstituting the phallus' to describe the Reagan administration's
attempt to shift the political discourse of sex equality. Its purpose
was to erode the progress made in the 1970s toward a sex equality
rooted in 'sameness' by substituting a sex equality rooted in difference (Eisenstein 1988: 116).

3 These quotations are typical, not in the sense that they appear in all
documents supporting the special rights strategy but in the sense
that they exhibit most vividly both the appeal and the danger of that
strategy. I have taken them from the works by Elizabeth Wolgast
and by Mary Midgley and Judith Hughes, since these are discussed
in this chapter.

4 The ERA is as follows:
    Section 1. Equality of rights under the law shall not be denied
    or abridged by the United States on account of sex.
    Section 2. The Congress shall have the power to enforce, by
    appropriate legislation, the provisions of this article.
    Section 3. This amendment shall take effect two years after
    the date of ratification.
  The article used by supporters and opponents of the ERA as the
authoritative interpretation of its likely effects is Barbara A. Brown
et al.(1971).

5 A local newspaper reported that the hospital took the less-than-
reassuring view that living human tissue cannot belong to anybody
(*Liverpool Echo* 1986). No doubt similar claims will be made in the
event of the unhappily labelled procedure of 'cadaver donation'.
This is where a woman becomes pregnant by posthumous *in vitro*
fertilisation with sperm or ovum from a deceased person to whom
she was not related by marriage. This method is only at the point of
discussion; certainly, it does not feature in the table of reproductive
options produced by Dickens in 1985. That, of course, is a measure
of the rapidity with which medical possibilities are ahead of common sense, never mind law.

Chapter 8

1 I have produced my own translations both of de Gouges' political writings and of the two Declarations. I have used de Gouges' texts as they are reproduced in the collection edited by Benoite Groult (1986). To preserve the greatest symmetry between the two Declarations, so that the differences between them are more visible, I have omitted the first two paragraphs of the 1791 document. I use the standard reproductions of the 1789 Declaration.

Bibliography

Abray, J. (1975) 'Feminism in the French revolution', *American History Review*, 80: 43–62.

Adams, P. and Minson, J. (1978) 'The "subject" of feminism', *m/f*, 2: 43–61.

Adlam, D. (1979) 'The case against patriarchy', *m/f*, 3: 83–102.

Adler, M. and Asquith, S. (1981) (eds.) *Discretion and Welfare*, London: Heinemann Educational Books.

Aitken-Swan, J. (1977) *Fertility Control and the Medical Profession*, London: Croom Helm.

Allen, I. (1981) *Family Planning, Sterilisation and Abortion Services*, London: Policy Studies Institute, No.595.

Arnaud, A-J. and Kingdom, E. (1990) (eds.) *Women's Rights and the Rights of Man*, Aberdeen: Aberdeen University Press.

Arnold, C. (1978) 'Analyses of rights', in E. Kamenka and A. Ehr-Soon Tay (eds.) *Human Rights*, London: Edward Arnold.

Association Choisir (1973) *The Bobigny Affair*, Introduction by Simone de Beauvoir, Sydney: Wild and Woolley.

Atiyah, P. S. (1987) *Pragmatism and Theory in English Law*, London: Stevens and Sons.

Atkins, S. and Hoggett, B. (1984) *Women and the Law*, Oxford: Blackwell.

Austerberry, H. and Watson, S. (1981) 'A woman's place', *Feminist Review*. 8: 49–62.

Bailey-Harris, R. (1990) 'Family law ... doctrine of unconscionability'. *Australian Law Journal*, 64, 6: 365–9.

Bainham, A. (1989) 'When is a parent not a parent?', *International Journal of Law and the Family*, 3, 2: 208–39,

Bankowski, Z. and Mungham, G. (1976) (eds.) *Essays in Law and Society*, London: Routledge and Kegan Paul.

— and Nelken, D. (1981) 'Discretion as a social problem', in M. Adler and S. Asquith (eds.).

Barrett, M. and McIntosh, M. (1982) *The Anti-Social Family*, London: Verso.

Barton, C. (1985) *Cohabitation Contracts*, Aldershot: Gower.

Bell, S. Groag and Offen, K. M. (1983) *Women, the Family and Freedom*, Volume One 1750–1880, Stanford, Calif.: Stanford University Press.

Beloff, M. J. (1976) *Sex Discrimination Act 1975*, Butterworths Annotated Legislation Service, Vol. 237, London: Butterworths.

— (1980) *The Observer*, 23 November.

Benton, S. (1988) 'Citizen Cain's silenced sisters', *New Statesman and Society*, 1, 26, 2 December: 18–19.

Bernard, J. (1973) *The Future of Marriage*, London: Souvenir Press.

Birth Control Trust (1978a) *Sterilisation and the National Health Service*.

— (1978b) *Abortion Ten Years On*.

Blake, S. (1982) *The Law of Marriage*, London: Barry Rose.

Bone, M. (1973) *Family Planning Services in England and Wales*, Social Survey Division, Office of Population Censuses and Surveys.

— (1978) *The Family Planning Services: changes and effects*, Social Survey Division, Office of Population Censuses and Surveys.

Bottomley, A. et al. (1981) *The Cohabitation Handbook*, London: Pluto.

Bradley, D. (1989) 'The development of a legal status for unmarried cohabitation in Sweden', *Anglo-American Law Review*, 18, 4: 322–34

Bradney, A. (1987) 'Transsexuals and the law', *Family Law*. 17: 350–3.

Brock, L. G. (1934) *Report of the Departmental Committee on Sterilisation* (Cmd. 4485).

Brophy, J. and Smart, S. (1984) (eds.) *Women in Law*, London: Routledge and Kegan Paul.

Brown, B. A. et al. (1971) 'The Equal Rights Amendment: a constitutional basis for equal rights for women', *Yale Law Journal*, 80, 5: 871–995.

Buckle, A. E. R. and Young, K. C. (1972) reported in *New Society* 24 February.

Burgess, A. (1983) 'Licensing your live-in lover', *Cosmopolitan*, November.

Byrne, P. and Lovenduski, J. (1978) 'Sex equality and the law in Britain', *British Journal of Law and Society*, 5: 148–65.

Cambridge Women's Studies Group (1981) *Women in Society*, London: Virago.

Campbell, B. (1980) 'Divorce', *Time Out*, 21 July: 11.

Carlen, P. and Collison, M. (1980) (eds.) *Radical Issues in Criminology*, Oxford: Martin Robertson.

Charter 88 (1988) *New Statesman and Society* special edition launching Charter 88, 1, 26, 2 December.

Clarke, L. (1989) 'Abortion: a rights issue?', in R. Lee and D. Morgan (eds.).

Clark-Kennedy, A. E. (1969) *Man, Medicine and Morality*, US Distribution: Shoe String Press Inc.

Cole, C. L. (1977) 'Cohabitation in social context', in R. W. Libby and R. N. Whitehurst (eds.).

Coussins, J. (1980) 'Equality for women', *Marxism Today*, January 6–11.

Coward, R. (1978) 'Rethinking Marxism', *m/f*, 2: 85–96.

Cranston, M. (1973) *What are Human Rights?*, London: Bodley Head.

Creighton, W. B. (1979) *Working Women and the Law*, London: Mansell.

Cuisine, D. (1977) 'Artificial insemination with the husband's semen after death', *Journal of Medical Ethics*, 3: 163–5.

Daly, J. (1989) 'Criminal justice ideologies and practices in different voices: some feminist questions about justice', *International Journal of the Sociology of Law*. 17: 1–18.

Davis, K. (1967) 'Population policy: will current programmes succeed?', *Science*, 158, 3802: 730–9.

DeCrow, K. (1975) *Sexist Justice*, New York: Vintage Books.

Deech, R. L. (1980) 'The case against legal recognition of cohabitation', *International and Comparative Law Quarterly*, 29: 480–97.

Denning, Lord (1980) *The Due Process of Law*, London: Butterworths.

Dewar, J. (1989) *Law and the Family*, London: Butterworths.

Dickens. B. M. (1985) 'Reproduction law and medical consent', *University of Toronto Law Journal*, 35, 255–86.

Edelman, B. (1979) *Ownership of the Image*, translated by E. Kingdom, with an Introduction by P. Q. Hirst, London: Routledge and Kegan Paul.

— (1980) 'The legalisation of the working class', extracts translated and with an Introduction by E. Kingdom, *Economy and Society*, 9 (1): 50–69.

Edwards, O. D. (1989) (ed.) *A Claim of Right for Scotland*, Edinburgh: Polygon.

Edwards, S. (1981) *Female Sexuality and the Law*, Oxford: Martin Robertson.

Eisenstein, H. (1984) *Contemporary Feminist Thought*, London: Allen and Unwin.

— (1988) *The Female Body and the Law*, Berkeley and Los Angeles: University of California Press.

Equal Opportunities Commission (1986) *Legislating for a Change: review of the sex discrimination legislation*, Manchester.

Equal Opportunities Review (1987) 'Equal opportunities review clause-by-clause guide to the Sex Discrimination Act 1986', 11, January/February.

Etzione, A. (1973) *Genetic Fix*, London: Macmillan.

Evening News (Edinburgh) (1990) 'No loos no excuse', 16 August.

Firestone, S. (1979) *The Dialectics of Sex*, London: The Women's Press.

Fleming, J. (1985) *The Law of Torts*, Oxford: Clarendon.

Frank, J. (1949) *Law and the Modern Mind*, London: Stevens and Sons.

Freeman, M. D. A.. (1988) 'Sterilising the mentally handicapped', in M. D. A. Freeman (ed.).

— (1988) (ed.) *Medicine, Ethics and the Law*, London: Stevens and Sons.

— and Lyon, C. M. (1983) *Cohabitation without Marriage*, London: Gower.

Fudge, J. (1987) 'The public/private distinction: the possibilities of and the limits to the use of *Charter* litigation to further feminist struggles', *Osgoode Hall Law Journal*, 25, 3: 485–554.

— (1989) 'The effect of entrenching a bill of rights upon political discourse: feminist demands and sexual violence in Canada', *International Journal of the Sociology of Law*, 17: 445–63.

Geiger, H. Kent (1970) *The Family in Soviet Russia*, Russian Research Center Studies, 56, Cambridge, Mass.: Harvard University Press.

Gelsthorpe, L. (1986) 'Towards a sceptical look at sexism', *International Journal of the Sociology of Law*, 14: 125–52.

General Household Survey 1987, London HMSO.

Gill, T. (1980) *New Society*, 14 August.

Gilligan, C. (1982) *In a Different Voice: psychological theory and women's development*, London: Harvard University Press.

Goldberg, S. (1977) *The Inevitability of Patriarchy*, London: Temple Smith.

de Gouges, 0. (aka Marie Gouze) (1791) *Les Droits de la Femme et de la Citoyenne*, in B. Groult (1986).

— (1788) 'Lettre au peuple ou projet d'une caisse patriotique par une citoyenne', in B. Groult (1986): 69–72.

Gray, P. N. (1973) 'A new lease of life', *New Law Journal*, 123: 596.

Graycar, R. (1990) 'Feminism and law reform: matrimonial property law and models of equality', in S. Watson (ed.)

Greenwood, K. and King, L. (1981) 'Contraception and abortion', in Cambridge Women's Studies Group (1981).

Greenwood, V. and Young, J. (1976) *Abortion in Demand*, London: Pluto.

Groult, B. (1986) *Olympe de Gouges: Oeuvres Présentées*, Paris: Mercure de France.

The Guardian (1980) 13 June.

Hampson, N. (1979) *The First European Revolution 1776–1815*, London: Thames and Hudson.

Hart, H. L. A. (1968) *Punishment and Responsibility*, Oxford: Clarendon University Press.

Harvard Law Review (1984) 'Anti-pornography laws and First Amendment values', Note, 9, 2: 460–81.

Hazard, J. (1951) *Soviet Legal Philosophy*, Cambridge, Mass.: Harvard University Press.

Henderson, S. and Mackay, A. (1990) (eds.) *Grit and Diamonds: women in Scotland making history 1980–90*, Edinburgh: Stramullion.

Hewitt, P. (1978) 'Women's rights and human rights', in Birth Control Trust (1978b): 29.

Hirst, P. Q. (1979) 'Introduction', in B. Edelman (1979).

— (1980) 'Law, socialism and rights', in P. Carlen and M. Collison (1980) (eds.).

— and Jones, P. (1987) 'The critical resources of established jurisprudence', *Journal of Law and Society*, 14: 21–32.

Hodson, D. (1990) 'The new partner after divorce', *Family Law*, 20: 27–30.

Holley, R. (1980) 'Abortion internationally', in National Abortion Campaign.

Honoré, T. (1978) *Sex Law*, London: Duckworth.

Howe, A. (1987) 'Social injury revisited: towards a feminist theory of social justice', *International Journal of the Sociology of Law*, 15: 423–38.

Hufton, 0. (1975) 'Women and the family economy in eighteenth century France', *French Historical Studies*, 9: 1–22.

— (1989) 'Voilà la citoyenne'. *History Today*, 39, May: 26–32.

Hutter, B. and Williams, G. (1981) (eds.), *Controlling Women*, London: Croom Helm.

The Independent (1990) 22 February.

Jaconelli, J. (1980) *Enacting a Bill of Rights*, Oxford: Clarendon.

Johnson, R. (1986) Cohabitation without formal marriage in England and Wales', *Family Law*, 16: 47–5.

Kamenka, E. and Tay, A. E-S (eds.) (1978) *Human Rights*, London: Edward Arnold.

— (1979) *Justice*, London: Edward Arnold.

Kelly. L., (1987) *Women of the French Revolution*, London: Hamish Hamilton.

Kingdom, E. (1980) 'Introduction', in B. Edelman (1980).

— (1987) 'Feminism and philosophy', in *Women and Philosophy*, Resources for Feminist Research, Toronto: Ontario Institute for Studies in Education: 8–9.

— (1990) 'Cohabitation and equality', *International Journal of the Sociology of Law*, 18: 287–98.

Knight, B. (1987) *Legal Aspects of Medical Practice*, London: Churchill Livingstone.

Kollontai, A. (1977) 'Marriage and everyday life', in *Selected Writings*, translated with an Introduction by Alix Holt, London: Allison and Busby.

Kuhn, A. (1978) 'Structures of patriarchy and capital in the family', in A. Kuhn and A. Wolpe (eds.).

— and A. Wolpe (1978) (eds.) *Feminism and Materialism*, London: Routledge and Kegan Paul.

Labour Party (1936) Report of the 36th Annual Conference.

Lacey, N. (1986) 'The rights we need', *New Society*, 7 February.

Laing, W. A. (1982) *Family Planning: the benefits and costs*, London: Policy Studies Institute, No. 607.

Lane Report (1974) *Report of the Committee on the Working of the Abortion Act* (Cmd. 5579).

Law Commission (1979) *Family Law: Illegitimacy*, Working Paper No. 74.

Leach, G. (1972) *The Biocrats*, London: Pelican.

Leathard. A. (1990) *Health Care Provision*, London: Chapman and Hall.

Lee, R. and Morgan, D. (1989) (eds.) *Birthrights: law and ethics at the beginning of life*, London: Routledge.

Leeson, J. and Gray, J. (1978) *Women and Medicine*, London: Tavistock.

Lester, A. (1990) *Times*, 22 May.

Levitt, R. and Wall, A. (1984) *The Reorganised Health Service*, London: Chapman and Hall.

Levy, D. G., Applewhite, H. B., and Johnson, D. G. (1979) *Women in Revolutionary France*, Urbana: University of Illinois.

Libby, R. W. and Whitehurst, R. N. (1977) (eds.) *Marriage and Alternatives*, Eurospan Ltd. Scott, Foresman.

Local Government Information Unit (1989) 'Women and the poll tax', London.

Liverpool Echo (1986) 19 May.

MacCormick, N. (1989) 'Discretion and rights', *Law and Philosophy*, 8, 1: 23–36.

MacKinnon, C. (1982) 'Feminism, Marxism, method and the state: an agenda for theory', *Signs*, 7, 3: 515–44.

— (1983) 'Feminism, Marxism, method and the state: toward feminist jurisprudence', *Signs*, 8, 4: 635–58.

— (1987) *Feminism Unmodified: discourses on life and law*, London: Harvard University Press.

McLean, S. A. M. (1981) (ed.) *Legal Issues in Medicine*, London Gower.

Marshall, K. (1982) *Real Freedom*, London: Junius Publications.

Martin, A. (1980), 'A question of balance', *Nursing Mirror*, 18 September.

Marx, K./Engels F. (1970) *Selected Works in One Volume*, London: Lawrence and Wishart.

Mason, J. K. and Smith, A. McCall (1987) *Law and Medical Ethics*, London: Butterworths.

Meron, T. (ed.) (1984) *Human Rights in International Law*. Oxford: Clarendon.

— (1986) *Human Rights Law-Making in the United Nations*, Oxford: Clarendon.

Metcalfe, O. K. (1962) *General Principles of English Law*, revised by J. Westwood, London: Donnington Press.

Midgley, M. (1978) *Beast and Man: the roots of human nature*, Ithaca NY: Cornell University Press.

— and Hughes, J. (1983) *Women's Choices*, London: Weidenfeld and Nicholson.

Minson, J. (1981) 'The assertion of homosexuality', *m/f*, 5 & 6: 19–39.

Morgan, D. (1989) 'Surrogacy: an introductory essay', in R. Lee and D. Morgan (eds.).

Mueller, G. O. W. (1960) *The French Penal Code*, London: Sweet and Maxwell.

National Abortion Campaign (1980) *Abortion: our Struggle for Control*, London.

National and Provincial Building Society (1987) *Occupational Lending Survey*.

Nationwide Building Society (1986) *Lending to Women – Nationwide*.

Naughton, J. (1990) 'Those surrogate baby blues', *Observer*, 12 August.

NCCL (1977) Re: Sterilisation, quoted by kind permission of the NCCL Women's Rights Unit.

— (1980) *Rights!*, special issue on unemployment, 4, May/June.

New Society (1972) 24 February.

— (1974) 18 July.

— (1975) 12 June.

— (1978) 23 February.

Oakley, A. (1975) 'Sex discrimination legislation', *British Journal of Law and Society*, 2: 211–17.

O'Donovan, K. (1985) *Sexual Divisions in Law*, London: Weidenfeld and Nicholson

— and Szyszczak., E. (1988) *Equality and Sex Discrimination*, Oxford: Blackwell.

Oliver, D. (1987) *Cohabitation: the legal implications*, Bicester: Commerce Clearing House Editions.

Olsen, F. (1983) 'The family and the market: a study of ideology and legal reform', *Harvard Law Review*, 96, 7: 1497–578.

Opit, L. J. and Brennan, M. E. (1974) reported in *New Society*, 18 July.

Parker, D. (1984) 'Cohabitants, their homes and and winds of change', *Family Law*, 14: 40

Parker, S. (1981) *Cohabitees*, London: Barry Rose.

— (1987) *Cohabitees*, London: Barry Rose.

Parry, M. L. (1988) *Cohabitation*, London: Sweet and Maxwell.

Pashukanis, E. B. . (1951) The General Theory of Law and Marxism, in

J. Hazard (ed.).

Pateman, C. (1988) *The Sexual Contract*, Cambridge: Polity Press.

Piachaud, D. (1984) *Round about Fifty Hours a Week*, Child Poverty Action group.

Pringle, R. (1990) Review of Smart 1989, *International Journal for the Sociology of Law*, 18, 2: 229–32.

Rae, M., Hewitt, P. and Hugill, B. (1979) *First Rights*, NCCL.

Rights of Women (1979–80) 'A rose by any other name ... cohabitation (= marriage?)', Newsletter, 11: 16.

Rights of Women, Family Law Subgroup (1985) 'Campaigning around family law'. in J. Brophy and C. Smart (eds.).

Roberts, Y. (1988) *Independent*, 18 May.

Rose, N. (1987) 'Beyond the public/private division: law, power and the family', *Journal of Law and Society*, 14: 61–76.

Rubenstein, M. (1984) *Equal Pay for Work of Equal Value*, London: Macmillan.

— (1989) *Discrimination*, London: Eclipse Publications.

Sachs, A. and Wilson, J. H. (1978) *Sexism and the Law*, London: Martin Robertson.

Scales, A. C. (1986) 'The emergence of a feminist jurisprudence: an essay', *Yale Law Journal*, 95: 1373–403.

Scorer, C. and Sedley, A. (1983) *Amending the Equality Laws*, NCCL.

Scott, J. W. (1989) 'French feminists and the rights of "man"', *History Workshop*, 28 1–21.

Scottish Law Commission (1990a) *Family Law: pre-consolidation reforms*, Discussion Paper No. 85.

— (1990b) *The Effects of Cohabitation in Private Law*, Discussion Paper No. 86.

Segal, L. et al. (1979) *Beyond the Fragments*, London: Merlin Press.

Sevenhuijsen, S. (1986) 'Fatherhood and political theory of rights: theoretical perspectives of feminism', *International Journal of the Sociology of Law*, 14: 329–40.

Sheffield Rights of Women (1980) *Women, Sexuality and the Law*, Sheffield: no longer available.

Simms, M. (1981) 'Abortion: the myth of the golden age', in B. Hutter and G. Williams (eds.).

Smart, C. (1977) *Women, Crime and Criminology*, London: Routledge and Kegan Paul.

— (1984) *The Ties that Bind*, London: Routledge and Kegan Paul.

— (1986) 'Feminism and law: some problems of analysis and strategy', *International Journal of the Sociology of Law*, 14: 109–23.

— (1989) *Feminism and the Power of Law*, London: Routledge.

— and J. Brophy (1984) 'Locating law' in J. Brophy and C. Smart (eds.).

Smith, G. (1985) 'Australia's frozen "orphan" embryos: a medical, legal and ethical dilemma', *Journal of Family Law*, 24: 27–41.

Sookias, M. J. et al. (1987) 'Conveyancers beware the co-habitee', *Law Society's Gazette*, 84: 1309.

Stark, B. (1990) Review of *Women's Legal Rights: international covenants, an alternative to ERA?*, (Halberstam and Defeis, Transnational Publishers 1987), *Women's Rights Law Reporter*, 12, 1: 51–7.

Stuchka, P. I. (1951) *The Revolutionary Part Played by Law and the State – a General Doctrine of Law*, in J. Hazard (ed.).

Sundberg, J. W. F. (1976) 'Recent changes in Swedish family law: experiment repeated', *American Journal of Comparative Law*, 23: 34–49.

Switzer, E. (1976) *The Law for a Woman*, New York: Charles Scribner's Sons.

Tay, A. E-S. (1979) 'The sense of justice in the common law', in E. Kamenka and A. Ehr-Soon Tay (eds.).

Taylor, B. (1983) *Eve and the New Jerusalem*, London: Virago.

Taylor, J. Leahy (1970) *The Doctor and the Law*, London: Pitman Medical.

Trubek, D. M. (1984) 'Economic, social and cultural rights in the Third World: human rights law and human needs programs', in T. Meron (ed.).

Tunkel, V. (1977) 'The law against family planning – a Commonwealth Survey', in *Abortion Laws in the Commonweath*, London: Commonweath Secretariat.

Usborne, D. (1989) *Independent*, 23 June.

Veitch, A. (1985) *Guardian*, 25 September.

Viel, B. and Walls, J. (1976) *The Demographic Explosion*, New York: Irvington.

Wallington, P. and McBride, J. (1976) *Civil Liberties and a Bill of Rights*, London: Cobden Trust.

Walton, T. (1974) 'When is a woman not a woman?', *New Law Journal*, 124, 30 May: 501–2.

Warnock, M. (1984) *A Question of Life*, Oxford: Blackwell.

Watson, S. (1990) (ed.) *Playing the State: Australian feminist interventions*, London: Verso.

Weeks, J. (1981) *Sex, Politics and Society*, London: Longman.

Weitzman, J. (1981) *The Marriage Contract*, New York: The Free Press.

Welstead, M. (1990) 'Mistresses in law: deserving of protection', *Family Law*, 20: 72–5.

Williams, G. (1958) *The Sanctity of Life and the Criminal Law*, London: Faber and Faber.

Wilson, S. and Fletcher, I. (1990) 'Getting it together', in S. Henderson and A. Mackay (eds.).

Wolgast, E. H. (1980) *Equality and the Rights of Women*, London: Cornell University Press.

Women's Claim of Right Group (1991) *A Woman's Claim of Right: essays on women and politics*, Edinburgh: Polygon.

A Woman's Claim of Right in Scotland (1989), submission to the Scottish Constitutional Convention, Edinburgh, June.

Women's Health and Reproductive Rights Information Centre (WHRRIC) (1990) Newsletter, May: 19.

Women's Reproductive Rights Campaign (WRRC) (1990) Newsletter, Summer: 4–5.

Women's Reproductive Rights Information Centre (WRRIC) (1986) Newsletter, August/September/October: 2–3.

Wright, M. (1984) 'Marriage: from status to contract', *Anglo-American Law Review*, 13, 1: 17–31.

Zander, M. (1985) *A Bill of Rights?*, London: Sweet and Maxwell.

Zuckerman, A. A. S. (1980) 'Formality and the family: reform and status quo', *Law Quarterly Review*, 96: 248–80.

Name index

Subject index